THE ORIGINS OF LIBERTY

THE ORIGINS OF LIBERTY

POLITICAL AND ECONOMIC
LIBERALIZATION IN
THE MODERN WORLD

Edited by

Paul W. Drake and Mathew D. McCubbins

PRINCETON UNIVERSITY PRESS   PRINCETON, NEW JERSEY

Library of Congress Cataloging-in-Publication Data

The origins of liberty : political and economic liberalization in the
modern world / edited by Paul W. Drake and Mathew D.
McCubbins.
p. cm.
Includes bibliographical references and index.
ISBN 0-691-05753-2 (cloth : alk. paper). — ISBN 0-691-05755-9
(pbk. : alk. paper)
1. Liberty. 2. Liberalism. 3. Free enterprise. I. Drake, Paul W.,
1944–. I. McCubbins, Mathew D. (Mathew Daniel), 1956–.
JC585.0695 1998
323.44—dc21   97-37205

This book has been composed in Sabon

Princeton University Press books are printed on acid-free paper and
meet the guidelines for permanence and durability of the Committee
on Production Guidelines for Book Longevity of the Council on
Library Resources

http://pup.princeton.edu

Printed in the United States of America

10 9 8 7 6 5 4 3 2 1

10 9 8 7 6 5 4 3 2 1
(Pbk.)

Dedicated to our Susans

Contents

Acknowledgments   ix

List of Contributors   xi

1. The Origins of Liberty
   Paul W. Drake and Mathew D. McCubbins   3

2. Limited Government and Liberal Markets: An Introduction
   to "Constitutions and Commitment"
   Douglass C. North and Barry R. Weingast   13

3. Constitutions and Commitment: The Evolution of
   Institutions Governing Public Choice in Seventeenth-Century
   England
   Douglass C. North and Barry R. Weingast   16

4. Democracy, Capital, Skill, and Country Size: Effects of
   Asset Mobility and Regime Monopoly on the Odds of
   Democratic Rule
   Ronald Rogowski   48

5. The International Causes of Democratization, 1974–1990
   Paul W. Drake   70

6. The Political Economy of Authoritarian Withdrawals
   Stephan Haggard and Robert R. Kaufman   92

7. When You Wish upon the Stars: Why the Generals (and
   Admirals) Say Yes to Latin American "Transitions" to
   Civilian Government
   Brian Loveman   115

8. Political Structure and Economic Liberalization: Conditions
   and Cases from the Developing World
   *William B. Heller, Philip Keefer, and
   Mathew D. McCubbins*   146

9. Afterword
   Paul W. Drake and Mathew D. McCubbins   179

References   181

Index   201

Acknowledgments _____

WE WISH to thank the Institute on Global Conflict and Cooperation at the University of California for a grant to study the international and national causes of democratization. These funds paid for a year-long seminar that produced most of the papers in this volume. In addition to the authors included here, D. Roderick Kiewiet, Roger Noll, Sharyn O'Halloran, Phil Roeder, Hilton L. Root, and Susan Shirk made valuable seminar presentations that helped shape our thinking on these issues. We thank *The Journal of Economic History* and Cambridge University Press for permission to reprint an article that appears in this volume as chapter 3. This endeavor also received support from the Project on Law and the Behavioral Sciences and from the Department of Political Science at the University of California, San Diego. We are grateful to them and to Jennifer Oh, who organized all the sessions.

List of Contributors _____

Paul W. Drake, Professor of Political Science and Dean of Social Sciences at the University of California, San Diego, and Institute of the Americas Chair for Inter-American Affairs

Stephan Haggard, Professor of International Relations and Pacific Studies at the School of International Relations and Pacific Studies at the University of California, San Diego

William B. Heller, Assistant Professor at University of Nebraska, Lincoln

Robert R. Kaufman, Professor of Political Science at Rutgers University

Philip Keefer, Economics in the Finance and Private Sector Development Division, Policy Research Division at the World Bank

Brian Loveman, Professor of Political Science at San Diego State University

Mathew D. McCubbins, Professor of Political Science at University of California, San Diego

Douglass C. North, Professor of Economics at Washington University and Nobel laureate in Economics

Ronald Rogowski, Professor and Chair of Political Science at University of California, Los Angeles

Barry R. Weingast, Professor and Chair of Political Science at Stanford University

THE ORIGINS OF LIBERTY

1

The Origins of Liberty

PAUL W. DRAKE AND MATHEW D. MCCUBBINS

WHY WOULD sovereigns ever grant political or economic liberty to their subjects? Under what conditions would a person or group that possesses ultimate authority over a society willingly give up any of that authority? What is the logic that leads power-and-purse-maximizing rational rulers to cede ground to other political and economic actors?

We will investigate both why a sovereign might liberalize and when. By "sovereign," we refer to the institutional locus of sovereignty. It is the supreme national political authority, with a monopoly on the legitimate use of force. That combination of state and regime can reside in a king, a dictator, an elected president or parliament, or any ruling body that exercises executive and legislative powers.

In this collection, our authors are usually asking what might motivate an authoritarian regime to make concessions to its subjects. We concentrate on autocrats as the toughest cases to explain because they are, by definition, the least likely to deliver liberties to their underlings. In a few instances, however, we will investigate the reasons why a democratic regime might expand the liberties of its citizens. We do so because liberalism is a continuum, not a dichotomous function, and we seek to explain why and whence it changes.

When discussing liberalization, we have in mind the standard concept of increasing the numbers and freedoms of competing participants in the political or economic system. This process involves opening the arena to a broader constellation of conflicting interests. We are discussing regimes that become more liberal—in the classic political or economic sense of expanding individual rights and freedoms—than they were before, without implying that they become paragons of liberalism. Of course, these are matters of degree. Despotic political systems may become less restrictive without becoming fully democratic in the historic Western mold of freely elected, representative, accountable institutions. Even if dictatorships do evolve into democracies, they may only meet

For comments on earlier drafts of this introduction, we wish to thank Bruce Bueno de Mesquita, Gary Cox, Peter Gourevitch, Eric Hershberg, Evelyne Huber, David Laitin, and Eduardo Silva.

the most narrow formal criteria for such systems. For example, they may recognize the people's rights to govern through elections, judicial procedures, and administrative processes, but they may retain severe constraints on those channels. To varying extents, all democracies are limited as to who can participate, who can govern, and what the governors can do.

Although most of the essays here concentrate on political changes, some—particularly that by Douglass North and Barry Weingast and that by William Heller, Philip Keefer, and Mathew McCubbins—also investigate economic reforms. Political liberalization and economic liberalization may or may not occur together. Economic liberalization usually includes the right to own private property and to exchange goods and services in markets relatively unencumbered by the state. However, few, if any, markets are totally free from government interference, although some are clearly less fettered than others. Moreover, we realize that political and economic organizations can offer greater equality of opportunity without improving social equity.

What are the central causes of liberalization? Obviously, it can be promoted by either the state or civil society, by elites or subordinates. Conceivably, openings can be generated from above or from below. Often the interaction, bargaining, tugging, and hauling between state power holders and other contenders determine the resulting degree of liberalization or even democratization. Scholars have argued frequently that political liberalization within authoritarian regimes depends on the balance of power and on negotiations—explicit or implicit—between dictators and democrats. Within that relationship, some analysts have shown that liberalization typically begins when the despots bestow some limited civil liberties on particular groups within society. This "top-down" approach was forcefully analyzed in the landmark multivolume study of transitions from authoritarian rule by Guillermo O'Donnell, Philippe C. Schmitter, and Laurence Whitehead (1986).

Our anthology carries that focus on elite-led cases a bit further by concentrating on the conditions under which ruling groups will initiate and carry out political or economic liberalization. In this volume, we are looking at the decisions and subsequent actions of sovereigns who preside over liberalization attempts. This book examines governments that are immune to revolutionary uprisings; they are too entrenched to be overthrown by force. When these rulers face conflict with their opposition, they can choose either to repress those that seek reform or to give in to demands to liberalize. They may choose liberalization for many reasons, including their own ideological propensities, reactions to exogenous shocks, or pressures from social or political movements. It goes without saying that one of the primary factors that policymakers take into account is the character and clout of their opponents.

Once liberalization is unleashed from above, it can take many courses. As it unfolds, the process can be reversed by reactionaries in the authoritarian camp, halted in midstream by clashing interests, or propelled on to full-blown democratization by reformers inside or outside the regime. Once in train, this process may go farther than the elites ever intended, perhaps damaging some of the interests they had thought they could preserve. Like anyone else, sovereigns can miscalculate, and they may have to recalculate as liberalization proceeds. These alternative outcomes assume that revolutionaries do not seize the initiative, for successful insurrections are few and far between.

As many scholars have established, even the triumph of democratization should not blind us to the limits and legacies left by authoritarians. Although the peaceful installation of representative, electoral democracy may be seen as a victory for democrats, it will seldom materialize except when it is also in the self-interest of the dictators. The essays in this volume argue that liberalization or democratization will rarely occur unless the authorities calculate that the expected benefits will exceed the costs for them and their preferences. As Alexis de Tocqueville in the 1830s observed about French politics from the twelfth to the nineteenth century:

> In the course of these seven hundred years, it sometimes happened that the nobles, in order to resist the authority of the crown, or to diminish the power of their rivals, granted some political influence to the common people. Or, more frequently, the king permitted the lower orders to have a share in the government, with the intention of depressing the aristocracy. In France, the kings have always been the most active and the most constant of levellers. (Tocqueville 1956, 27)

When will sovereigns conclude that they can maximize their benefits or minimize their costs by opening up spaces for their subjects to exercise political or economic freedoms? From the point of view of the logic of power holders, what analysis might convince them to cede some control over resources, whether people or property? Sovereigns have a certain amount of power and security, and when they decide to liberalize it is because they believe that this stock of leverage and safety will increase more or decrease less under a more liberal system. This collection proposes that peaceful transitions to less authoritarian political and economic systems are most likely to transpire when the existing autocrats are reaping some gains while retaining some protections of their welfare, rights, privileges, and interests.

Whenever the question of liberalization comes up, the chief of state will be wise to calculate carefully the potential costs and benefits. Some of the costs of liberalization a ruler might pay include increased risk of personal injury or death, less control over policy implementation, and uncertainty or losses in the economic sector. The benefits are more subtle, but they can include less political unrest, a more robust economy, and more efficient production of social services. Whatever the particular costs and benefits the sovereign envisions, his analysis is crucial to the inauguration and implementation of liberalization.

When choosing to reinforce or relax controls, the ruler's considerations reflect five main concerns. Conceivably, either repression or liberalization might be the best alternative for heads of state to attain their five goals:

(1) Personal welfare: When weighing a decision to intensify or relieve pressure, sovereigns will first evaluate which choice is best for their personal situation. Rulers have to preserve their own welfare in order to retain their power, maintain order, and enact policies. Above all, they will seek to avoid being punished—for example, by trial, imprisonment, exile, or execution. They will also try to enhance and insure their personal gains and safety, whether by exterminating their enemies or turning power over to their least hostile adversaries. During liberalization, the supreme authorities may structure the incentives created by the new institutions in such a way as to safeguard their lives and honor.

(2) Personal power: The ruler will also seek to obtain or retain as much personal power as possible. Either tightening or loosening the screws could conceivably incur the following costs: dividing the ruling coalition, alienating the security forces, weakening the rule of law, losing legitimacy, or forfeiting the office entirely. Only repression would entail the additional cost of paying the internal security forces and perhaps the added benefits of satisfying them and monopolizing resources. By contrast, only liberalization would carry the risks of having to share some resources and perhaps even turn power over to an unacceptable alternative. Despite those dangers, dictators might decide to lighten their hands in order to broaden the ruling coalition, reduce the cost and clout of the security forces, preserve some resources, or pass power on to a tolerable successor.

(3) Internal order: Either coercion or concessions, sticks or carrots could spread disobedience, conflict, violence, rebellion, or revolution. Conversely, both strategies have the potential to diminish and moderate the government's opponents, to mitigate strife and bloodshed, and to encourage obedience. Under varying circumstances, intimidation or co-optation might be equally effective at establishing tranquillity and avert-

ing upheaval. Improving civil liberties might have the added virtue of generating information and feedback from the citizenry as well as nurturing the consent of the governed.

(4) External order: The quest for national security, international respect, and peace abroad are all manifestations of the sovereign's desire for external order. An iron fist might be an effective means to those ends because it could frighten outsiders as well as insiders. However, a velvet glove might be more effective at defusing foreign animosity, attracting external cooperation, and convincing other democracies not to go to war against a fellow liberal state.

(5) Policy preferences: Policy goals would presumably include control over the government budget as well as over a host of public issues. The substantive agendas of particular sovereigns might be benevolent or malevolent for the rest of society. In most cases, the rulers' highest priority will be a healthy, stable, growing economy that pleases investors as well as consumers. Economic crises and downturns will render all other objectives less attainable, since depressions damage all governments, and no regime can survive without revenues.

A sovereign's reliance on either bullets or ballots could help or harm the economy. Brutality seems more likely to guarantee the hegemon almost exclusive domain over the budget and policies, whereas mercy could require the ruler to share fiscal resources and modify the policy choices available. Nevertheless, the autocrats as well as their subjects might see some economic advantages in liberalization. These positive features could include economic freedom, rule of law, sanctity of contracts and private property from government whims, checks and balances on arbitrary actions, vetoes against extreme policy shifts, less uncertainty about alternative rulers and programs, transparency of transactions, and reliable income for the state.

As sketched above, there are certain outcomes authorities want to achieve and others they want to avoid. In order to realize their five main objectives, they must always make a delicate calculation of the relative strengths of their proponents and opponents and the likely risks of alternative strategies. Thus, they must decide whether to repress or liberalize.

Since the potential benefits are greater, repression is usually tempting as the first option, especially when there is still some chance of maximizing gains. In most cases, only a heavy hand will allow the sovereign to optimize personal welfare, sustain a narrow governing coalition with whom to share spoils, satisfy the repressors, monopolize resources, extract maximum obedience, and implement budgets and policies without significant modifications or concessions. Most other benefits discussed in the preceding paragraphs could conceivably be obtained through either closing or opening the polity or economy, depending on the balance of forces between the ruler and the ruled.

Liberalization becomes more attractive to the sovereign when the odds are in favor of merely minimizing losses. The leader becomes willing to give up some assets so as not to sacrifice more, believing that benefits are more likely to be realized from lifting up rather than from clamping down the lid. In other words, toleration appears less expensive than persecution. One of the main attractions of opening safety valves is that it may allow the sovereign to rule with the consent of more of the governed, thus slashing police and transaction costs. However, letting off steam is extremely unlikely to be chosen voluntarily if it seems destined to lead to anarchy or to severe personal or policy losses for the ruler. Therefore, authoritarians will frequently try to build in safeguards to assure that liberalization does not result in chaos or regicide.

After balancing the costs and benefits inherent in all five categories and deciding that liberalization is a sound policy, when will a sovereign opt to carry out these changes? Four necessary conditions will have to be met. The first fundamental requirement is the existence and maintenance of order. It is a sine qua non for the survival of society, political or economic liberty notwithstanding.

Protection from the Hobbesian war of all against all—rampant disorder—is the root of the power of a sovereign, as the monopolist of legitimate force within a country. The authority to enforce laws and defend borders is a by-product of this monopoly. Government in general enjoys a comparative advantage in the production of force, and the ruler controls when and how this weapon is used. If the necessary order can be sustained without the application of massive firepower, then the extension of liberties may occur if three other conditions hold.

The second requirement is that the sovereign must possess unified power and purpose. To succeed at liberalization, the ruling body cannot be divided against itself. Even an absolute monarch with the desire and knowledge to liberalize might not be in a position to do so, such as when there is more than one decisive group within the country. Even in totalitarian regimes, factions within the governing strata can often act to oppose any attempt to liberalize the political or economic system.

In many nations, sovereign power is held by a group. How these people exercise authority is determined in part by how they make decisions. The institutional structures—the rules of the game—can shape outcomes. For example, if the dominant clique makes decisions by unanimous rule, then the decisive group is the entire sovereign. If, however, a sovereign legislature such as the English Parliament makes decisions by majority rule, then the decisive group is a little more than half of the membership. If there is no decisive group within the government who desires liberalization, then it will not occur.

In democracies, divided and coalitional government can lead to effective resistance to change. If, however, the sole source of force or authority resides within one decisive group, they can liberalize whenever they see fit. The converse of this premise is that policy losers are either not decisive or can be bought off. In the first instance, it must be the case that losers neither hold a veto position over policy change nor possess enough strength to hold the decisive group hostage. If losers from policy change are capable of exerting influence, then they must agree to go along with proposed changes. Losers of this type (who by virtue of their influence are important actors) can often be compensated for their losses with side payments.

Third, in order to liberalize, the sovereign must be capable of enforcing his policies within his own country. The sovereign must be a privileged group capable of supplying a public good, in this case liberty, of its own accord. We have previously discussed how the ability to prevent or end the Hobbesian war of all against all is the source of the sovereign's authority. The top decision maker must consolidate his or her own power before attempting to liberalize, but then he or she must also insure that he or she commands sufficient force to eliminate threats to this authority both at home and abroad.

Not all attempts to liberalize succeed, even in the presence of all the necessary conditions discussed above, as a ruler must satisfy a fourth condition: a credible commitment not to renege. In order to achieve this commitment, a chief executive may sometimes give up some political power for economic advancement, in effect selling off political assets for capital. In some cases, when rulers are insolvent, the only collateral or guarantee they can offer is their office. Credible commitments receive the most attention in this book in the essays by North and Weingast and by Heller, Keefer, and McCubbins, and to a lesser extent in the article by Loveman.

In selecting the chapters for this volume, we sought an unusual mixture of theoretical and empirical approaches to the question of why sovereigns might liberalize. Some authors employ abstract models of decision making, some statistical analysis, and some historical methods. We believe that this diversity of approaches is the most effective way to uncover the many different origins of liberty. Looking at this central question from a number of fresh perspectives helps to elucidate and debate the sufficient conditions for liberalization.

We realize that trying to generalize and theorize about this complex issue across centuries and borders slights many significant contextual, historical, regional, social, and cultural differences, contradictions, and nuances. Obviously, liberalization in seventeenth-century England had different meanings and imperatives than in twentieth-century Chile. Nevertheless, we feel that a broad sweep is necessary in order to abstract a model using simplifying assumptions. We have tried to balance those generalizations with enough case studies to show that our theory can be applied in the real world and has to be qualified there.

The authors vary as to which aspects of top-down liberalization they examine and highlight. All of the chapters offer both theoretical claims and empirical findings. Some tilt more toward abstractions, while others lean more toward case materials. Theoretically inclined social scientists may be more satisfied with the essays that emphasize principles and axioms, while area or historical specialists may be more pleased with the contributions that spotlight the idiosyncrasies and complexities of time and place. Combined, these approaches provide both grand generalizations and rich examples. In our view, these two approaches are necessary, complementary, and too seldom brought together. Whether concentrating more on the forest or the trees, all of the chapters address and illuminate the unifying question of why and when rulers are prone to liberalize.

In their chapters, Douglass North and Barry Weingast ask why a king would choose, however reluctantly, to yield to subjects demanding participation and rights. The authors unveil the conditions that favored liberalization in England in the seventeenth century. As in many of our cases, exogenous factors provided important motivations for changing the rules of the game in the direction of liberalization. Britain and France were at war, and the English monarch needed money to defend the realm. In order to secure this capital, the monarch needed to make a commitment to pay back all debts. If he could not commit himself in some credible way, then the interest rates would be too high and the amount too small. This commitment was made credible by liberalizing the political institutions of England. In short, the Stuart king abdicated some of his political power to insure his safety and well-being. The crown created an independent judiciary and legislature in what has become known as the bloodless revolution. This accomplished his principal goal of personal security at the expense of the secondary goal of personal power. Like several of our authors, North and Weingast emphasize the role of institutions, demonstrating that new institutional arrangements helped a government to make credible commitments to restrain its own behavior and thus facilitated tandem political and economic liberalization.

Ronald Rogowski's contribution to this volume addresses the question of why the rulers of some types of countries are more likely to liberalize and democratize than others. He explains why democracy is more prevalent in nations blessed with abundant physical and human capital but that have small populations. A key factor is a sovereign's reaction to capital flight. A credible commitment to secure property rights is necessary to encourage investment. In particular, Rogowski focuses on human-capital flight and the development of democracy as a response to the expanding needs of the labor market. As the populace grows wealthier and better educated, its human capital becomes more valuable. In order to maintain high levels of human capital, an authoritarian regime may well liberalize rather than risk losing its most precious assets, the people.

Paul Drake analyzes the issue of why so many despots relinquished perquisites and power in the tidal wave of democratization from the 1970s to the 1990s. He argues that the effect of the international climate on their options and decisions has been underestimated. He studies two types of external factors. First, some conditions, such as economic downturns, could have disrupted order under any kind of regime, but in this historical cycle they mainly undermined dictatorships; these elements provoked regime alterations without determining the direction of change. Second, other factors, such as ideological influences, encouraged a particular type of change, in this period inducing tyrants to liberalize instead of lash out. In another era, such as the 1930s, economic crises could topple democracies, which foreign ideologies could promote replacing with dictatorships. With an emphasis on Latin America, Drake illustrates the significance of such global forces in recent years by showing their impact on Chile's Augusto Pinochet, a dictator who seemed exceptionally impervious to outside pressures.

Exploring similar questions in the same decades of democratization, Stephan Haggard and Robert Kaufman disaggregate that global phenomenon. They investigate which types of authoritarian regimes were most susceptible to international forces and others encouraging transitions toward democracy. They underscore the differential impact of economic trends and crises on varying configurations of authoritarian institutions and coalitions. Concentrating on Latin America and Asia, Haggard and Kaufman conclude that divided military governments were more likely to acquiesce in liberalization than were unified military regimes or dominant party systems. They warn, however, that democratic sovereigns are also vulnerable to exogenous shocks.

Looking at a subset of authoritarian rulers, Brian Loveman inquires as to why Latin American militaries, despite their ability to rule by force, are willing to give ground to civilians. He shows that the armed forces, like other sovereigns, may promote democracy out of their own personal, institutional, and programmatic self-interests. Lacking legitimacy as permanent rulers, the military grants liberties to civilians but only within limits and only with guarantees for its own institutional protection, needs, and values. Loveman reminds us that since the armed forces left office largely on their own terms, they can also return to power for their own reasons.

Addressing a somewhat different puzzle about liberalization by sovereigns, William Heller, Philip Keefer, and Mathew McCubbins explain why both authoritarian and democratic governments in developing countries have become surprisingly willing to shrink themselves in the interest of economic liberalization. These leaders divest themselves of certain powers in the pursuit of economic efficiency and growth. Drawing on examples from Latin America and Asia, the authors establish that a sovereign needs the desire, ability, and knowledge to open up the economy. These reforms succeed only when policy makers want change, control the necessary political and institutional resources, and possess adequate expertise to make the new laws produce the desired results. Further, they show how institutional variations play an important role in determining the nature and extent of liberalization. Finally, Heller, Keefer, and McCubbins underscore how a credible commitment to carry out and maintain the proposed reforms is necessary to make the transition permanent.

As all our authors show, the origins of liberty usually lie in the calculations of its supposed enemies. It is often a self-interested sovereign, fearing losses, disorder, insurrection, revolution, or foreign defeat, that institutes liberal political or economic policies. Liberalization and democratization can also emerge from the grass roots, but that is only part of the story and perhaps not the decisive part. In their struggle for liberty, its champions should realize that, since they lack superior force, they are more likely to succeed if they can convince the ruler that concessions are in his self-interest. In order to explain why and when sovereigns will decide to liberalize, it is necessary to explore further the logic of liberalization from their perspective.

2

Limited Government and Liberal Markets

AN INTRODUCTION TO "CONSTITUTIONS
AND COMMITMENT"

DOUGLASS C. NORTH AND BARRY R. WEINGAST

THE ARDUOUS struggle over economic and political reform in the former socialist states demonstrates that governments cannot legislate the creation of free markets and political participation without limiting their own power to change this legislation at their convenience. Enforcing the limits inherent in markets and democracy requires that political officials find it in their own interest to abide by these limits—that is, that these limits be self-enforcing (North and Weingast 1989, Ordeshook 1993, Przeworski 1991, and Weingast 1995). Here, we will explain that the English monarch's creation of an independent judiciary and legislature in 1688 was an attempt to produce self-enforcing limits on his own actions in order to commit himself credibly to the market reforms he desired. These reforms were necessary for the crown to borrow the capital that England needed to prosecute a war with France.

The ability of a government to borrow depends on the security and stability of the debt instruments it can provide. In effect, a government trades certain property rights (such as the enforcement of debt instruments) for revenue. The availability of capital to the sovereign from the market is a direct function of the commitment a monarch has to the property rights of all who reside or trade within his or her influence of power. In order to ensure property rights, a sovereign has two possible strategies. First, the sovereign can establish a reputation for fulfilling obligations and paying debts. Alternatively, he or she can constrain himself in such a way as to make reneging on public debts expensive or impossible. The two strategies are functionally equivalent—in both cases, the ruler guarantees property rights and receives the benefits of increased access to capital—but they differ in practice.

If a sovereign relies on a good reputation as a commitment to fulfill his or her end of the bargain, there are several pitfalls. Even the most benevolent sovereign, who not only desires a good reputation but would pay heavily to ensure it, cannot commit future sovereigns to this same path. Thus, access to capital depends on the health and safety of the monarch. Ironically, the times when a monarch needs access to capital the most are when his or her security is the most threatened (war, famine, or natural disaster). Thus, even the most benevolent sovereign cannot depend on reputation to provide the needed access to capital. A second pitfall comes when the ruler is not so benevolent. The value of his or her reputation is worthless if he or she is deposed, so when funds are needed, the short-term benefits of seizing property (reneging on the promise to provide property rights for income) outweigh the long-term benefits of a good reputation. Thus, while a good reputation is valuable, the commitment it entails is not credible to investors.

Under the second option, in which a monarch's power is constrained in such a way as to make reneging expensive or impossible, the commitment becomes credible. If the penalties for reneging are greater than the benefits, there is little doubt that the sovereign will fulfill his or her end of the bargain and uphold property rights. The external security of property rights makes the investment attractive to financiers, allows a greater access to public funds, and lowers the sovereign's transaction costs (in the form of economies of scale, lower interest rates, and greater national security).

The two divergent paths can be seen in the cases of England and France in the seventeenth century. In both cases, the monarch was faced with the need for capital to fight a war, in this case with each other. Both monarchs secured finances on the benefits of their reputations, in England in the form of forced loans and in France in the form of selling titles and granting monopolies. In both cases, the incentive to defect was too great, and accordingly each monarch seized property rights: In England, the loan payments were delayed, reduced, and sometimes ignored; in France, contrary to the monarch's promise, more titles were sold, reducing the value to current officeholders.

By reneging on their contracts, both monarchs achieved short-term gain at the expense of long-term considerations. We characterize any contract with a monarch as an iterative prisoner's dilemma with complete information. The more often a monarch reneges, the less likely anyone will be to invest because there is no guarantee he or she will not defect after you cooperate. Therefore, since the incentive to defect will always be present, the more iterations there are—that is, the more often a monarch tries to borrow money—the less likely he or she will be able to do so. Both monarchs were in this position when they chose to adopt a strategy of self-constraint.

The difference between France and England was that France had a standing army, while England did not. When the English monarch was faced with pressure to constrain himself, there was no army to quell the revolution, and the monarch was deposed. In France, there was no real threat of revolution, so the monarch was safe. Because the French king was safe, he sold monopoly rights to corporations and guilds in order to secure loans, allowing the king to borrow much more than before (Root 1989). His commitment to the corporations made his commitment to property rights credible. In England, however, even after the revolution, there was no credible way to constrain the monarch, and thus the king was reinstated so the state could borrow from his reputation again. However, the Glorious Revolution of 1688 allowed monarchal constraint by creating an independent judiciary immune from any reprisals from the king and a separate legislature that was no longer dependent on royal whims. By instituting a representative government with internal checks against reneging on contracts, the English government was able to secure huge sums of money from creditors at favorable interest rates.

In both cases, the monarch could not depend on reputation to borrow money and attempted to make a credible commitment to repay debts by constraining the possibility of reneging. In France, this was done by creating a powerful class of corporate financiers, and in England by democratization. The most efficient method was England's, which allowed an astounding increase in the amount of credit available to the monarch. Both monarchs traded some of their power for capital: France traded it to elite creditors, England traded it to the populace. England's monarch abdicated, allowing his country to win the war. In the next chapter, we explore the nature of the Glorious Revolution of 1688 with respect to the financing of loans and the credibility of the English King's commitment to repay these loans.

3

Constitutions and Commitment

THE EVOLUTION OF INSTITUTIONS GOVERNING PUBLIC
CHOICE IN SEVENTEENTH-CENTURY ENGLAND

DOUGLASS C. NORTH AND BARRY R. WEINGAST

THIS ARTICLE focuses on the political factors underpinning economic growth and the development of markets—not simply the rules governing economic exchange, but also the institutions governing how these rules are enforced and how they may be changed. A critical political factor is the degree to which the regime or sovereign is committed to or bound by these rules. Rules the sovereign can readily revise differ significantly in their implications for performance from exactly the same rules when not subject to revision. The more likely it is that the sovereign will alter property rights for his or her own benefit, the lower the expected returns from investment and the lower in turn the incentive to invest. For economic growth to occur, the sovereign or government must not merely establish the relevant set of rights, but must make a credible commitment to them.

A ruler can establish such commitment in two ways. One is by setting a precedent of "responsible behavior," appearing to be committed to a set of rules that he or she will consistently enforce. The second is by being constrained to obey a set of rules that do not permit leeway for violating commitments. We have very seldom observed the former, in good part because the pressures and continual strain of fiscal necessity eventually led rulers to "irresponsible behavior" and the violation of agreements. The latter story is, however, the one we tell.

The Journal of Economic History, Vol. XLIX, No. 4 (Dec. 1989) © The Economic History Association. All rights reserved. ISSN 0022-0507. Reprinted with the permission of Cambridge University Press.

The authors gratefully acknowledge the helpful comments of Robert Bates, Gary Cox, Paul David, Aaron Director, John Ferejohn, Jack Goldstone, Max Hartwell, Derek Hirst, Leonard Hochberg, Paul Milgrom, Glenn Nichols, Roger Noll, Alvin Rabushka, Thomas Sargent, Kenneth Shepsle, Gordon Tullock, and David Weir. They also thank Elisabeth Case for her editorial assistance. Barry Weingast thanks the National Science Foundation (grant no. SES-8617516) for partial support.

We attempt to explain the evolution of political institutions in seventeenth-century England, focusing on the fundamental institutions of representative government emerging out of the Glorious Revolution of 1688—a Parliament with a central role alongside the Crown and a judiciary independent of the Crown. In the early seventeenth century fiscal needs led to increased levels of "arbitrary" government, that is, to expropriation of wealth through redefinition of rights in the sovereign's favor. This led, ultimately, to civil war. Several failed experiments with alternative political institutions in turn ushered in the restoration of the monarchy in 1660. This too failed, resulting in the Glorious Revolution of 1688 and its fundamental redesign of the fiscal and governmental institutions.

To explain the changes following the Glorious Revolution, we first characterize the problem that the designers of the new institutions sought to solve, namely, control over the exercise of arbitrary and confiscatory power by the Crown.[1] We then show how, given the means, motives, and behavior of the king during this century, the institutional changes altered the incentives of governmental actors in a manner desired by the winners of the Revolution. These changes reflected an explicit attempt to make credible the government's ability to honor its commitments. Explicit limits on the Crown's ability *unilaterally* to alter the terms of its agreements played a key role here, for after the Glorious Revolution the Crown had to obtain Parliamentary assent to changes in its agreements. As Parliament represented wealth holders, its increased role markedly reduced the king's ability to renege. Moreover, the institutional structure that evolved after 1688 did not provide incentives for Parliament to replace the Crown and itself engage in similar "irresponsible" behavior. As a consequence the new institutions produced a marked increase in the security of private rights.

As evidence in favor of our thesis, we study the remarkable changes in capital markets over this period. After the first few years of the Stuarts' reign, the Crown was not able systematically to raise funds. By the second decade of the seventeenth century, under mounting fiscal pressure, the Crown resorted to a series of "forced loans," indicating that it could not raise funds at rates it was willing to pay. Following the Glorious Revolution, however, not only did the government become financially solvent, but it gained access to an unprecedented level of funds. In just nine years (from 1688 to 1697), government borrowing increased by more than an order of magnitude. This sharp change in the

---

[1] Our discussion of the events prior to the Glorious Revolution (1603 to 1688) simply characterizes this period; it does not model or explain it. Moreover, since our history emphasizes the problems the winners (the Whigs) sought to solve, it necessarily contains strong elements of "Whig" history.

willingness of lenders to supply funds must reflect a substantial increase in the perceived commitment by the government to honor its agreements. The evidence shows that these expectations were borne out, and that this pattern extends well into the next century.

Since we focus on the evolution and impact of the political institutions, of necessity we slight the larger economic and religious context, even though in many specific instances these larger religious and economic issues were proximate sources of actions and policies that we describe. Indeed, no history of the seventeenth century is complete that does not describe both the growing markets and the evolving organizations that accompanied economic expansion as well as the persistent religious tensions, particularly between Catholic and Protestant. A more thorough study, one far too big for this essay, would attempt to integrate the change in opportunity costs of both the economic and *religious* actors as they intermingled with the immediate political issues on which we concentrate. But having said that, it is important to stress that our central thesis is a key part of the whole process by which an institutional framework evolved in England. We contend that while the English economy had been expanding and its markets growing, in order for economic development to continue the constraints described below had to be altered.

This essay proceeds as follows. Section I develops the importance of political institutions and the constitution and their relevance for the sections that follow. Sections II and III develop the narrative of the period, focusing respectively on England under the Stuarts and on the evolution of new institutions and secure rights following the Glorious Revolution. Section IV contains the central part of our analysis and reveals why these institutions made *credible* the government's commitment to honoring its agreements. Sections V and VI present our evidence from public and private capital markets.

I. The Role of Political Institutions and the Constitution

The control of coercive power by the state for social ends has been a central dilemma throughout history. A critical role of the constitution and other political institutions is to place restrictions on the state or sovereign. These institutions in part determine whether the state produces rules and regulations that benefit a small elite and so provide little prospect for long-run growth, or whether it produces rules that foster long-term growth. Put simply, successful long-run economic performance requires appropriate incentives not only for economic actors but for political actors as well.

Because the state has a comparative advantage in coercion, what prevents it from using violence to extract all the surplus?[2] Clearly it is not always in the ruler's interests to use power arbitrarily or indiscriminately; by striking a bargain with constituents that provides them some security, the state can often increase its revenue. But this alone is insufficient to guarantee consistent behavior on the part of the ruler.

The literature on transactions costs and institutions emphasizes that while parties may have strong incentives to strike a bargain, their incentives after the fact are not always compatible with maintaining the agreement: compliance is always a potential problem. This literature also notes that when ex post problems are anticipated ex ante, parties will attempt to alter incentives, devising institutions or constitutions that promote compliance with bargains after the fact. Oliver Williamson says:

> Transactions that are subject to ex post opportunism will benefit if appropriate actions can be devised ex ante. Rather than reply to opportunism in kind, the wise [bargaining party] is one who seeks both to give and receive "credible commitments." Incentives may be realigned and/or superior governance structures within which to organize transactions may be devised.[3]

Problems of compliance can be reduced or eliminated when the institutions are carefully chosen so as to match the anticipated incentive problems. Under these circumstances, parties are more likely to enter into and maintain complex bargains that prevent abuse of political control by the state.

To succeed in this role, a constitution must arise from the bargaining context between the state and constituents such that its provisions carefully match the potential enforcement problems among the relevant parties. The constitution must be *self-enforcing* in the sense that the major parties to the bargain must have an incentive to abide by the bargain after it is made.[4]

---

[2] Throughout late medieval and early modern times, if rulers did not maintain a comparative advantage in coercion, they soon failed to be rulers. See William McNeill, *Pursuit of Power* (Chicago, 1983); Douglass North, *Structure and Change in Economic History* (New York, 1981); and Gordon Tullock, *Autocracy* (Dordrecht, 1987).

[3] Oliver Williamson, *Economic Institutions of Capitalism* (New York, 1985), pp. 48–49.

[4] Our formulation of the problem draws on the "new economics of organization." Application of this approach to political problems—and especially to the problem of providing institutions to enforce bargains over time—is just beginning. See, however, Barry R. Weingast and William Marshall, "The Industrial Organization of Congress; or Why Legislatures, Like Firms, Are Not Organized as Markets," *Journal of Political Economy*, 96 (Feb. 1988), pp. 132–63; and Terry Moe, "The New Economics of Organization," *American Journal of Political Science*, 28 (Aug. 1984), pp. 739–77.

Consider a loan to a sovereign in which the ruler promises to return the principal along with interest at a specified date. What prevents the sovereign from simply ignoring the agreement and keeping the money? Reputation has long been noted as an important factor in limiting a sovereign's incentive to renege, and this approach has recently been formalized in the elegant models of modern game theory. The "long arm of the future" provides incentives to honor the loan agreement today so as to retain the opportunity for funds tomorrow. In many of the simple repeated games studied in the literature, this incentive alone is sufficient to prevent reneging.

Yet it is also well known that there are circumstances where this mechanism alone fails to prevent reneging.[5] In the context of current Third World debt, Jeremy Bullow and Kenneth Rogoff show that repeat play alone is insufficient to police reneging, and that more complex institutional arrangements are necessary. Similarly, in the medieval context, John Veitch has recently shown that medieval states had strong but not unambiguous incentives to develop reputations for honoring debt commitments, and that by and large they did so. Nonetheless, a series of major repudiations occurred when a second and typically more plentiful source of funds emerged. Edward I confiscated the wealth of the Jews in the late thirteenth century once the Italian merchants began operating on a larger scale; Philip IV confiscated the wealth of the Templars under similar circumstances.

One important context in which repeat play alone is insufficient to police repudiation concerns variations in the sovereign's time preference or discount rate. States in early modern Europe were frequently at war. Since wars became increasingly expensive over the period, putting increasingly larger fiscal demands on the sovereign, the survival of the sovereign and regime was placed at risk. When survival was at stake, the sovereign would heavily discount the future, making the one-time gain of reneging more attractive relative to the future opportunities forgone. Indeed, there is a long history of reneging under the fiscal strain accompanying major wars.[6]

---

[5] Paul R. Milgrom, Douglass C. North, and Barry R. Weingast, "The Role of Institutions in the Revival of Trade, Part I: The Medieval Law Merchant," Mimeo., Hoover Institution, Stanford University, 1989. Jeremy Bullow and Kenneth Rogoff, "A Constant Recontracting Model of Sovereign Debt," *Journal of Political Economy*, 97 (Feb. 1989), pp. 155–78; John M. Veitch, "Repudiations and Confiscations by the Medieval State," *Journal of Economic History*, 46 (Mar. 1986), pp. 31–36.

[6] Joseph Schumpeter, "Fiscal Crises and the Tax State," in Richard A. Musgrave and Alan T. Peacock, eds., *Classics in the Theory of Public Finance* (London, 1962). John Hicks, *A Theory of Economic History* (Oxford, 1969). North, *Structure and Change*, and Veitch, "Repudiations and Confiscations." This is not to say that the sovereign will *never* honor commitments, only that he will not *always* do so.

The insufficiency of repeat play and reputation to prevent reneging provides for the role of political institutions. If the problem of variable discount rates is sufficiently important, individuals have an incentive to devise institutions to protect against reneging. It is important to observe that these institutions do not substitute for reputation-building and associated punishment strategies, but complement them.[7] Appropriately chosen institutions can improve the efficacy of the reputation mechanism by acting as a constraint in precisely those circumstances where reputation alone is insufficient to prevent reneging. The literature on the theory of the firm is replete with illustrations of how specific institutional features of the firm are necessary to mitigate an incentive problem that is insufficiently policed by reputation.[8]

This view provides an endogenous role for political institutions. Restrictions on the ex post behavior of the state improve the state's ability to maintain its part of bargains with constituents, for example, not to expropriate their wealth.[9] As we show below, this logic can be used to interpret the institutional changes at the time of the Glorious Revolution.

Our view also implies that the development of free markets must be accompanied by some credible restrictions on the state's ability to manipulate economic rules to the advantage of itself and its constituents. Successful economic performance, therefore, must be accompanied by institutions that limit economic intervention and allow private rights and markets to prevail in large segments of the economy. Put another way, because constitutional restrictions must be self-enforcing, they must serve to establish a credible commitment by the state to abide by them. Absolutist states which faced no such constraint, such as early modern Spain, created economic conditions that retarded long-run economic growth.

The ability of a government to commit to private rights and exchange is thus an essential condition for growth. It is also, as we shall see, a central issue in the constitutional debate in seventeenth-century England.

[7] Weingast and Marshall, "Industrial Organization of Congress"; Milgrom, North, and Weingast, "The Role of Institutions."

[8] Vertical integration is the standard example: because of potential transactions problems due to "asset specificity" or "appropriable quasi-rents," firms that internalize the problem via vertical integration outperform those which do not. See Williamson, *Economic Institutions*.

[9] In this sense our argument parallels that of James Buchanan and Geoffrey Brennan, who argue that the "recognition of the temporal dimensionality of choice provides one 'reason for rules'—rules that will impose binding constraints on choice options after the rules themselves have been established." James Buchanan and Geoffrey Brennan, *Reason of Rules* (Cambridge, 1981), p. 67.

II. England under the Stuarts: Limited Credible
Commitment to Rights

After the Crown passed from the Tudors to the Stuarts in 1603, revenue problems and their consequences become increasingly important. At this time the king was expected to "live on his own," that is, to fund the government in the manner of an extended household. The execution of public laws and expenditures was not subject to a public budgetary process, and Parliament played only a small role in the decisions over expenditure and investment. The Crown therefore had considerable discretionary power over how and on what the money was spent. Parliament's main source of influence over policy resulted from its power to provide the Crown with tax revenue, typically for extraordinary purposes such as various wars. Parliament was also responsible for granting the Crown its revenue from other sources, such as customs, but in practice, the Stuarts, particularly Charles I, continued to collect the revenue without parliamentary consent.

Throughout the Stuart period revenue from traditional sources did not match expenditures. While figures for government expenditures during the Stuart period have not been collected as systematically as for the period following the Glorious Revolution, the following picture emerges.

At the beginning of the Stuarts' reign, Crown lands produced roughly half the annual revenue. To make up annual shortfalls, the Crown regularly resorted to sale of these lands.[10] Following the war with Spain in 1588, Elizabeth had sold 25 percent of the lands, raising £750,000. Still, James I inherited sizable debts from Elizabeth's war. Over his reign (1603–1625), another 25 percent of Crown lands were sold, and the remainder went during the reign of his son, Charles I (1625–1641). Sale of a major portion of a revenue-producing asset for annual expenses indicates the revenue problem was endemic. It also implies that over time the revenue problem had to get worse, for with every sale the expected future revenue declined. And, indeed, as Table 3.1 shows, for the year 1617 total revenue did not match expenditures, leaving a deficit of £36,000 or of just under 10 percent of expenditures.

Under the Stuarts, therefore, the search for new sources of revenue became a major priority. An important new source which produced conflict between the Crown and Parliament was the raising of customs revenues through new "impositions." Indeed, in the 1630s such in-

---

[10] See, for example, Derek Hirst, *Authority and Conflict: England, 1603–1658* (Cambridge, MA, 1986), chap. 4, and Lawrence Stone, *The Crisis of the Aristocracy, 1558–1641* (Oxford, 1965).

TABLE 3.1
Revenue Sources and Expenditure Levels, 1617

Revenue Source	Amount (£/year)
Crown Lands	£80,000
Customs and "new impositions"	190,000
Wards and so forth (besides purveyance)	180,000
Total Revenue	450,000
Total Expenditures	486,000
Deficit	36,000

Source: David Hume, *The History of England* (Indianapolis, 1983), appendix to "The Reign of James I."

creases almost brought financial solvency, and with it the ability of the Crown to survive without calling Parliament.

Another method used by the Crown to raise revenue was to demand loans. The Crown did not, however, develop a systematic, regular relationship with moneyed interests, negotiating a series of loans in which it honored today's agreements because it wanted to avail itself of future loan opportunities. Indeed, just the opposite occurred. The Stuarts secured most of their loans under threat; hence they are known as "forced loans," of which more later. Repayment was highly unpredictable and never on the terms of the original agreement. In the forced loan of 1604/5 the Crown borrowed £111,891, nominally for one year; "although . . . ultimately repaid, £20,363 . . . was still due as late as December 1609."[11] The forced loan of 1617 (just under £100,000) was not repaid until 1628. The Crown behaved similarly on loans from 1611 and 1625. As time went on, such loans came to look more and more like taxes, but because these were nominally loans the Crown did not need parliamentary assent.[12]

The Crown's inability to honor its contractual agreements for borrowed funds is a visible indicator of its readiness to alter the rights of private parties in its own favor. Despite the significant incentive provided by the desire to raise funds in the future, the Crown followed its

[11] Robert Ashton, *The Crown and the Money Market, 1603–1640* (Oxford, 1960), p. 35.

[12] Ashton, *Crown and the Money Market*, p. 36. Richard Cust, in his recent study of the 1626 forced loan, provides several instances of sanctions imposed on individuals refusing to provide funds: leading refusers were "either committed to prison or pressed in readiness for service abroad." Richard Cust, *The Forced Loans and English Politics* (Oxford, 1987), p. 3.

short-run interests, reneging on the terms to which it had agreed. As noted above, this type of behavior was not unique to England.

A second revenue-raising method was the sale of monopolies. While not the most important source of new revenue, it is particularly instructive because of its economic consequences.[13] In order to raise revenue in this manner, the Crown used patents in a new way. Originally designed to protect and promote the invention of new processes, patents came to be used to "reduce settled industries to monopolies under cover of technical improvements."[14] From a revenue standpoint, the best sources of new monopoly rights involved an economic activity that was profitable and whose participants were not part of the king's constituency. This led to a systematic search for and expropriation of quasi-rents in the economy. Moreover, as we will see in the next section, the Crown utilized a different system for enforcing these grants than that used for the older mercantilist controls, and one that was considerably more responsive to the Crown's interests. The system involved circumventing existing rights and the institutions designed to protect these rights.

Grants of monopoly clearly disrupted both existing economic interests in the targeted activity and those who depended on it (for example, suppliers and consumers). Monopoly grants thus acted as a tax that, since it expropriated the value of existing investment as well as future profits, was considerably greater at the margin than a 100 percent tax on profits. This risk lowered the rewards from all such new investments and hence discouraged their undertaking.

Beyond grants of monopoly, James, and especially Charles, used a variety of other, more subtle forms of expropriation of wealth. Because so many dimensions of public policy were involved, the political risk to citizens increased substantially over previous times. One important example was expansion of the peerage by the Crown, again in exchange for revenue.[15] While this expansion had broad social, cultural, and ideological implications, it also had significantly negative effects on existing peers. Expansion of the size of the House of Lords altered the value of an existing seat since it limited the ability of existing lords to protect themselves against the Crown.[16] Between the coronation of James I and

---

[13] Robert B. Ekelund and Robert D. Tollison, *Mercantilism as a Rent-Seeking Society* (College Station, 1981).

[14] W. Price, *English Patents of Monopoly* (Boston, 1906). Examples include soap, tobacco, and starch.

[15] F. W. Maitland, *Constitutional History of England* (Cambridge, 1908); Wallace Notestein, *The Winning of the Initiative by the House of Commons* (London, 1924); and Stone, *Crisis of the Aristocracy*.

[16] There were two separate reasons for this: the total number of voters was increasing, and the expansion added new members whose views systematically differed from those of

the outbreak of the Civil War, the Stuarts' sale of peerages doubled the number of lay peers.

Governmental power was used in other ways to raise revenue. Employing the ancient power of purveyance, agents of the Crown seized various goods for "public purposes," paying prices well below market. Purveyance brought in an annual "unvoted" tax of £40,000 in the 1620s.[17] James also put hereditary titles up for sale: for example, offering to sell the title of baronet for £1,095 and promising that only a fixed number would be sold. This brought in £90,000 by 1614. But James soon reneged on this, lowering the price and selling more than the promised number. By 1622, the price had fallen to £220.[18] Through the court of wards, the Crown managed the estates which had passed to minors. These were often openly run for the advantage of the Crown, not infrequently extracting the full value of the estate.[19] The Crown put "dispensations" up for sale, that is, the use of its powers to allow specific individuals to dispense with a specific law or restriction. "Sale" of this power was often used in conjunction with the enforcement or threat of enforcement of regulations that had not been enforced for years. At times the Crown simply seized the property of citizens. An especially egregious example occurred in 1640 when "the government seized £130,000 of bullion which private merchants had placed in the Tower for safety, causing numerous bankruptcies."[20]

This clash of interests between the king on the one hand and wealth holders and taxpayers on the other was a major reason why the Crown failed to obtain grants from Parliament. In exchange for grants, Parliament demanded conditions and limits on the king's power that he was unwilling to accept. Parliamentary interests thereby exacerbated the problem they were attempting to eliminate. Withholding funds worsened the Crown's fiscal problems and intensified its search for alternative sources of revenue.

Institutional Basis of Stuart Policymaking

Both Parliament and the common law courts fought the Crown's use of monopolies and other changes in rights in its search for revenue. Parlia-

---

existing nobles. The exchange that brought new nobles to the Lords undoubtedly entailed a commitment of support for the king.

[17] Hirst, *Authority and Conflict*, p. 103; and C. Hill, *Century of Revolution, 1603–1714* (2nd edn., New York, 1980), chap 4. See also John Kenyon, *Stuart England* (2nd edn., New York, 1985).

[18] Hirst, *Authority and Conflict*, pp. 113–14.

[19] Ibid., p. 103.

[20] C. Hill, *Century of Revolution*, p. 103.

ment regularly presented the king with "grievances," lists of problems caused by the king that it wanted addressed.[21] Grievances were part of a larger bargaining process in which Parliament attempted, in exchange for revenue, to limit the Crown's power and its use of policymaking to expropriate wealth. Because of ever-present revenue problems, the Stuarts often called on Parliament for additional revenue. Parliamentary interests regularly demanded that in exchange for revenue the Crown respect traditional property rights and institutions: for example, that it cease declaring new monopolies. The Crown, in turn, was evidently unwilling to accept these restrictions and hence Parliament was often dissolved without having come to an agreement with the Crown.[22]

Attempts were also made to prevent the Crown's using the law to further its objectives. In 1624 Parliament passed the much-noted Statute of Monopolies prohibiting the use of patents to grant monopolies to existing businesses in exchange for revenue. In this manner it attempted to assert the traditional rights of secure property. In addition common law courts handed down the famous "Case of Monopolies" in 1601, making the Crown's use of monopolies illegal in common law. The Crown, however, was able to evade these restrictions. While these evasions often took forms of questionable legality, so long as the Crown did not depend on Parliament for revenue, it was able to use them in practice.

Understanding the subsequent institutional reaction to these royal policies requires that we study the institutional means by which the Crown ran the government. For our purposes three elements of the royal powers and institutions were central to the Crown's success. First, a major source of power for the Crown was the royal prerogative, by which the Crown issued proclamations or royal ordinances. By this means it could issue new rules; that is, it had quasi-legislative powers without recourse to Parliament. Crown rules were enforced, not through the common law court system, but through the prerogative courts and included the power to suspend laws and to dispense with laws for specific individuals.[23]

---

[21] For details, see Notestein, *The Winning of the Initiative*.

[22] Part of the Crown's motivation appears to have been a desire to move toward the absolutism prevalent on the continent, notably in France and Spain. As Kenyon observes, at the onset of the seventeenth century, "any further adjustments [in the balance of power between Parliament and the Crown] were likely to be at the expense of Parliament" (Kenyon, *Stuart England*, p. 43). It almost succeeded. Hirst describes debates in Parliament in which the participants were explicitly concerned with this possibility (Hirst, *Authority and Conflict*, chap. 3).

[23] Dispensations for individuals, like most powers under the Stuarts, were put up for sale (Maitland, *Constitutional History*, pt. IV).

Second, the Star Chamber, combining legislative, executive, and judicial powers, played a key role. On issues concerning prerogative, the Star Chamber had come to have final say, and could in certain circumstances reverse judgments against the Crown.[24]

Finally, since the Crown was personally responsible for day-to-day government operations, it paid the judges, who served at its pleasure. Increasingly the Stuarts used their power over judges to influence their judgments. Judges—Chief Justices Coke (1616/17) and Crew (1627)—were openly fired for ruling against the Crown. Ultimately this tactic produced judges who by and large supported the Crown.[25]

The effect of these institutions was to combine in the Crown executive, legislative, and judicial powers, limiting external institutional checks. While royal proclamations did not have the same legal status as an act of Parliament, they were enforced directly through the common law courts. While these courts did not have to go along with the king—and often did not—ultimately he won through the higher court, the Star Chamber. Thus, while the common law was often against the king, the king could alter the jurisdiction of a dispute by issuing proclamations. The expanded use of the Star Chamber and the successful running of the government for substantial periods without Parliament limited the ability of traditional institutions to constrain the Crown. Effective possession of legislative and judicial powers also gave the Crown the ability to alter economic and political rights when it was convenient to do so. In comparison with the previous century, the rights that Parliament and other institutions were designed to protect were considerably less secure.

In response, a coalition formed against the Crown, seeking to preserve personal liberties, rights, and wealth. This raised the stakes of the political game to the various economic interests—in particular the value of opposing the king rose. Moreover, because the Crown attempted to extract from its own constituents a major portion of the advantages it had bestowed on them, the value of supporting the king declined. It is clear, however, that the opposition would have been unlikely to succeed, had the English Crown, like its French or Spanish counterpart, had a standing army with which to quell the initial uprising.

[24] The Star Chamber, in which the most egregious examples of arbitrary power occurred, became a regular feature of Stuart England. See Maitland, *Constitutional History*, and Friedrich A. Hayek, *Constitution of Liberty* (Chicago, 1960), chap. 11.

[25] Coke's dismissal, "the first of a judge in over thirty years, ushered in a period of increasing royal pressure on the bench: in Charles's reign two other chief justices, Crew and Heath, and one chief baron of the exchequer court, Walter, were to follow Coke" (Hirst, *Authority and Conflict*, p. 121). See also Hayek's excellent and extensive discussion, in *Constitution of Liberty*, chap. 11.

Civil War to Glorious Revolution

Eventually the opposition openly challenged the king, leading the country into civil war. But the ultimate opposition victory was not inevitable.

After seizing power, the opposition modified the institutions underpinning the Crown's most egregious behavior. Not surprisingly, the Star Chamber was abolished in 1641 by an act requiring that all cases involving property be tried at common law, thus adding another milestone along the route toward supremacy of the common law, so favorable to property rights. Restrictions against monopolies were now enforced. In an attempt to prevent the Crown from ruling for substantial periods without calling a Parliament, Parliament passed the Triennial legislation, which called for regular standing of the Parliament. The royal administrative apparatus was dismantled, and with it the royal ability to impose regulatory restrictions on the economy in conflict with the rights enforced by the common law courts.

Important changes reduced restrictions on labor mobility. Land tenure modifications simultaneously favored the development of private rights and markets and reduced the Crown's political hold over this once-important part of its constituency.[26] New and profitable opportunities resulted from lifting restrictions on land use and improving markets.

After the Civil War a number of political innovations occurred, including the abolition of the monarchy and the House of Lords. Their failure led to pressure to bring back the king. With the Restoration of the monarchy in 1660, England was once again ruled by the Stuarts. It is critical for understanding the next series of events to notice a striking limitation of the institutional changes prior to the Restoration. While the details differ considerably, the next twenty-five years repeated the events of the earlier Stuarts' reign in one important respect. Political struggle with constituents resulted in the king's arbitrary encroachment. By far the most important instance of this—indeed, the one resulting in a nation united against the Crown—concerned the rechartering of local governments and political power. Rechartering came in reaction to the Whig-led "Exclusion Crisis"; it allowed the Crown to disenfranchise much of the opposition and thereby reduce impediments to its exercise of power. Of the 104 members of Parliament returned in the mid-1680s

---

[26] See H. J. Perkins, "The Social Causes of the British Industrial Revolution," *Transactions of the Royal Historical Society*, 18 (1968). Hill, discussing the 1660 Act confirming the abolition of feudal tenures, notes that in the eighteenth century Blackstone called this Act a greater boon to property owners than the Magna Carta itself (*Century of Revolution*, p. 127).

by the boroughs receiving new charters, only one Whig was elected. This converted "what had been a formidable, aggressive and highly organized opposition party into an impotent collection of a few individuals."[27]

Had the Crown succeeded in this political maneuver, there would be few checks on its powers, because it allowed the Crown to disenfranchise *any* opposition. But between 1686 and 1688, James II, having disenfranchised the Whig opposition, turned on his own supporters, causing his own constituents to join the opposition to remove him in the Glorious Revolution of 1688.

III. Institutional Changes Following the Glorious Revolution

At the same time it extended the Crown to William and Mary, Parliament restructured the society's political institutions in the Revolution Settlement. To understand the new institutions it is necessary to see clearly the problem the parliamentary interests sought to solve. The early Stuarts' use of the Star Chamber and the rechartering of the later Stuarts threatened the liberties and wealth of citizens, leaving them with little protection against Crown attempts to appropriate their wealth. But experience showed that simply removing the powers underpinning arbitrary behavior was insufficient to prevent abuse. Controlling Crown behavior required the solving of financial problems as well as appropriate constraints on the Crown. So the Glorious Revolution also ushered in a fiscal revolution.[28] The main features of the institutional revolution are as follows.

First and foremost, the Revolution initiated the era of parliamentary "supremacy." This settled for the near future the issue of sovereignty: it was now the "king in Parliament," not the king alone.[29] No longer would the Crown, arguing the "divine rights of kings," claim to be above the law. Parliamentary supremacy established a permanent role for Parliament in the on-going management of the government and hence placed a direct check on the Crown. The Crown no longer called or disbanded Parliament at its discretion alone.

Parliament also gained a central role in financial matters. Its exclusive

[27] Jones, *Revolution of 1688*, pp. 47, 50. As B. W. Hill observes, James's efforts to repack the constituencies "came near to success in every respect but one: they alarmed landed society, Tory as well as Whig." See B. W. Hill, *The Growth of Parliamentary Parties: 1689–1742* (Hamden, 1976).

[28] P. G. M. Dickson, *The Financial Revolution in England* (New York, 1967).

[29] See, for example, Maitland, *Constitutional History*, pp. 298–301, or David Keir, *The Constitutional History of Modern Britain Since 1485* (London, 1966).

authority to raise new taxes was firmly reestablished; at the same time the Crown's independent sources of revenue were also limited. For the Crown to achieve its own goals this meant it had to establish successful relations with Parliament. Shortly thereafter, Parliament gained the never-before-held right to audit how the government had expended its funds. Parliamentary veto over expenditures, combined with the right to monitor how the funds they had voted were spent, placed important constraints over the Crown.

Another important institutional change focused on the royal prerogative powers. These were substantially curtailed and subordinated to common law, and the prerogative courts (which allowed the Crown to enforce its proclamations) were abolished. At the same time the independence of the judiciary from the Crown was assured. Judges now served subject to good behavior (they could only be removed if convicted for a criminal offense or by action of both houses of Parliament) instead of at the king's pleasure. The supremacy of the common law courts, so favorable to private rights, was thereby assured.

Because the Stuarts had violated the personal liberties of their opponents (excessive bail, no writ of Habeas Corpus) as a means of raising the cost of opposition, reducing the arbitrary powers of the Crown resulted not only in more secure economic liberties and property rights, but in political liberties and rights as well. Political rights were seen as a key element of protection against arbitrary violations of economic rights.

Two final points are worth emphasizing. First, part of the glue that held these institutional changes together was the successful dethroning of Charles I and, later, James II. This established a credible threat to the Crown regarding future irresponsible behavior. The conditions which would "trigger" this threat were laid out in the Revolution Settlement, and shortly thereafter in the Declaration of Rights. Second, although parliamentary supremacy meant that Parliament dictated the form of the new political institutions, it did not assume the sole position of power within the government, as it did after the Civil War or in the nineteenth century. While substantial constraints were placed on the king, these did not reduce him to a figurehead.

IV. The Glorious Revolution and England's Credible Commitment to Secure Rights

The institutional innovations increased dramatically the control of wealth holders over the government. Since fiscal crises inevitably produced pressure on the Crown to break its agreements, eliminating unilateral control by the Crown over key decisions was a necessary component of the new institutions. As previously described, this occurred in two ways. First, by requiring Parliament's assent to major changes in policies (such as changing the terms of loans or taxes), the representatives of wealth holders could veto such moves unless they were also in their interest. This allowed action in times of crisis but eliminated the Crown's unilateral action. Second, several other ways for the Crown to renege on promises were eliminated, notably its ability to legislate unilaterally (through the prerogative), to by-pass Parliament (because it had an independent source of funds), or to fire judges who did not conform to Crown desires.

Two factors made the new arrangements self-enforcing. First, the credible threat of removal limited the Crown's ability to ignore the new arrangements. Second, in exchange for the greater say in government, parliamentary interests agreed to put the government on a sound financial footing, that is, they agreed to provide sufficient tax revenue. Not only did this remove a major motive underlying the exercise of arbitrary power, but for the new King William it meant he could launch a major war against France. The arrangement proved so satisfactory for the king that a host of precedents were set putting the new division of powers on a solid footing. As a consequence of these institutional changes, private rights became fundamentally more secure.[30]

Institutional and Political Constraints on Parliament

The triumph of Parliament raises the issue of why it would not then proceed to act just like the king? Its motives were no more lofty than those of the Crown. But the institutional outcome effectively deterred Parliament from similar behavior. Robert Ekelund and Robert Tollison provide the following general analysis:

> Higher costs due to uncertainty and growing private returns reduced industry demands for regulation and control in England. All this strengthened the emergent constitutional democracy, which created conditions making rent-seeking activity on the part of both monarch and merchants more costly. When the locus of power to rent-seeking shifted from the monarch to Parliament . . . the costs of supply of regulation through legislative enactment rose.[31]

[30] Jones, on p. 6 of the *Revolution of 1688*, concludes: "None of its architects could have predicted its effectiveness in securing the liberties, religion, property and independence of the nation after so many previous attempts had failed."

[31] Ekelund and Tollison, *Mercantilism*, p. 149.

They suggest that the natural diversity of views in a legislature raises the cost of supplying private benefits in the form of favorable regulation.

The framework of institutional evolution we have described complements their story. The embedding of economic and political freedoms in the law, the interests of principals (for example, merchants) in a greater measure of freedom, and the ideological considerations that swept England in the late seventeenth century combined to play a role in institutional change. The new constitutional settlement endowed several actors with veto power, and thus created the beginnings of a division or separation of powers.[32] Supplying private benefits at public expense now required the cooperation of the Crown, Parliament, and the courts. Only the Crown could propose an expenditure, but only Parliament could authorize and appropriate funds for the proposal, and it could do so solely for purposes proposed by the Crown. Erskin May summed up this procedure as, "The crown demands, the Commons grants, and the Lords assent to the grant." A balance of power between the Crown and Parliament significantly limited publicly supplied private benefits.[33]

Three other political factors help explain why the new era of parliamentary supremacy did not simply transfer power from the Crown to Parliament. In 1641 the centralized administrative apparatus which enforced royal attempts to alter rights and property was destroyed. The absence of such a structure prevented either the Crown or Parliament from similar encroachment. Because a new apparatus—even one that was initially quite limited—would allow its future expansion, many interests could be counted upon to oppose its initiation.

Second, the commercially minded ruling Whig coalition preferred limited government and especially limited political interference with the common law courts. Parliament was thus *politically* constrained from intervention in the courts. As R. Braun observes:

> the Whig oligarchy was anxious to avoid encroachment upon the privacy of the business of those groups from which it drew its support. Not only the constitutional and institutional framework, but also the prevailing ideological basis of the [Whigs and their constituents] prevented the central administrative apparatus of the British government from developing [a major regulatory and control function].[34]

---

[32] We emphasize, however, that this division of powers was not a clear-cut system of checks and balances. Nor can it be considered a true separation of powers. The designers of the new institutions were far more worried about constraints on the Crown than on protecting the Crown from encroachments by Parliament. Thus in the latter half of the eighteenth century, the power of the Crown diminished, and with it the constraints (or checks) on Parliament. See A. F. Pollard, *The Evolution of Parliament* (London, 1926).

[33] Erskin May, *Parliamentary Practice* (17th edn., London, 1966; 1st edn., 1844). Further investigation of the procedures devised at this time is called for.

[34] R. Braun, "Taxation, Sociopolitical Structure, and State-Building: Great Britain and

Widespread regulation of markets by Parliament along the line of Colbert in France (or the Stuarts) would have led to a clash with the common law courts. Thus the political independence of the courts limited potential abuses by Parliament. Combined with the explicit institutional limits on Crown intervention, this assured the courts important and unchallenged authority in large areas of economic activity.

Third, the creation of a politically independent judiciary greatly expanded the government's ability credibly to promise to honor its agreements, that is, to bond itself. By limiting the ability of the government to renege on its agreements, the courts played a central role in assuring a commitment to secure rights. As we will see, this commitment substantially improved the government's ability to raise money through loans.

Thus the institutional and political changes accompanying the Glorious Revolution significantly raised the predictability of the government. By putting the government on a sound financial basis and regularizing taxation, it removed the random component of expropriation associated with royal attempts to garner revenue. Any interest group seeking private gain had now to get approval from both the Crown and the Parliament.

V. The Fiscal Revolution

To see the profound effects of the Glorious Revolution, we focus on one important element of public finance, government borrowing. Since capital markets are especially sensitive to the security of property rights, they provide a unique and highly visible indicator of the economic and political revolution that took place. Indeed, they are one of the few means for empirically evaluating the effects of the Glorious Revolution.

Prior to the Glorious Revolution, payments on loans were subject to manipulation by the Crown; rescheduling and delays in payments were common. As indicated in Table 3.2, money was raised through forced loans in 1604/5, 1611/2, 1617, and 1625. In each instance the Crown did not honor its terms. In the loan of 1617, for example, James I raised £100,000 in London at 10 percent for the period of one year. At the end of the year, although James paid the interest, he refused to repay the principal and demanded that the loan be renewed. No interest was paid over the next several years, and each year another renewal was "agreed" to. In 1624 Charles I lowered the interest rate to 8 percent; however, he

---

Brandenburg-Prussia," in Charles Tilly, ed., *Formation of National States in Western Europe* (Princeton, 1975).

TABLE 3.2
Forced Loans by the Early Stuarts, 1603–1625

Year	Amount	Rate (percent per year)	Repayment
1604/5	£111,891	10%	£20,362 unpaid as of Dec. 1609
1611/2	116,381	10	£112,000 unpaid as of Jul. 1616
1617[a]	96,466	10[b]	Unpaid until 1628
1625[c]	60,000	8	Unpaid until 1628

[a]Extension in 1624 secured by Crown lands.
[b]Unilaterally lowered by Charles I in 1624 to 8%.
[c]Secured by Crown lands.
Source: Robert Ashton, *The Crown and the Money Market, 1603–1640* (Oxford, 1960), chaps. 2 and 5.

did not pay any interest, nor did he repay the principal until 1628. Such behavior was hardly designed to gain the confidence of potential sources of loans. As Robert Ashton concludes, the "cavalier treatment which the Crown meted out to its creditors, and more especially to those most unwilling lenders who made more or less compulsory contributions through the medium of the Corporation of London" helps explain why London and the money interests supported the parliamentary cause.[35] Nor did the Stuarts attempt to develop a major international source of loans.[36]

Several financial innovations occurred under the late Stuarts, including some that were to play a key role in the "financial revolution" after 1688, for example, making notes "assignable," thus allowing them to be sold. The recent work of Glenn Nichols suggests that financial arrangements under the late Stuarts were far superior to those under the early Stuarts. Nonetheless, fiscal stress pressed the system to its limits, and led to a partial repudiation in the famous "stop the exchequer" in 1672. The debt in question, over a million pounds, shows that the late Stuarts' until that time, at least—could raise substantial sums.[37]

[35] Ashton, *Crown and the Money Market*, p. 113.

[36] Ashton reports only two such loans, the second of which (£58,400 in 1616) was still outstanding in 1636. Here too the Stuarts failed to develop a reputation for honoring agreements. By the 1630s, the Crown was unable to borrow at all from either international sources or London.

[37] See Glenn O. Nichols, "English Government Borrowing Before the Financial Revolution," manuscript, Anderson College, 1988. For details about the stop of the exchequer, see Dickson, *Financial Revolution*. In exchange for its short-term notes, the Crown gave new long-term loans. Much of the interest from the latter was still unpaid at the time of the Glorious Revolution, however.

Institutional Innovations

A series of institutional innovations during the war with France (1689–1697) changed the way the government sought credit, facilitating the regularization of public finance. First, the government began as a regular practice to earmark new taxes, authorized by statute for each new loan issue, to pay the interest on all new long-term loans. By earmarking taxes beforehand, parliamentary interests limited the king's discretion each year over whether to pay bondholders their interest.

Second, the first large, long-term loan (£1,000,000) secured by new taxes took place in 1693. By 1694, however, these funds were exhausted. When the government sought a new large loan, it invited the subscribers to incorporate as the Bank of England. The Bank was responsible for handling the loan accounts of the government and for assuring the continuity of promised distributions. Certain restrictions were also imposed: the Bank could not lend the Crown money or purchase any Crown lands without the explicit consent of Parliament. As Macaulay observed over a century ago, this created a strong instrument of the Whig party (and hence of commercial interests). Since loans to the Crown went through the Bank, "it must have instantly stopped payment if it had ceased to receive the interest on the sum which it had advanced to the government."[38] The government had thus created an additional, private constraint on its future behavior by making it difficult to utilize funds of a current loan if it failed to honor its previous obligations.

Two other changes are worth noting. In 1698 the government created a separate fund to make up deficiencies in the event that the revenue earmarked for specific loans was insufficient to cover the required distributions (as was the case for several loans). This explicitly removed the component of risk associated with each loan due to its ties to a specific tax.[39] Second, during this period the milling of coins began, reducing the debasement of the currency due to shaving of coins.

Government Loans, 1688–1740

Thus were the institutional foundations of modern capital markets laid in England. These institutional changes were more successful than their

[38] Lord Macaulay, *The History of England* (London, 1914), vol. V, p. 2438.

[39] As David Ogg explains: "Thenceforth, the investor knew that, in lending money on a specified tax, he had parliamentary guarantee for the security of this investment, based not only on the particular fund, but on the whole of the national revenue." David Ogg, *England in the Reigns of James II and William III* (Oxford, 1955), p. 413. Regarding the second, see pp. 422–25.

TABLE 3.3
Growth of Government Debt, 1618–1740 (£ million)

Year	Governmental Expenditure[1]	Debt[2]	Prices[3] (1701 = 100)
Stuart England			
1618[4]	£0.5	£0.8	
mid-1630s[5]	1.0	1.0	
1680[6]	1.4		113
1688[6]	1.8	1.0[7]	99
Post–Glorious Revolution			
1695	6.2	8.4	116
1697	7.9	16.7	122
1700	3.2	14.2	115
1710	9.8	21.4	122
1714	6.2	36.2	103
1720	6.0	54.0	102
1730	5.6	51.4	95
1740	6.2	47.4	100
1750	7.2	78.0	95

Note: Because these figures are obtained from a variety of sources, they are intended solely to provide an indication of underlying trends. Figures for expenditures and debt after the Glorious Revolution are most reliable.

Sources: 1 Government Expenditure, post-1688: B. R. Mitchell, British Historical Statistics (Cambridge, 1988), chap. 11, table 2.

2 Debt, post-1688: Mitchell, British Historical Statistics, chap. 11, table 7.

3 Prices: Mitchell, British Historical Statistics, chap. 14: 1680–97, table 1, part A, "consumer goods"; 1697–1750, part B, "consumer goods."

4 Government Expenditure and Debt, 1618: David Hume, The History of England (Indianapolis, 1983), "Appendix to the Reign of James I."

5 Government Expenditure and Debt, mid-1630s: Derek Hirst, Authority and Conflict: England, 1603–1658 (Cambridge, MA, 1986), p. 174.

6 Government Expenditure, 1680 and 1688: C. D. Chandaman, The English Public Revenue, 1660–1688 (Oxford, 1975), appendix 2, table 7, "Total Available for Ordinary Purposes."

7 Debt, 1688: H. Fisk, English Public Finance (New York, 1920), p. 93.

originators had hoped. The original subscription to the Bank of England, for instance, was expected to be slow and possibly unsuccessful. In actuality, one-third of the loan was subscribed on the first day and another third during the next two days. Ten days later the loan was fully subscribed.

To see the dramatic results of the fiscal revolution, we turn to the public finances during this period. Table 3.3 provides information on governmental expenditures and debt. On the eve of the Revolution, governmental expenditures were about £1.8 million, reflecting a slow but steady increase over two decades.[40] Government debt was limited to about £1 million, or between 2 and 3 percent of GNP (estimated to be £41 million). Moreover, at a time when Holland was borrowing £5 million long term at 4 percent per year, the English Crown could only borrow small amounts at short term, paying between 6 and 30 percent per year.[41]

The Revolution radically altered this pattern. In 1697, just nine years later, governmental expenditures had grown fourfold, to £7.9 million. The immediate reason for the rise was the new war with France. But importantly, the government's ability to tap the resources of society increased. This is evidenced by the increase in the size of government debt, which grew during the nine years of war from £1 million to nearly £17 million. This level of debt—approximately 40 percent of GNP— was previously unattainable. Moreover, the ability of the new government to finance a war at unprecedented levels played a critical role in defeating France. To put these figures in modern perspective, a trillion-dollar economy would have begun the period with $25 billion of debt, which in just nine years would grow to approximately $400 billion.

Following the war, both government expenditures and the amount financed through debt were substantially higher than previous levels. By 1720 government debt was over fifty times the 1688 level and on the order of GNP. Financing wars by borrowing had another remarkable benefit. Previous instances of unexpected large wars were nearly always accompanied by large fiscal demands, the search for sources of revenue, and consequently unfavorable demands on wealth holders. Such demands were virtually eliminated by the new methods of finance. Another evidence of the new regime's increased predictability is indicated by the series of price changes. Despite sustained deficits resulting in the enormous increase in debt, government policy did not result in inflationary finance.[42]

[40] C. D. Chandaman, *The English Public Revenue, 1660–1688* (Oxford, 1975).

[41] For figures on government debt and GNP estimates, see B. R. Mitchell, *British Historical Statistics* (Cambridge, 1988). On interest rates, see Sidney Homer, *A History of Interest Rates* (New Brunswick, 1963), p. 149.

[42] Prices rose a little over 20 percent between 1690 and 1710 (and then fell again between 1710 and 1730). But the enormous increase in debt during this period suggests that the government did not attempt to meet its debt obligations through inflationary finance. The modern view of inflation suggests two further inferences (see, for example, Thomas Sargent, *Rational Expectations and Inflation* [New York, 1986]). Since inflation in part reflects expectations about future governmental finance of deficits, the lack of major increases in prices suggests that the market did not expect inflationary finance. Since this pattern was maintained for several decades, it indicates that these expectations were "con-

TABLE 3.4
Government Long-term Borrowing: Interest Rates, 1693–1739
(Selected Loans)

Date[a]	Amount	Interest	How Funded
Jan. 1693	£ 723,394	14.0%	Additional excise
Mar. 1694	1,000,000	14.0	Duties on imports
Mar. 1694	1,200,000	8.0	Additional customs and duties
Apr. 1697	1,400,000	6.3	Excise and duties
July 1698	2,000,000	8.0	Additional excise duties
Mar. 1707	1,155,000	6.25	Surplus from funds of five loans from 1690s; duties
July 1721	500,000	5.0	Hereditary revenue of Crown
Mar. 1728	1,750,000	4.0	Coal duties
May 1731	800,000	3.0	Duties
June 1739	300,000	3.0	Sinking fund

[a]Date of royal assent to loan act.
Source: P. G. M. Dickson, The Financial Revolution in England (New York, 1967), tables 2, 3, and 22.

At the same time that the scope of governmental borrowing increased, however, the market rate charged the government fell. Its initial long-term loans in the early 1690s were at 14 percent (see Table 3.4). By the end of the 1690s the rate was about half, between 6 and 8 percent. The rate continued to fall over the next two decades so that, by the 1730s, interest rates were 3 percent.

These numbers are impressive in two ways. First, the amount of wealth now available for use by others increased tremendously. Second, at the same time as governmental borrowing increased, the interest rate fell. Sharp increases in demand accompanied by decline in rates indicate that the overall risk associated with governmental behavior decreased considerably despite the enormous increase in the size of the debt. As the society gained experience with its new institutions, particularly their predictability and commitment to secure rights, expectations over future actions began to reflect the new order.

These changing expectations were directly reflected in the capital market response. The new institutional underpinnings of public finance provided a clear and dramatic credible commitment that the govern-

---

firmed" in the sense that new information about current governmental behavior did not change expectations. Robert Barro provides evidence that budget deficits had almost no effect on prices from 1700 until the Napoleonic campaigns. Robert Barro, "Government Spending, Interest Rates, Prices, and Budget Deficits in the UK, 1701–1918," Journal of Monetary Economics, 20 (Sept. 1987), pp. 221–48.

ment would honor its promises and maintain the existing pattern of rights. While underlying economic conditions were surely an important component of the large increase in debt, they alone can not explain the *suddenness* with which the debt increased, nor its magnitude. Even though the later Stuarts were more financially successful than their predecessors, nothing that came before the Glorious Revolution suggests the dramatic change in capital markets that it unleashed.

VI. Implications for Private Capital Markets

Our thesis is that the credible commitment by the government to honor its financial agreements was part of a larger commitment to secure private rights. The latter was clearly a major factor for the institutional changes at the time of the Glorious Revolution. Data on general economic activity are sparse, so we cannot perform a major test of our thesis, but we can provide some support. As evidence we turn to the development of private capital markets and the necessary evolution of the financial foundation of long-run economic success.

While it is clear that the institutions underlying private capital markets go back at least several centuries, it is widely agreed among economic historians that private capital markets date from the early eighteenth century.[43] The rise of banks and an increasingly differentiated set of securities, providing a relatively secure means of saving, brought individual savings into the financial system. Ashton reports that this "meant that men were less concerned than their fathers . . . to keep quantities of coin, bullion, and plate locked up in safes or buried in their orchards and gardens."[44]

The institutions leading to the growth of a stable market for public debt provided a large and positive externality for the parallel development of a market for private debt. Shortly after its formation for intermediating public debt, the Bank of England began private operations. Numerous other banks also began operations at this time. This development provided the institutional structure for pooling the savings of many individuals and for intermediation between borrowers and lenders. A wide range of securities and negotiable instruments emerged

[43] This section summarizes the conclusions of the literature on the early eighteenth century. See, for example, T. S. Ashton, *An Economic History of England* (London, 1955); John Clapham, *The Bank of England* (New York, 1945); Phyllis Deane, *The First Industrial Revolution* (2nd edn., Cambridge, 1979); Dickson, *Financial Revolution*; Peter Mathias, *The First Industrial Nation* (2nd edn., London, 1983); and E. Powell, *The Evolution of the Money Market: 1385–1915* (London, 1966).

[44] Ashton, *Economic History*, p. 178.

in the early eighteenth century and these were used to finance a large range of activities.[45]

Phyllis Deane summarizes the development of private capital markets alongside that for public capital:

> The secondary effects of the Bank's financial transactions on behalf of the government stemmed from the new financial instruments which were thus created . . . and because [the instruments] issued by a credit-worthy borrower are themselves readily saleable, the effect was further to lubricate the channels linking savings and investment by creating a large stock of negotiable paper assets which new savers could buy. Similarly, the deposits from private sources could also be used as a basis for further credit to the private sector.[46]

As a consequence, private capital markets flourished.

Several sources of evidence support our claims. First, research on interest rates for various forms of private credit reveals that these roughly parallel rates on public credit.[47] Falling private rates increased the range of projects and enterprises that were economically feasible, thus promoting the accumulation of capital. As L. S. Pressnell concludes, the "accumulation of capital in the 18th century, which the declining trend of interest rates . . . clearly indicates, appears in this light as a major social and economic achievement."[48] Unfortunately the data from the first half of the eighteenth century, in contrast to those from the second half, are sketchy, and for the period prior to the Glorious Revolution, almost nonexistent.

Second, large-scale trading in private securities dates from this period.[49] Figure 3.1 shows the growth of one component of the market, short-dated securities. In the early 1690s the volume of these securities averaged £300,000 per year. Ten years later, volume averaged £3,400,000 per year, and by the early 1710s, £11,000,000 per year. While growth trailed off after the collapse of the South Sea Bubble, the market from 1715 to 1750 was far larger than that prior to the Revolution.

Third, the period saw the growth and development of banks. The

---

[45] "The essence of the financial revolution of the early 18th century was the development of a wide range of securities in which new mercantile and financial companies—the chartered trading companies, the partnership banks, the insurance companies, etc.—could flexibly and safely invest and disinvest" (Deane, *Industrial Revolution*, p. 185).

[46] Ibid., pp. 184–85.

[47] Clapham, *Bank of England*; L. S. Pressnell, "The Rate of Interest in the 18th Century," in L. S. Pressnell, ed., *Studies in the Industrial Revolution* (London, 1960), p. 181; and Homer, *A History of Interest Rates*.

[48] Pressnell, "Rate of Interest," p. 181.

[49] As Dickson notes, "The development of a market in securities in London in the period 1688–1756 was one of the more important aspects of the Financial Revolution." Dickson, *Financial Revolution*, p. 457.

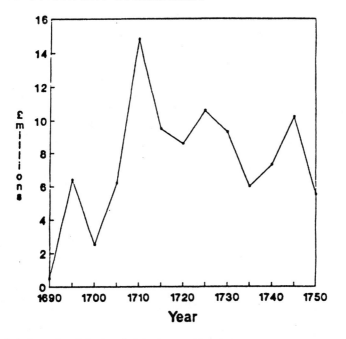

Figure 3.1 Growth of the Stock Market, 1690–1750

Source: P. G. M. Dickson, *The Financial Revolution in England* (London, 1967), Appendix C.

Bank of England was followed shortly by numerous other banks in London. By the 1720s these numbered about 25. By 1750 there were 30; by 1770, 50; and by 1800, 70. While banks in areas outside London began to appear in large numbers only after 1750, Ashton argues that many of these areas were integrated into a national capital market much earlier.[50] "Inland bills and promissory notes played a considerable part in the trade of all parts of England and Wales. But nowhere had their use extended so far as in the north-west. The ubiquity of the bill was probably the reason why in this area formal banking made its appearance relatively late."[51]

[50] See Charles P. Kindleberger, *Financial History of Western Europe* (London, 1984), p. 74; and Mathias, *Industrialized Nation*. The earliest provincial bank cited by Mathias was in Bristol (1716), and there were not more than a dozen in 1750. By 1784, however, there were 120, and by 1800, 370 (Mathias, p. 151).

[51] Ashton, *Economic History*, p. 185. Ashton's claim is also supported by the study of credit instruments other than those provided by banks. B. L. Anderson, discussing the rise of inland bills, notes that their legal status was markedly improved in the first years of the

The final set of evidence centers on the Bank of England's private activities in three areas. (1) Discounted bills. Systematic data on the Bank's discounting operations apparently do not survive. Nonetheless, sporadic reports are available and indicate a considerable growth of activity during the first few decades of the Bank's operations. For 1699 data reveal the following volume of notes discounted: 13–31 June, £8,534; 27 June–4 July, £14,000. By 1730 the *median* day's volume was over £10,000, and by 1760 days over £100,000 were common.[52] (2) Notes in circulation. During the eighteenth century the Bank's notes became a major medium of exchange, first in London, and then throughout England.[53] In the first two years of the Bank's operations the volume of notes grew to about £760,000 (see Table 3.5). By 1720 they numbered £2,900,000, and they were above £4,500,000 by 1730 and for the next few decades. (3) Drawing accounts. This early form of demand deposit seems to have become systematized about twenty years after the Bank's founding.[54] As shown in Table 3.5, drawing accounts were quite modest in the late 1690s. By 1720 they numbered more than a million pounds, growing to over two million by 1730. To summarize, the Bank expanded operations over several types of private credit. By 1720, a little over 25 years after the Bank's establishment, these sums reached substantial levels, showing the steady growth in financial services for private economic activity.

Thus, it appears that the growth of private capital markets paralleled that of public capital markets. This development mobilized the savings of large numbers of individuals and, by mid-century, provided financial services in an integrated, national market. These funds appear to have financed a large variety of business activities and played a necessary role in the economic expansion throughout this century.[55] While these activ-

---

eighteenth century. "This recognition of the bill as a transferable means of payment was a decisive turning point in the development of the English credit system. . . . [The] English practice made it an instrument of credit in a system of accommodation paper that was highly responsive to the community's demand for money." B. L. Anderson, "Money and the Structure of Credit in the 18th Century," *Business History*, 85 (No. 1, 1970), p. 90.

[52] Clapham, *Bank of England*, p. 126.

[53] While other banks issued notes, by far the largest source for most of the period we are studying are those of the Bank of England. Throughout this period, these notes were convertible to gold. See D. M. Joslin, "London Private Bankers, 1720–1785," in E. M. Carus-Wilson, ed., *Essays in Economic History*, vol. 2, pp. 340–59.

[54] The only year before 1720 reported by Clapham is 1698.

[55] An additional piece of evidence concerns investment in transportation infrastructure, which also increased at this time. By 1724 there were over 1,160 miles of river open to navigation, double that of a century earlier. See Ashton, *Economic History*, p. 73; Mathias, *Industrial Nation*, p. 100. While the "canal age" is usually dated at mid-century, it "did not spring to life in 1750" but was the "conclusion of a mounting momentum of effort"; Mathias, *Industrial Nation*, p. 100. Both Ashton and Mathias noted that there

TABLE 3.5

The Bank of England's Notes and Drawing Accounts, 1698–1750
(£ thousands)

Year	Notes in Circulation	Drawing Accounts
1698	£1,340	£100
1720	2,900	1,300
1730	4,700	2,200
1740	4,400	2,900
1750	4,600	1,900

Note: Figures for 1720–1750 are averages for the five-year period beginning with the year listed.

Source: John Clapham, The Bank of England: A History (New York, 1945), vol. 1: 1694–1797.

ities have not been studied in detail as they have for the period following 1750, 1688 appears to be a more abrupt break with the past than 1750. Returning to our main thesis, this growth indicates that the attempts to maintain secure private rights were largely successful. Although the evidence cannot be used to discern the precise level of security, it shows that it was substantial. A more systematic test awaits future research on these markets.

Conclusion

In this essay we have provided a brief account of the successful evolution of institutional forms that permitted economic growth to take place in early modern England. It is clear from this discussion of a century of civil war and revolution, however, that these institutional innovations did not arise naturally. Rather they were forced, often violently, upon the Crown. The Crown, however, nearly won the struggle. Had a standing army existed in England, it would have been under the control of the Crown, and the political and economic future of England would very likely have been different, potentially more in keeping with that of France and Spain.

We have shown how the political institutions governing society can be considered endogenously. Fiscal constraints and a revenue-seeking Crown, problems exacerbated by an uncooperative Parliament, created a situation of insecure rights in which the wealth and welfare of individual citizens were at risk. Prior to the Glorious Revolution, institutions

were two big booms in improving rivers during this period, one at the turn of the century and one between 1718 and 1720.

such as the Star Chamber enabled the Crown to alter rights in its favor in a manner that parliamentary interests were hard pressed to resist.

Given their means and motives, the triumph of parliamentary interests in the Glorious Revolution led to five significant institutional changes. First, it removed the underlying source of the expediency, an archaic fiscal system and its attendant fiscal crises. Second, by limiting the Crown's legislative and judicial powers, it limited the Crown's ability to alter rules after the fact without parliamentary consent. Third, parliamentary interests reasserted their dominance of taxation issues, removing the ability of the Crown to alter tax levels unilaterally. Fourth, they assured their own role in allocating funds and monitoring their expenditure. The Crown now had to deal with the Parliament on an equal footing—indeed, the latter clearly had the advantage with its now credible threat of dethroning a sovereign who stepped too far out of line. Fifth, by creating a balance between Parliament and the monarchy—rather than eliminating the latter as occurred after the Civil War—parliamentary interests insured limits on their own tendencies toward arbitrary actions. In combination, these changes greatly enhanced the predictability of governmental decisions.

What established the government's commitment to honoring its agreements—notably the promise not to appropriate wealth or repudiate debt—was that the wealth holders gained a say in each of these decisions through their representatives in Parliament. This meant that only if such changes were in their own interests would they be made. Increasing the number of veto players implied that a larger set of constituencies could protect themselves against political assault, thus markedly reducing the circumstances under which opportunistic behavior by the government could take place.

In the story we have told, the emergence of political and civil liberties was inextricably linked with economic freedom. Opportunistic behavior on the part of the Crown was often accompanied by abuse of the opposition's political rights. The Crown had jailed people without charge or for lengthy periods prior to trial, and had required excessive bail to raise the costs of opposition. Hence protection of political liberties emerged as a component of the political protection of economic rights.

The principal lesson of our article is that the fundamental institutions of representative government—an explicit set of multiple veto points along with the primacy of the common law courts over economic affairs—are intimately related to the struggle for control over governmental power. The success of the propertied and commercially minded interests led to institutions that simultaneously mitigated the motive underlying the Crown's drive to find new sources of revenue and also greatly constrained the behavior of the government (now the "king in

Parliament" rather than the king alone). Though these institutional innovations failed to anticipate the decline of the power of the Crown and ascendancy of Parliament in the latter half of the eighteenth century, the system successfully balanced power for well over sixty years. In comparison with the previous century or with the absolutist governments of the continent, England's institutional commitment to secure rights was far stronger. Evidence from capital markets provides a striking indication of this.

Recent research that has significantly upgraded France's economic performance before the French Revolution has led to an overhauling of traditional interpretations of British as well as French economic history.[56] If England and France were almost at parity in economic performance, the clear implication is that institutions per se—and in particular, the institutional changes we have described—were not so revolutionary after all. Similarly, the elaborate bureaucratic structure inherited from Louis XIV was not such a hindrance to economic growth. But that conclusion ignores the consequences that followed. It is clear that the institutional changes of the Glorious Revolution permitted the drive toward British hegemony and dominance of the world. England could not have beaten France without its financial revolution, and the funds made available by the growth in debt from 1688 to 1697 were surely a necessary condition for England's success in this war with France as well as the next one (1703–1714), from which England emerged the major power in the world.[57]

France, like England, had an ongoing fiscal crisis; and Louis XIV did come to terms with his constituents to gain more revenue early in his reign. But his success was temporary, not rooted in fundamental institutional change, and it was outdistanced by the magnitude of the English success. France's economy lived on borrowed time, and ultimately the unresolved institutional contradictions resulted in bankruptcy and revolution.[58]

The comparison of growth rates alone is therefore insufficient to judge economic parity. While in 1690 France was the major European power, it declined in power and stature relative to England over the

[56] See, for example, F. Crouzet, "England and France in the Eighteenth Century," in Max Hartwell, ed., *Causes of the Industrial Revolution in England* (London, 1967).

[57] Dickson, *Financial Revolution.*

[58] See David Bien, "Offices, Corps, and a System of State Credit: The Uses of Privilege under the Ancient Regime," in K. Baker, ed., *The French Revolution and the Creation of Modern Political Culture* (New York, 1987), vol. 1, pp. 89–114; Philip Hoffman, "Taxes, Fiscal Crises, and Representative Institutions: The Case of Early Modern France," manuscript, California Institute of Technology, 1988; and Hilton Root and Daniel Ingberman, "Tying the King's Hands," manuscript, University of Pennsylvania, 1987.

next century. More wars followed those at the turn of the eighteenth century, so that in 1765—at the end of the Seven Years War, in which France suffered a humiliating defeat—it had lost its New World colonies (Canada and Louisiana) and was in financial peril from which it did not recover until after the revolution. The contrast between the two economies in mid-century is striking: in 1765 France was on the verge of bankruptcy while England was on the verge of the Industrial Revolution.[59]

It is always tempting to claim too much. Would Britain really have followed the path of continental countries if the Stuarts had won? Would there have been a first Industrial Revolution in England? One could tell a plausible counterfactual story that put more weight on the fundamental strength of English property rights and the common law that had evolved from the Magna Carta and which would have circumscribed royal behavior and ultimately forced "responsible government." One could point to the robust economy (particularly at the local level) that existed in seventeenth-century England despite the uncertainties we have described. There exists neither a definitive theory of economic growth which would define for us the necessary and sufficient conditions nor the evidence to reconstruct the necessary counterfactual story. But we are convinced from the widespread contemporary Third World and historical evidence that *one* necessary condition for the creation of modern economies dependent on specialization and division of labor (and hence impersonal exchange) is the ability to engage in secure contracting across time and space. That entails low transaction costs per exchange. The creation of impersonal capital markets is the single most important piece of evidence that such a necessary condition has been fulfilled. And we have told a story of how these institutions *did* come about in England.

As evidence against the counterfactual thesis, we again point to the financial revolution. A change of this magnitude in such a short period clearly hinged on the underlying constitutional reorganization. Because the financial revolution played a critical role in England's long-run success, the implication is that even if other forces would ultimately have

---

[59] Jeffrey Williamson's recent, if controversial, work provides further support for this thesis. It suggests that British growth rates rose substantially once the long series of wars with France, ending with the Napoleonic campaign, were over. If during this period England's growth rates were not substantially larger than France's, its ability to spend more on war without bringing financial peril meant at most lower domestic consumption and investment, and hence came at the expense of growth. France's near bankruptcy shows that, in comparison, it was living on borrowed time. See Jeffrey G. Williamson, "Why Was British Growth so Slow During the Industrial Revolution?" *Journal of Economic History*, 64 (Sept. 1983), pp. 687–712.

led England to success under the Stuarts, they would have done so more slowly and probably less decisively.

We have thus shown how institutions played a necessary role in making possible economic growth and political freedom. Furthermore, it appears from our survey of seventeenth-century England, from the historical performance of other economies, and from performance records of current Third World economies, that the circumstances fostering secure rights and hence economic growth are relatively rare and deserve further exploration.

4

Democracy, Capital, Skill, and Country Size

EFFECTS OF ASSET MOBILITY AND REGIME MONOPOLY ON THE ODDS OF DEMOCRATIC RULE

RONALD ROGOWSKI

FOLLOWING almost universal scholarly convention (e.g., Gastil 1986), I define full democracy as the regular reallocation of political power by equal and effective vote of the entire adult population and admit that systems of rule may be more or less democratic according to what share of the adult population has an equal and effective vote—that is, how broad the franchise is.[1] Then among the riddles that any adequate explanation of democracy must address are these:

1. Why are rich countries more democratic than poor ones?

2. Why are the few rich but undemocratic countries (e.g., Saudi Arabia, Bahrain) abundant in resources rather than human or physical capital?

3. Why have the few democracies that emerged at early stages of economic development often been in "frontier"—that is, sparsely settled—societies (the early United States, Canada, Australia)?

4. Why has the effective franchise, not only in democracies, often been restricted according to criteria that were either immutable (race, gender, ancestry, year of birth) or socially ascribed (religion, in most cases wealth), and why have such barriers fallen, and fallen successively, as societies have grown wealthier?

5. Why have changes in the franchise—expansions in ancient Greece and in the modern world, contractions at the dawn of feudalism—often occurred with remarkable rapidity, and are historians right in linking these sudden changes, as they often have (e.g., Forrest 1966, White 1962), to shifts in the technology of war or in the pattern of trade?

6. Finally, why is it the franchise—the right to vote—that is so salient an object in constitutional struggles? Would most people not prefer an authori-

[1] Because in modern-day practice even grotesque tyrannies often practice a nominally universal franchise, proxy indicators of the extent of the real franchise must be employed. See below, n. 29.

tarian state bound by the rule of law to an arbitrary and capricious democracy?

I develop here a simplified model of the interactions between rulers and ruled that offers plausible answers to each of these questions and is compatible with present-day and historical evidence. In crucial respects, I shall try to show, the model's implications are sustained by a broad cross-national analysis of recent data. Basically, the model pursues fundamental insights of the theory of monopoly (e.g., Varian 1992, chap. 14), of exit (Hirschman 1970), of industrial organization (Williamson 1985), and of the state (North 1981, Bates and Lien 1985) to argue that the extent to which democracy prevails in a country varies directly with its endowments of physical and human capital and interactively with plausible measures of its populace's ability to emigrate. In short, a country that is either economically advanced or well educated will be democratic regardless of its size, but so will only moderately advanced or moderately educated nations whose subjects can easily escape. Along the way, I argue that the otherwise plausible and illuminating theory of Bates and Lien (1985) that suggests a negative correlation between "trapped" physical capital and democracy is properly understood as a partial equilibrium, which is supplemented but not supplanted by the general equilibrium that I develop here.

Theoretical Argument

Historians and political scientists often regard democratization as simply a struggle between rulers and ruled: democratic participation is always wrested from benighted autocrats. But we can gain more by thinking about why rulers find it in their interest to grant or withhold participation. We should, in short, focus less exclusively on the demand for and more on the supply of democratic rule. Surely democracy is most secure where self-interest animates rulers to supply it.

The neoclassical theory of the state, as pioneered by North (1981, esp. chap. 3), takes precisely this demand-and-supply perspective, regarding governments as monopolistic purveyors of public goods that their subjects demand, including crucially defense and justice—that is, protection against external predators and adjudication of domestic disputes.[2] I here extend the standard neoclassical analysis in two directions, considering first not only the market for the public goods them-

---

[2] In a more general sense, governments lower transaction costs (e.g., Weingast and Marshall 1988). I propose here to explore the different and less-researched aspect of government's monopoly power.

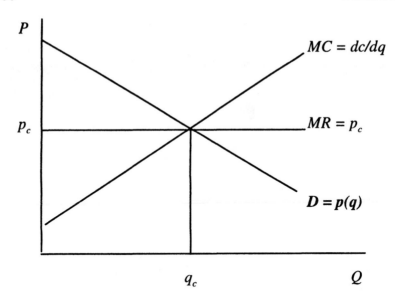

Figure 4.1 Demand and Supply of Influence under Perfect Competition

selves but also the secondary market for influence over their distribution and finance, and second the broader implications of government's monopoly over both public goods and influence.[3]

Subjects seek influence—a share of power over governmental decisions. They do so because they want access to the goods that governments provide (or, equivalently, shelter from the costs that they impose). We assume for now that demand for and marginal cost (i.e., supply) of influence obey the usual constraints:[4] the former is monotonically decreasing in price, the latter monotonically increasing.[5] At a lower price, subjects will demand more influence but less will be supplied; at a higher price, the converse will obtain. Thus, we obtain the conventionally sloped demand and supply curves of figure 4.1.

[3] The argument on this point is suggested by that of Lake 1992, 25. Max Weber (1968 [1922]) first argued that in all but the most primitive economies the supply of "core" public goods—or of the means of organized violence required for their provision—is a natural monopoly. That is, over any given territory only one government normally prevails. North (1981) and others have rightly attributed the natural monopoly to the classical cause—namely, high fixed and low marginal costs of provision.

[4] If price exceeds marginal cost, more units will be supplied; if not, not. Supply therefore expands until price exactly equals marginal cost and the supply curve is identical to that of marginal cost.

[5] For now I leave vague the precise meaning of "price," or at least of the currency in which it is denominated. Money, loyalty, and military service are all possibilities. See the further discussion below.

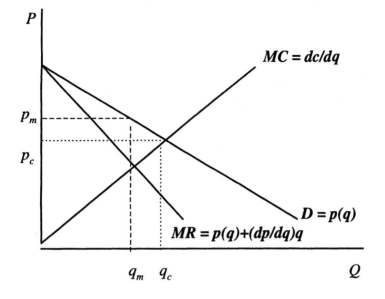

Figure 4.2 Demand and Supply of Influence under Monopoly

Figure 4.1 also illustrates the conventional result. If the market for influence were perfectly competitive, price and quantity would equilibrate where demand exactly equaled marginal cost, assuring a Pareto-optimal social outcome. (The resultant pure-competition price and quantity are here labeled respectively p_c and Q_c.) Individual suppliers, lacking market power, would face a "flat" (infinitely elastic) demand curve,[6] hence also constant marginal revenue (equal to prevailing price), and would produce at the level that equates price with marginal cost.

Government, however, is a monopoly. Controlling the supply of public goods and the allocation of public burdens, it develops secondary (and equally monopolistic) markets in access to relevant decision makers (i.e., influence). And monopoly leads (again, in entirely conventional analysis) to quite a different result from figure 4.1, illustrated in figure 4.2. Government, like any other monopolist, faces not a flat demand curve but the downward-sloping one actually given by the market; and because the monopoly's production does affect price, its marginal-reve-

[6] In a perfectly competitive market, a firm that sets its price above that of any competitor's loses all custom; one that underbids all competitors will capture the entire market. Hence, the firm's derivative of quantity with respect to price, dQ/dp, may be regarded as (negatively) infinite; this entails that price elasticity of demand, defined as $\epsilon = (dQ/dp)$ (p/Q), is also infinite. (Because ϵ is always negative, it is notationally more convenient to take its absolute value, $|\epsilon|$, and to speak of demand as "more elastic" when $|\epsilon|$ is greater.)

nue function lies everywhere below the demand curve.[7] Hence when government, or any other monopolist, equates marginal cost with marginal revenue, it produces less than the competitive market (Q_m rather than Q_c), charges a higher price (p_m, not p_c),[8] extracts monopoly rents equivalent to Q_m times the difference between p_m and average cost (c/Q), and inflicts social deadweight costs. Government in short sells influence too dearly, to too narrow a circle, with results that are Pareto suboptimal.

The puzzle, however, is that governments do not equally restrict access. Authoritarian regimes supply little and price influence dearly; democracies supply a lot rather cheaply. Why this variation?

In general, the extent to which a good is suboptimally restricted varies inversely with $|\epsilon|$, the price elasticity of demand, or (roughly) the "flatness" of the demand curve.[9] Inelastic demand implies restricted access; elastic demand, broad access.

So, rephrasing the question, What causes variation, over time and across states, in the elasticity of demand for influence? In traditional economic analysis, applied in North's model of government (1981, 24), it is above all availability of "close substitutes": If gas can replace oil at slightly higher cost, an oil monopoly can extract few rents; similarly, a monopolistic ruler with attractive rivals, internal or external, will grant wider access than one who is unchallenged. Yet the fact that government is a natural monopoly means that it ordinarily has few effective internal rivals; paradoxically, it is generally accepted that regimes with fewer external rivals (the island United Kingdom, mountain-ringed Switzerland, long-isolated America) are likelier to be democratic.

The crucial point, as Hirschman (1970) first observed, is rather that close substitutes permit exit: if, for example, I am dissatisfied with one American long-distance telephone company, I can now move to another.

---

[7] If we regard price as a function of quantity, $p(Q)$, then total revenue R must amount to $R = Qp(Q)$; hence, marginal revenue is $MR = dR/dQ = p(Q) + (dp/dQ)Q$. That the demand curve is downward sloping means that dp/dQ must be negative, so the MR curve lies everywhere below the inverse demand curve described by $p(Q)$. A standard treatment is Varian 1992, chap. 14.

[8] Assume for now that the monopolist must charge a single price and cannot practice price discrimination. I consider other possibilities below.

[9] Marginal revenue MR can readily be shown to be equivalent to $p[1 - 1/|\epsilon|]$, which in equilibrium must equal marginal cost; hence, the extent to which p exceeds MC is seen to be $p/MC = [1 - 1/|\epsilon|]^{-1} = |\epsilon|/(|\epsilon| - 1)$, which decreases with increasing $|\epsilon|$, going to unity as $|\epsilon|$ grows very large. (The flat demand curve of infinite price elasticity entails equality of price and marginal cost.) Since the extent to which production is suboptimal—the ratio of competitive to monopoly production—varies directly with p/MC, it also varies inversely with $|\epsilon|$. Cf. Varian 1992, chap. 14.

The political analogue is thus the ease with which subjects can leave an oppressive regime (cf. Tiebout 1956) or can transfer out of it their most important assets (Bates and Lien 1985). In short, a crucial element that increases elasticity of demand for influence, and hence induces rulers to grant it more widely, is the possibility of emigration, of literal exit from an unsatisfactory government.

What, then, makes exit easier or more costly? The cost of exit is affected, in politics as in markets, by at least two things: actual conversion costs (acquiring new equipment or skills), and write-off of nonredeployable assets (incompatible or highly specific equipment). A computer user who leaves his or her Macintosh for a Windows-based system must learn a new "language" and other skills, bear the cost of the new equipment, and write off existing hardware.[10] A Salvadoran who migrates to the United States must learn English; bear the costs of (often illegal) transport and of search for new job and housing; and abandon, at whatever the home market will yield, such fixed assets as land and housing.[11]

In partial equilibrium, then—and we shall see momentarily how the general equilibrium differs—we expect price elasticity of demand in political and in economic markets to vary inversely with conversion costs, inversely with ownership of relevant nonredeployable assets, and directly (but interactively with conversion costs) with ownership of relevant redeployable assets. In other words, to the extent that conversion costs are high and relevant assets are "trapped" with existing rulers or vendors, provision of influence, as with goods, will be suboptimally restricted. Let us consider each aspect in turn.

Obviously, conversion costs will vary inversely with one's "fluency" in alternative operating systems: knowing both WordPerfect and Microsoft Word or both stick shift and automatic opens more possibilities. Much less obviously, conversion costs in equilibrium will also vary directly with the size of the existing base of customers or subjects. More users ordinarily implies higher costs of conversion.

Think again of computer operating systems. A user of some very narrow "niche" system (such as NeXT or Amiga) will find it necessary to learn others, to become "multilingual." A DOS or Windows user, by

---

[10] This example is perhaps too obvious. More subtle is the situation of American automobile owners who, in the 1960s, were increasingly dissatisfied with the ludicrously priced trash that Detroit's oligopoly produced. Exit to non-U.S. products then often required mastering previously unfamiliar techniques of driving and maintenance.

[11] Portable assets, such as currency and valuables, incur at most the costs, or risks, of smuggling. But this matters only to the extent that conversion costs are low—i.e., that the potential emigrant can actually leave.

contrast, may never learn even the rudiments of how to run a Macintosh.[12] Hence the paradoxical (but as every computer user will recognize, true) result that users of Windows incur higher conversion costs, are therefore more exploitable, and are often more exploited, than users of systems with smaller customer bases.

The same point applies to language, the most significant aspect in which countries' "operating systems" differ.[13] The smaller one's own linguistic group, the likelier one is, out of day-to-day necessity, to know other languages. Virtually all native speakers of Dutch and Danish (not to mention Icelandic), many speakers of French and German, but a much smaller fraction of Anglophones are fluent in something other than their native tongue; most often this will be a "world language" such as English.[14] Plausibly, the same principle governs crucial nonlinguistic aspects of culture.[15] Chinese or Americans, precisely because their domestic operating systems are shared by such huge numbers, are on average less cosmopolitan and adaptable than Swedes or Belgians; hence, in any weighing of potential emigration, they face higher conversion costs.[16]

I propose, then, to examine both the share of population fluent in a "world language" and inverse population size as reasonable proxies of low political conversion costs.

In general, assets are specific or nonredeployable to the extent that their value in their present use outweighs that in any second-best use (cf. Klein, Crawford, and Alchian 1978), where their resale price is considerably lower than their income stream's present value. Stamping dies for a particular automobile, for example, have no use in the manufacture of any other make; hence, their resale value is only their price as scrap metal. At the opposite extreme, trucks and office equipment are of equal use to many buyers and have "thick" resale markets; such assets are nonspecific or transferrable.

Virtually all investments in physical capital are nonredeployable be-

[12] Similarly, virtually every user of the Dvořak keyboard knows QWERTY, but the converse is certainly not the case.

[13] And why do operating systems differ between countries? As David Friedman (1977) has noted, rulers are motivated to align culturo-linguistic borders with state borders when their revenues depend heavily on labor taxes. Such an alignment always increases monopoly rents.

[14] Apparently, the recent expansions of the European Union have occasioned enormous difficulties in finding people who can translate simultaneously between, e.g., Danish and Greek or Finnish and Portuguese. It is obviously more sensible for a Dane or a Greek to learn English or French than for either to master the other's tongue.

[15] A shared language eases but rarely renders costless movement to another culture.

[16] That high costs are sometimes borne by successful Chinese emigrants does not prove that they are not high.

tween countries, either in the sense that they are physically immobile (imagine the cost of transporting an existing automobile factory to a different country) or that governments can interdict their export. More concretely, owners of such assets cannot expect to move them to another jurisdiction if government becomes oppressive. As an indicator of average ownership of nonredeployable assets, I shall seek to measure physical capital per capita.

Redeployable assets, in contrast, are those that can find a nearly equal second use and that therefore command strong resale markets. Given the ability of governments to interdict most physical exports, virtually the only asset assured of value outside its existing jurisdiction is one's own capabilities and skills—that is, human capital. A good indicator of assets redeployable across borders is therefore human capital per capita, conventionally measured as mean years of education in the adult population.[17] Such capital will, however, have "exile" value only to the extent that conversion costs are low: advanced medical skills in a person who speaks only Mongolian are of little value outside Mongolia.

In partial equilibrium, then, elasticity of demand for access, and hence the level of access that monopolistic government provides, is expected to vary among countries directly with ease of exit, inversely with per capita endowment of physical capital, and directly (but interactively with ease of exit) with per capita endowment of human capital.[18]

As soon as we admit that people choose and alter their investments, however, we see why this equilibrium—which regards portfolios as exogenous—is only partial. To move to a more general understanding, we must recognize that barriers to exit become barriers to entry and that people demand particular kinds of guarantees, and a particular sort of influence, before they will invest in nonredeployable (and therefore more easily expropriated) assets.

Our best insights into investment in specific, nonredeployable assets come from a generation of studies of investment in firms.[19] These have shown repeatedly that people put their money into firm-specific assets— that is, ones that have little or no value outside the firm—not as loans but only in the form of equity shares, whose crucial characteristic is that they carry voting control over the firm's direction.

Trucking firms, for example, are typically financed by contractual

[17] A worthy effort to measure quality, instead of merely quantity, of education is Barro and Lee 1993.

[18] We interact human capital with ease of exit to get an estimate of the productive assets that the average subject might hope to take along. Because most physical capital cannot be removed, there is no point in interacting it with ease of exit.

[19] The seminal paper is Alchian and Demsetz 1972; another landmark is Williamson 1985, esp. 304–6.

debt because their chief asset, trucks, can readily be resold. Default entails simple forfeiture and resale of collateral, and lenders' risk is correspondingly limited. At the opposite extreme, computer and pharmaceutical firms are overwhelmingly financed by equity, for they necessarily invest in technologies and expertise that cannot be resold—assets that, as Williamson (1985, 306) puts it, "are numerous and ill-defined and cannot be protected in a well-focused, transaction-specific way."[20] To protect such "trapped" assets, investors insist on a definite voice in management—a system of "one share, one vote" that looks surprisingly like democracy.

Why do investors insist on the voting control? In Williamson's analysis, the fundamental difficulty with specific assets is incomplete contracting or, more precisely, a situation in which no conceivable contract could cover all eventualities. Where a single principal must contract incompletely with many agents, the answer lies in establishing what March and Simon (1958; cited in Williamson 1985, 218ff.) call the "zone of acceptance": a bounded authoritarian rule of employer over employee. Where many principals must contract incompletely with one or a few agents, the answer is voting power to supervise and, if necessary, to dismiss the agent or agents.

Now comes the crucial point. Anticipating this aspect of capital markets, firms pursue financing by equity rather than by debt precisely to the extent that the assets they need to finance are nonredeployable. It is the essence of becoming a public joint-stock corporation that managers widen access to corporate decision making in the specific form of granting voting control to "outsiders." And managers expand access in this way not because they prefer shared governance to unchallenged control or because they think the joint-stock corporation morally superior, but because, in the market situation they face, shared control benefits them by increasing their profits.

Precisely because, in partial equilibrium, nonredeployable assets would be trapped in the firm, in general equilibrium investment in such assets occurs only at the price of voting control. In partial equilibrium, firms with the least redeployable assets would exploit their investors most; in general equilibrium, it is precisely such firms that exhibit the most "democratic" control by investors.[21] To push the point even far-

---

[20] Williamson goes on to conjecture that countries with ill-developed equities markets will force some firms into suboptimal investment in redeployable assets and discourage altogether ones that must make nonredeployable investments.

[21] What happens if such shareholder control is for some reason impossible, e.g., local laws burden or prohibit joint-stock organization of firms? Williamson (1985, 306) provides the obvious answer; investment in nonredeployable capital will be suboptimal, investment in nonspecific assets will be superoptimal. Extending this insight yields an in-

ther: Given that firms with fully redeployable assets face perfectly elastic demand for influence,[22] ones with specific assets seek in essence to make their own demand curves more elastic through commitments to one share–one vote corporate governance.

From this point the extension to state structure is easy, if hardly indisputable. Rulers forgo potential monopoly rents from restricted sale of influence in order to attract and retain the physical capital that makes their economies prosper and thus expands their revenue base.[23] They do so in the same way as corporate managers do, by committing themselves to submit periodically to voting control by the relevant "shareholders"; doing so increases effective elasticity of demand and hence both lowers the price and increases the level at which access is supplied.[24] To a lesser extent, subjects adjust their linguistic and cultural "portfolios" to insure against predatory rule.[25]

In general equilibrium, then, we expect access to governmental decision making, particularly as entrenched in the franchise, to vary inversely with ease of exit, directly with per capita endowment of physical capital, directly (but interactively with ease of exit, proxied either as fluency in a world language or as smallness of population) with per capita endowment of human capital (proxied as mean years of education in the adult population).[26]

---

triguing (and, so far as I know, untested) corollary: Subjects of nondemocratic regimes overinvest in human capital, underinvest in physical capital.

[22] This assumes thick and well-functioning secondary markets in firms' obligations, which in effect minimize costs of conversion—i.e., of "dumping" the bonds of a badly performing firm. To the extent that funds could not flow freely among distinct markets (e.g., among localities or clans), investors would be more exploitable. For evidence that national boundaries still segregate in this way, see Feldstein and Horioka 1980 and Feldstein 1995. Greater cross-border capital mobility—according to one estimate almost $1 trillion daily by 1992 and growing geometrically (Keohane and Milner 1996, introduction)—will work powerfully to guarantee human freedom but paradoxically may eventually undermine democracy.

[23] This trade-off suggests an optimal value for |ε|, but I have not yet specified the model well enough to set out anything like first-order conditions.

[24] Could subjects of large states not adjust similarly, learning additional languages and cultures as a way of insuring against domestic tyranny? Presumably in general equilibrium they do, but only slightly: This is too expensive an insurance against too distant a risk. Only the more immediate inducements of professional necessity lead to a broader linguistic portfolio. (I owe this point to an anonymous referee.)

[25] Familiar cases include German Jews who intensified their learning of English or French after 1933 to ease emigration, or Russians or Chinese who learned English specifically with an eye to eventual exit; but already high costs of learning other languages are then often raised by distrustful rulers (restricting access to "enemy" languages, jamming foreign broadcasts, etc.).

[26] See above, n. 18.

There remains at least one potentially telling objection. Why is governmental access granted on the basis of one person, one vote, rather than (as in corporations) "one share, one vote" or in differing amounts at different prices? In the nineteenth century, partially democratized regimes often coupled the franchise with a property requirement, and a few weighted votes differently according to wealth (the Prussian three-class system, Belgium's multiple votes). In earlier centuries, governments actually sold offices of varying influence at different prices, such as the *venalité des charges* of prerevolutionary France (cf. Anderson 1974).

At least as a plausible conjecture, suppose that there is only one significant currency for which modern rulers will trade access, namely, some finite but ex ante unspecifiable probability of being able to conscript the subject for total service (military or other) during wartime (cf. Ginsberg 1982, chap. 1). Given that one person can provide only one body, there is little reason to grant different levels of access; rather, the sole "pricing" issue becomes one of how far to extend the franchise into groups with low probabilities of service. According to this interpretation, the various quasi-ascriptive characteristics that have delimited the franchise (ancestry, property, sex, age) have served as proxies for those probabilities,[27] and each extension of the vote has involved inclusion of a group perceived as having lower probability of serving.[28]

Whatever the precise mechanism, the fact is that in modern societies the issue is how far to extend and how effective to make the equal franchise. The theory as I have so far outlined it suggests strong cross-sectional links between democracy and three specific, measurable variables. Do these links in fact obtain?

Data from Ninety-seven Countries

As a preliminary test of plausibility, we investigate the correlates of democratic rule among the almost two hundred independent countries ranked on the Gastil–Freedom House scoring of "political rights," equivalent in present circumstances to democracy as defined earlier.[29] In essence, we estimate the model that

[27] Our modern assumption that the poor will bear the brunt of the fighting dates only from the French Revolution. Until then, and long after in more conservative states, rulers feared to arm the poor and relied as much as possible on bourgeois and aristocratic forces.

[28] Rulers do not, however, restrict the franchise to those who are on active service (e.g. the Roman *comitia centuriata*) or who have served because they would thereby lose the loyalty, or precipitate the emigration, of subjects who knew privately that they were unlikely to serve.

[29] Since even the most oppressive modern dictators (such as Ceauşescu, Saddam Hus-

$$\text{democracy} = a + b_1 \text{ (physical capital)} + b_2 \text{ (human capital)} + b_3$$
$$\text{(ease of exit)} + b_4 \text{ (human capital * ease of exit)} + \epsilon.$$

That is, cross-sectionally democratic rule will vary directly with a given country's endowment of physical capital and ease of exit and interactively with endowment of human capital and ease of exit.[30] To allow for the possibility that intercept, as well as slope, varies with human capital, we introduce mean education (the proxy for human capital) as a separate, as well as an interactive, term.

Because the Gastil ranking is a constrained and categorical-dependent variable (1 = most democratic, 7 = least democratic), ordinary least-squares (OLS) estimation is inappropriate (see, e.g., Hanushek and Jackson 1977, chap. 7). Given, however, that the categories have a definite ranking, one suitable method of estimation is ordered probit (Dubin and Rivers 1988, 62).[31] In view of the very sparse population of some of the Gastil categories (see table 4.1), it seems worth the slight loss of information to collapse the seven-point ranking into a four-point one.[32] Rankings 3, 4, and 5 are merged, as are 6 and 7, yielding in essence categorizations of "fully democratic," "mostly democratic," "somewhat democratic," and "undemocratic." The probit procedure thus estimates predictors of the probabilities that a given country will fall into one or another of these four categories.

Data on the variables regarded here as exogenous are drawn from four standard sources. Human capital is operationalized as mean years of education in the year 1992 in the population aged twenty-five and over, as reported in United Nations Development Program 1992 (136–37, 190).[33] A proxy for physical capital is given in table 9 of World Bank 1993. Because good data on physical capital are available for

---

sein, Mobutu) almost always carry out sham elections, the issue is not the extent of the nominal franchise but whether voting effectively chooses leadership. Two of Gastil's indicators (chief authority elected by a meaningful process; legislature recently elected by a meaningful process) ask whether rulers are elected at all; one (multiple parties) whether elections offer choice; one (fair election laws, campaign opportunities, and polling procedures) whether choice is free; and two (recent shifts in power through elections; significant opposition vote) whether choice is effectively exercised. (Civil liberties comprise a separate index not referenced here.) The weaker a country's score for "political rights" on the Gastil index, the likelier it is that the effective franchise is confined to a small elite. See Gastil 1986, 9–10, 11–18.

[30] See above, n. 18.

[31] I am grateful to Mathew McCubbins for guidance on these points.

[32] The essential findings reported here were robust under other mergers into three or five categories. The probit routine failed to converge after sixteen iterations when all seven original categories were included.

[33] Such a measure ignores differences in quality of education but is readily available for a large set of states. See above, n. 17.

TABLE 4.1

Distribution of Cases among Ranks on Gastil Political Freedom Index

	Freedom House Political Rank							
Freedom	1	1.5	2	3	4	5	6	7
Count	38	1	28	9	13	9	41	19
Percent	24.05	0.63	17.72	5.70	8.23	5.70	25.95	12.03

Note: 158 valid observations. 1 = most democratic, 7 = least democratic.

only a few countries (most of them economically advanced),[34] I use information on 1991 per capita investment[35]—that is, accumulation of new capital.[36]

As noted earlier, I employ two proxies for ease of exit, both imperfect. The first, compiled by Hall and Jones (1996, data appendix), is the share of the country's population for whom a "world language" is "the primary language spoken at home."[37] The less direct but broader indicator of culturo-linguistic versatility is simply the inverse of population size, and for this I also employ the data reported by the World Bank (1993). Probably because second languages do not register in the Hall-Jones measure—for example, Denmark, India, the Netherlands, and Sweden all are classified as having no speakers of English—these two proxies turn out to be very weakly correlated ($r = .19$). In all, data on the four variables are available for a total of ninety-seven countries.

---

[34] "The available data on physical capital seem unreliable, especially for developing countries and even in relation to the measures of human capital, because they depend on arbitrary assumptions about depreciation and on inaccurate measures of benchmark stocks and investment flows" (Barro and Lee 1993, 374).

[35] The numbers used here are products of two figures reported by the World Bank, namely gross domestic investment as a share of GDP and (dollar) GNP per capita (World Bank 1993, table 1). The product approximates (dollar) investment per capita, since (investment/GDP) (GDP/population) = investment/population.

[36] Declining marginal productivity of capital would of course imply a higher return to, and thus higher investment in, regions less abundant in physical capital. In practice, however, new investment seems to correlate cross-nationally with existing investment (cf. Barro 1991). For fifty-four of the countries examined here, the Penn World Tables (on-line database, May 1996) offer estimates of capital stock per worker for at least one year in the period 1990–1992 at 1985 international prices. The correlation between those values and the ones for investment per capita used here is $r = .93$.

[37] These languages include Arabic, Chinese, English, French, German, Portuguese, Russian, and Spanish. The classification is taken over by Hall and Jones from Gunnemark (1991) and allegedly comprises the languages that "carry the bulk of international communication." "Data on second languages are available in some countries, but collection is not uniform and interpretation is much more subjective" (Hall and Jones 1996, 12m 22).

TABLE 4.2

Human Capital, Physical Capital, and Command of World Language as Predictors of Democracy: Ninety-seven Countries (Probit estimation. Dependent variable: Gastil political-freedom index)

Value	Label	Count	Percent	Upper Threshold
1	fully democratic	26	26.80	0.000
2	mostly democratic	20	20.62	0.333
4	somewhat democratic	24	24.74	0.588
6	undemocratic	27	27.84	

At convergence grade * dir = 0.000685

Independent Variable	Estimated Coefficient	Standard Error	t-Statistic
constant	3.10130	0.33074	9.37696
physical capital[a]	−0.404908	1.64066e-004	−2.46796
human capital[b]	−0.23477	6.62308e-002	−3.54465
% w/world language	0.27375	0.75709	0.36159
humcap*lang	−0.23167	0.14502	−1.59752
Threshold 1	1.28712	0.17713	7.26636
Threshold 2	2.39777	0.20976	11.43123

auxiliary statistics	at convergence	initial
log likelihood	−82.738	−150.77
number of observations	97	
percent predicted correctly	61.856	

[a]1992 investment in thousands of dollars per worker.
[b]Mean years of education, citizens aged twenty-five or higher, 1992.

A first test is reported in table 4.2. Recalling that lower rankings mean a higher degree of democracy, we see that, as anticipated, democracy increases with physical capital, with human capital, and with the product of human capital and linguistic expertise. Against our initial expectations, linguistic expertise appears to have no direct effect—the estimated coefficient b_3 does not differ significantly from zero. In table 4.3, we therefore reestimate, eliminating the direct term. All variables appear to be significant at well over the .05 level.[38]

[38] It should be noted that education is collinear with physical capital (r = .73). We should expect this to introduce a larger standard error, and hence a lower t-score, for the estimated coefficient of one or both variables (see, e.g., Pindyck and Rubinfeld 1991, 83–85). In other words, the coefficients estimated here are probably more significant than their t-scores suggest. Education, however, is but weakly associated with command of a

TABLE 4.3

Human Capital, Physical Capital, and Command of World Language as
Predictors of Democracy: Ninety-seven Countries, Modified Specification
(Probit estimation. Dependent variable: Gastil political-freedom index)

Value	Label	Count	Percent	Upper Threshold
1	fully democratic	26	26.80	0.000
2	mostly democratic	20	20.62	0.333
4	somewhat democratic	24	24.74	0.588
6	undemocratic	27	27.84	

At convergence grade * dir = 0.000520

Independent Variable	Estimated Coefficient	Standard Error	t-Statistic
constant	3.13857	0.30820	10.18356
physical capital[a]	−0.39526	1.61506e-004	−2.44736
human capital[b]	−0.24349	6.12562e-002	−3.97497
humcap*lang	−0.18415	6.12977e-002	−3.00424
Threshold 1	1.27629	0.17595	7.25369
Threshold 2	2.39077	0.21038	11.36432

auxiliary statistics	at convergence	initial
log likelihood	−82.805	−150.77
number of observations	97	
percent predicted correctly	62.887	

[a]1992 investment in thousands of dollars per worker.
[b]Mean years of education, citizens aged twenty-five or higher, 1992.

Table 4.4 presents the analogous initial specification substituting inverse of population as the proxy for ease of exit.[39] Again, we observe that physical capital, human capital, and the product of human capital and our measure of ease of exit appear to have significant effects, while ease of exit by itself does not. Reestimating in table 4.5, we again find all variables significant at the .05 level.

To interpret the coefficients, recall that probit estimates (normally distributed) probabilities that a given case will fall into one category or another. Consider the average country in our set of ninety-seven. It has $1,776 of "capital" (new investment in 1992) per worker, 3.64 years of education in the typical citizen aged twenty-five or over, 35.6 percent of its citizens speaking chiefly a world language at home, and a population

---

world language ($r = .36$).

[39] Parenthetically, human capital is only weakly correlated with human capital/population ($r = .16$).

TABLE 4.4

Human Capital, Physical Capital, and Inverse of Population as Predictors of Democracy: Ninety-seven Countries (Probit estimation. Dependent variable: Gastil political-freedom index)

Value	Label	Count	Percent	Upper Threshold
1	fully democratic	26	26.80	0.000
2	mostly democratic	20	20.62	0.333
4	somewhat democratic	24	24.74	0.588
6	undemocratic	27	27.84	

At convergence grade * dir = 0.000625

Independent Variable	Estimated Coefficient	Standard Error	t-Statistic
constant	2.93222	0.37505	7.81829
physical capital[a]	−0.34657	0.161326	−2.14830
human capital[b]	−0.25222	0.072195	−3.49353
1/pop (m)	1.29391	1.58684	0.81540
humcap/pop (m)	−0.55497	0.35907	−1.54557
Threshold 1	1.23789	0.17047	7.26149
Threshold 2	2.31750	0.20257	11.44056

auxiliary statistics	at convergence	initial
log likelihood	−85.042	−150.77
number of observations	97	
percent predicted correctly	52.577	

[a]1992 investment in thousands of dollars per worker.
[b]Mean years of education, citizens aged twenty-five or higher, 1992.

of 5.24 million. Plugged in to the estimated formulas of tables 4.3 and 4.5, these figures would give our average country respective scores of 1.353 and 1.285. This says, in essence, that the probability that our average country will fall into the "most democratic" category is the area under the unit normal curve between $-\infty$ and the given number of standard deviations from the mean: in the first case about .09, in the second almost exactly .10. The probability that such a case will fall into either the most or the second most democratic category is the area under the normal curve left of the point defined by "Threshold 1" minus the calculated value: in the first case $1.276 - 1.353 = -.077$, in the second $1.237 - 1.285 = -.048$ standard deviations. This turns out to be .47 or .48; hence, the probability that our average case will fall into category 2 is .38 by either reckoning. Proceeding in this way, we can say that our average country has approximately a probability of .10 of fall-

TABLE 4.5

Human Capital, Physical Capital, and Inverse of Population as Predictors of
Democracy; Ninety-seven Countries, Modified Specification (Probit estimation.
Dependent variable: collapsed [four-category] Gastil index)

Value	Label	Count	Percent	Upper Threshold
1	fully democratic	26	26.80	0.000
2	mostly democratic	20	20.62	0.333
4	somewhat democratic	24	24.74	0.588
6	undemocratic	27	27.84	

At convergence grade * dir = 0.000602

Independent Variable	Estimated Coefficient	Standard Error	t-Statistic
constant	3.11599	0.30270	10.29409
physical capital[a]	−0.32204	0.15753	−2.04427
human capital[b]	−0.28886	0.05697	−5.07057
humcap/pop (m)	−0.29890	0.15278	−1.95642
Threshold 1	1.23698	0.17023	7.26641
Threshold 2	2.31538	0.20242	11.43821

auxiliary statistics	at convergence	initial
log likelihood	−85.387	−150.77
number of observations	97	
percent predicted correctly	52.577	

[a]1992 investment in thousands of dollars per worker.
[b]Mean years of education, citizens aged twenty-five or higher, 1992.

ing into the "fully democratic" category, .38 of being in the "mostly democratic" group, .37 or .38 of entering the "somewhat democratic" category, and .15 of being in the "least democratic" group.[40]

What, then, is the marginal change that more physical or human capital, a greater command of world languages, or a smaller population would make on the democratic chances of such an average country? Under the first specification (table 4.3), an additional $1,000 per worker in physical capital would by itself raise the odds of being fully democratic from .09 to .17; an additional year of education, from .09 to .15; an additional tenth of the population mastering a world lan-

[40] To compare, India is classified by Gastil as a "3" on the political freedom category, hence in our terms as only "somewhat democratic." With 2.4 years of mean education, $3,500 per capita annual investment, allegedly no primary speakers of a world language, and a population of 849.5 million, it achieves a predicted score of 1.173 by our first specification and 1.298 by our second, hence a predicted probability of between .12 and .10 of ending up in the "most democratic" category.

guage, from .09 only to .10. Under the second specification (table 4.5), either the additional $1,000 per worker in physical capital or the additional year of education per citizen would bring odds of being fully democratic from .10 to .17; halving the country's population (again, independent of other changes) would increase the odds to .19.[41] To look at the matter a different way, to raise our middling country's odds of full democracy from .1 to .5, we could do any one of the following: increase its flow of new investment to almost $6,000 per worker, raise mean education to a bit over eight years, or cut population to about 15 percent of its current level (to a total of around 850,000). But even teaching everyone a world language would not suffice; that would bring the odds only to about .18.

As we would expect, the marginal effects are stronger in countries already near a .5 probability, weaker in those at one of the tails of the distribution. An advanced country with, say, $10,000 per worker in physical capital and on average ten years of education would have odds of better than .999 of falling into the most democratic category even if its population were 1 billion and all of them spoke only Rhaeto-Romansch. At the other extreme, a nation with but $100 of physical capital per worker and an average of 0.1 years of education, even if its population were only a million and all spoke French, would have odds of about .0012 of achieving the most democratic ranking. In these circumstances, small changes in population, education, physical capital, or linguistic repertoire would manifestly achieve very little. Yet even a large or linguistically isolated country with much physical and little human capital, or vice versa, could sharply raise its odds by gaining more of either.

Under the specification of table 4.3, $8,000 in physical capital per worker, no human capital at all, and no primary mastery of a world language would imply odds of about .51 of falling into the most democratic category; adding even a single year of education to the average citizen would raise that probability to about .60. Similarly, no physical capital and an average of twelve years of education (again, under linguistic isolation) would mean odds of about .41 of being most democratic; adding even $1,000 of new physical capital per worker would raise that probability to .57.

In so preliminary an exercise, we can take the precise estimates as only blurry outlines of reality. The more important point is that physical capital, human capital, and size all affect the probability of democratic rule, in each case in the theoretically anticipated direction.

---

[41] Alternatively, lowering the population of our average country by 1 million (from 5.24 to 4.24 million) would raise the odds of its being in the most democratic category to .154.

Implications

The argument sketched out and briefly tested above suggests answers to the specific questions stated at the outset of this essay. The answers, in turn, indicate further possible tests of the theory.

1. Why are rich countries more democratic? With rare exceptions, as we have seen, rich countries are abundant in physical and human capital. The combination inevitably leads to democracy.

2. Why are the few rich but undemocratic countries often resource abundant? Where wealth derives from resources rather than physical or human capital, as in many of the oil-rich Gulf states, demand will be inelastic and little access will be granted.[42]

3. Why were the few countries that adopted democracy early in their economic development sparsely settled "frontier" societies (the United States, Canada, Australia)? First, exit is easier in frontier societies.[43] Second, scarce (and therefore expensive) labor in such societies encourages heavy investment at an early stage in physical and human capital, thus creating the preconditions for democracy even at low levels of wealth.[44]

4. Why has the franchise often been restricted along ascriptive or quasi-ascriptive criteria, and why have those quasi-ascriptive barriers fallen successively as societies have grown wealthier? Such criteria serve as useful proxies for price—that is, what the average member of the given group offers in terms of potential service to the state, especially in wartime (see above, p. 58). Hence, rulers rely on them to delimit the franchise; when they are impelled to expand access, they do so according to such criteria.

---

[42] Saudi Arabia has on average 3.7 years of education among its population aged twenty-five and over (among females, 1.5 years; among males, 5.9), Iraq 4.8, Iran and Bahrain each 3.9, Oman 0.9. (The population-weighted world average is 5.0 years, the developing-country average 3.7.) The World Bank data permit calculation of per capita investment for only one of these countries, Iran, where the amount is $498—just over half the world population-weighted average of $882. All educational data are from United Nations Development Program 1992, 136–37; investment data are calculated from World Bank 1993, tables 1 and 10.

[43] I owe this point to David Lake.

[44] This is elementary microeconomics. Given a fixed isoquant from prevailing production technology, a higher price for one factor of production encourages substitution of (and raises returns to) other factors. Where labor is expensive, more capital and skill will be employed; and returns to capital and skill will rise. According to one empirical estimate (Maddison 1995, 143), in 1890 the United Kingdom had $3,438 in gross fixed nonresidential capital per capita (1990 PPP [purchasing-power parity] dollars), while the United States had $10,355, just over three times as much. Obviously, not all sparsely settled regions achieve such investment. Political instability, in particular, discourages investment in physical capital; in primitive technologies, serfdom and slavery have provided alternative answers to scarcity of labor (cf. Wallerstein 1974).

5. Why has the franchise often changed rapidly and in conjunction with changes in war or trade? Unanticipated shifts in the cost of cross-border trade can enrich or impoverish particular groups within societies (cf. Stolper and Samuelson 1941, Kindleberger 1951, Milner 1988, Rogowski 1989, Frieden 1991), thus shifting the demand for participation and the probability of contributing effectively to defense. Trade's beneficiaries employ some part of their new wealth to bid more for participation, as European workers and middle classes did in the later nineteenth century; trade's victims can pay less and may find their supply of participation swiftly curtailed, as European workers did in the 1930s.

Historians are virtually unanimous that changes in the technology of war often shift markedly the marginal value of particular participants' contributions to rulers' capacity for combat. The rapid development of more labor-intensive warfare in ancient Greece and again in nineteenth-century Europe and North America made raw manpower more valuable and devalued aristocratic expertise; the similarly rapid evolution of skill- and capital-intensive equestrian warfare around 750 C.E. made rulers rely on well-trained and expensively equipped knights.[45] Rulers, just as in the case of trade-induced changes but with even greater immediacy, alter the strategies by which they grant and price access.

6. Why does the franchise loom so large in constitutional struggles? The franchise is important for exactly the same reason as in corporate governance, namely, incomplete contracting in a situation of multiple principles and few agents. Reliance only on rule of law is an effort at complete contracting. The crucial insight of Alchian and Demsetz, Williamson, and others in the industrial-organization tradition is that no complete contract can be written, either for the typical firm or for the typical government.

Conclusion

We have long known that wealth and education are conducive to democratic rule.[46] The present analysis helps to explain the link and to account for the exceptions. More surprising is the effect demonstrated here, conditional on endowment of human capital, of linguistic open-

[45] A superb introduction to this whole topic is North 1981, esp. 104–9, 135–38. On classical Greece, see Forrest 1966, esp. chap. 3, and Burn 1982, 121ff.; on the rise of feudalism, see White 1962. When, as in ancient Greece, changes in trade and war benefit the same group, participation shifts with particular rapidity. Historians of the period without exception emphasize the stunning speed with which democracy emerged.

[46] Lipset's summary (which so far as I am aware remains unrefuted by subsequent research) is still worth emphasizing: "All the relevant studies indicate that education is more important [as a predictor of within-country variations in support for democracy] than either income or occupation" (Lipset 1960, 56; see also esp. chap. 2).

ness and country size.[47] Language and size exert greatest influence at moderate levels of wealth. The most technically advanced and best educated societies will almost always be democratic in any event; the least advanced and worst educated will be authoritarian. At middling levels of physical capital, however, the combination of easy exit and considerable education offers advantages for democratic rule. This may explain why in nineteenth-century Europe it was often the smaller and more linguistically diverse of the more literate states (Belgium, the Netherlands, Switzerland, and the Scandinavian countries, in contrast to equally literate Germany) that moved earliest toward parliamentary rule and a broader franchise.[48] It also offers insights on the seeming imperative of "hard" authoritarian or totalitarian regimes, particularly at middling levels of development, to pursue cultural hegemony, conquest, and expansion (cf. the classical analysis of Arendt 1951 and 1966).

More speculatively, we can use this approach to think through the political implications of three major developments: the end of the Cold War, the entrenchment of a liberal order in international trade, and the rise of a service economy.

Historically, the two chief reasons for large states were defense and a guaranteed home market—as answers, respectively, to international anarchy and international protectionism (see Tilly 1975 and Gourevitch 1979). When every state faced major military threats, small states survived mostly as "buffers" or protectorates; when the world was protectionist, small states could guarantee their producers only a limited home market and could issue no threats of tariff retaliation that might induce rivals to open their markets. To the extent that both constraints are waning—military threats are less, the successive GATT rounds have guaranteed much more open international markets—smaller states have much brighter prospects of survival. Because few states countenance secession, the birth pangs of such smaller states may be severe (as with Bangladesh or Eritrea). Over the longer term, however, their emergence may entail greater democracy, particularly among economies of moderate wealth and education.[49]

[47] Looking at prodemocratic attitudes rather than democratic performance and survival, Dahl and Tufte (1973) found little support for classical arguments about the link between size and democracy.

[48] Katzenstein (1985, chap. 4) argues in essence that such a connection arises from an omitted historical variable: A weak feudal tradition led to both early democratization and small states. The breadth of the present finding, however, including many states and regions where European-style feudalism was never an issue, weighs against Katzenstein's interpretation.

[49] It may, however, turn out that, among the most advanced manufacturing economies, increasing returns to scale require even larger political units, such as the European Union. Cf. Krugman 1991, esp. chap. 3.

The analysis advanced here may however be time bound; or, more precisely, the most economically advanced small states may in future decades turn out to be *less* democratic. If small states, as I have conjectured, encourage mobility, then they will attract the burgeoning service industries rather than manufacturing, and these sectors are in many cases (banking, insurance, law, system design and engineering, software) intensive in human rather than physical capital. For the highly trained, intelligent, and mobile employees of these sectors, exit may prove so easy an option that voice will hardly be an issue. If Singapore proves repressive, the businesses in question may move to Hong Kong or Vienna; if Hong Kong's public services are poor, the answer is not political activism but another move—to Kuala Lumpur, London, Los Angeles, or some other center of the given activity.

Some forty years ago, the brilliant political economist Charles Tiebout (1956) foresaw the political consequences of such perfect mobility. Just as Williamson and Hirschman contend that where customers can exit costlessly to other firms voice is unnecessary—if six groceries are located conveniently to my home, I require no voting power over the management of the nearest to make it serve my needs—so, in Tiebout's analysis, truly costless exit to other political jurisdictions obviates the need for democratic control. Just as the grocer performs best when driven solely by the profit motive, the small-state government with perfectly mobile subjects may provide collective goods most efficiently if it is proprietary—that is, the residual claimant to any surplus of revenues over costs.

Purely as speculation, I am suggesting that the effects of human capital and mobility we have observed here may be only one side of what is really an inverted "U": after some peak, still higher levels of human capital, particularly in very small states with extremely footloose subjects, may be associated with *lower* levels of democracy. A first test of this conjecture will likely come at the level of local government within countries. Do the smallest cities with the most mobile residents (e.g., in larger conurbations where movement across boundaries need not affect employment) either show less-democratic systems of government or display a negative correlation between degree of democracy and plausible measures of performance (e.g., efficient provision of collective goods)?

This is a hunch for future research to follow. Here, it suffices to reemphasize that democratic rule is best guaranteed by material wealth, high levels of education, and—at least among educated populations—easy exit.

5

The International Causes of Democratization, 1974–1990

PAUL W. DRAKE

WHAT WERE the major causes of the democratic "tsunami" that engulfed the globe from 1974 to 1990? In much of the literature on these transitions to democracy ("transitology"), analysts have concluded that outside forces had a marginal impact, especially in Latin America. By contrast, I will argue that international causes must be given high priority. This argument will focus mainly on the Western Hemisphere and particularly on Chile, since multinational factors in regime change were more obviously significant in southern and Eastern Europe.

Introduction

In the Chilean and many other cases, investigators have concluded that external forces played a very limited role. They arrived at this conclusion because they were searching mainly for the results of direct, concrete, intentional, and official policies of foreign governments and agencies. However, a different conclusion can be reached by asking a different question: What was the impact of general tendencies in the global context?[1] In other words, what international factors created an international democratic conjuncture? In this time period, why did democratic regimes become the norm in many parts of the world? To answer this question, it will be necessary to concentrate on broad currents more than precise actions. The emphasis will be on international or multina-

For suggestions for this paper, I am indebted to Ellen Comisso, Peter Evans, Peter Gourevitch, Stephan Haggard, Miles Kahler, David Lake, Sanford Lakoff, Robin Linsenmeyer, Brian Loveman, Victor Magagna, José María Maravall, David Mares, Mathew McCubbins, Eduardo Silva, Peter Smith, Barbara Stallings, and Laurence Whitehead. I am also indebted to the following works: Whitehead in O'Donnell, Schmitter, and Whitehead 1986, 3–46; Diamond 1988; Diamond, Linz, and Lipset 1988; Lowenthal 1991, especially the articles by Whitehead, 356–82, Sheahan, 331–55, and Lowenthal, 383–406; Levine 1988; Karl 1990; Remmer 1991b; Pastor 1989.

[1] Muñoz in Lowenthal 1991, 161–74; Portales in Drake and Jaksic 1991, 251–75; Muñoz and Portales 1987.

tional causes rather than on national processes, without forgetting that the impact of trends varied enormously from country to country.

Two types of international factors must be taken into account. First, some global forces caused disorder, undermined dictatorships, and/or strengthened oppositions, thus requiring sovereigns to repress or liberalize. Second, other international currents created incentives for dictators to liberalize or even democratize. They also made more likely successful democratization without chaos.

Through this international lens, this chapter will try to explain the transition to democracy of over thirty countries in sixteen years. It is untenable to argue that a cycle of change in regimes so vast, rapid, and uniform was a coincidence. It could not have been merely the fortuitous result of myriad national, local, individual, and idiosyncratic decisions. Very few social scientists could believe that so many countries changed their political systems in the same direction at the same time by chance. Profound common causes must be found, without being deterministic.[2]

During a worldwide trend, domestic factors can determine the reception, the transmission, the translation, the character, the form, the pace, the timing, the mechanisms, the actors, the direction, and the outcome of political change in a particular country. In an individual nation in an international period of regime transitions, crucial factors may include the actions of a social group, the rules for an election, the ideology of a political party, or the decisions of a leader. Moreover, the correlation of forces in some countries will produce resistance and rejection of the global propensity, which is not an unavoidable whirlpool but rather a probable tendency in a specific historical epoch.

Principally because of the occidental culture of its elites, its vulnerable peripheral position in the international arena, and its subordination to Great Powers, Latin America has frequently reflected tendencies in Europe and the United States, albeit within its own framework. These external forces have been strategic, political, economic, social, intellectual, and cultural. Near the end of the twentieth century, international factors had an extraordinary impact, partly because of the globalization of capitalism and communications, eroding national barriers to penetration.

Years of perspective on multinational events often lead scholars to deemphasize local factors and to highlight broader, shared elements. It is harder for us to see the big picture, the forest instead of the trees, for events occurring in the 1990s than in the 1890s. Fifty years from now, a

---

[2] Smith 1991; Fukuyama 1992; Huntington 1991; Diamond and Plattner 1993, especially ix–xxvi; Baloyra 1987; Pridham 1991; Whitehead in Pastor 1989 and in Pridham 1991, 45–61; Stepan in O'Donnell, Schmitter, and Whitehead 1986, 64–84; Frohmann 1993.

historian might be more likely to perceive the prevalent trends in our era. To underscore the significance of hindsight to discern global patterns, it is worthwhile to look briefly at the causes of two previous liberalization periods in Latin American political regimes. In large part, both occurred as reactions to huge transformations in the international system, similar to the economic crisis and the end of the Cold War in the 1980s.[3]

In the first instance, why did the diverse Latin American colonies struggle for independence from various crowns from 1808 to 1824? From today's perspective, it seems obvious that those movements would not have caught fire in the early years of the nineteenth century without the winds of change from overseas. External factors fomented disorder, and the New World elites perceived benefits from abandoning the sovereign. When the king chose to repress rather than liberalize, the colonists mounted sufficient force to break his grip.

In the latter years of the eighteenth century, the administrative and economic reforms of the Bourbon monarchs had displeased some Creole elites in the New World. In the beginning of the nineteenth century, the wars in Europe, especially the invasion of Iberia by the French, who deposed the Spanish and Portuguese monarchs, eventually drove many Latin Americans to declare their independence. Among economic factors pulling the Creoles in a liberal direction was the expansion of commerce between Europe and Latin America. Imperial pressures in favor of free trade and democracy emanated from Great Britain and the United States. The ideological influence of new liberal beliefs was propelled by the French and U.S. revolutions. And the domino effect swept the hemisphere as one colony after another broke away from their mother countries.[4]

In the second instance, why did most Latin American countries experience an opening to democracy and the left between 1944 and 1946? Again, many historians would emphasize international forces. One of the basic causes was the widespread pent-up hope—fueled by propaganda and assistance from the Allies—for a postwar bonanza of democracy and prosperity. The victory in World War II of the democratic and leftist countries and the brief cooperation between capitalist and com-

---

[3] In this chapter, all of the discussions about regimes in the Western Hemisphere apply only to the Latin American countries. All the statements about democracy refer simply to a narrow definition of the political processes, rules, and institutions normally associated with elected, representative, civilian governments. This definition says nothing about social or economic justice. Schmitter and Karl in Diamond and Plattner 1993, 39–52; Dahl 1971.

[4] Lynch 1973.

munist powers made it attractive to Latin Americans to get on the bandwagon.

After this democratic spring, most Latin American countries switched abruptly to more autocratic and rightist political systems—in several cases military dictatorships—from 1946 to 1956. Without a doubt, the intensified global struggle between capitalists and communists had an enormous impact economically, strategically, and ideologically. The United States changed its relations with the rest of the hemisphere to align with almost any type of government—in many cases authoritarian regimes—willing to combat the "Red menace."[5]

The Democratic Tsunami

The democratic deluge between 1974 and 1990 was the biggest in history. The flood started in southern Europe, continued in Latin America, and reached high tide in Russia and Eastern Europe. This period saw the establishment of the following new democratic governments:

1974: Portugal, Greece
1976: Spain
1979: Ecuador
1980: Peru
1982: Honduras, Bolivia
1983: Argentina, Turkey, Grenada
1984: El Salvador, Uruguay, Nicaragua
1985: Brazil, Guatemala
1986: Philippines
1987: South Korea
1988: Pakistan
1989: Paraguay, Taiwan, Poland, Hungary, East Germany, Panama, Czechoslovakia, Bulgaria, Romania, Albania
1990: Yugoslavia, Russia, Latvia, Estonia, Lithuania, Mongolia, Chile, Nicaragua, Haiti

In sixteen years, more than thirty countries adopted democratic forms of government. And the trend continued thereafter.[6]

---

[5] Bethell and Roxborough 1992; Rock 1994; Huntington 1991, 18–19; Whitehead in O'Donnell, Schmitter, and Whitehead 1986, 34–35.

[6] Although no one doubts that a democratic impulse circled the globe, this is not a perfect list. Some of these so-called democracies are flimsy at best and riddled with authoritarian remnants. Particularly dubious regimes can be found in Central America, Mexico, and the remains of the Soviet empire. The roster here emphasizes cases in Europe

Without question, in 1990 Latin America displayed the highest number of formal democracies in its history. That wave started in the Andes. Before the general economic crisis of the early eighties, the authoritarian governments in Ecuador and Peru experienced grave problems with sluggish economies and burgeoning foreign debts. Partly for that reason, they turned over power to elected successors at the end of the 1970s. The ability of those rickety civilian administrations to survive during the economic disaster of the 1980s testified to the strength of the international democratic trend. In Ecuador and Peru after democratization, citizens expressed discontent with the struggling economy through electoral changes of governments rather than through unconstitutional changes of regimes. During the economic downturn, voters also used ballots to overturn unpopular governments in the continuing democracies of Colombia, Venezuela, Costa Rica, and the Dominican Republic.

After the economic collapse of most of Latin America in 1981 and 1982, some despotic governments quickly turned over the reins to democratic leaders between 1982 and 1986 (Honduras, Bolivia, Argentina, El Salvador, Uruguay, Nicaragua, Brazil, Guatemala). Other dictatorships held out longer, clashing with protests against economic and political hardships and then leaving office between 1987 and 1990 (Panama, Paraguay, Chile, Nicaragua, Haiti). In the hemisphere, only two authoritarian regimes survived the stampede of democratization during the "lost decade" of economic misery: Mexico and Cuba. Both survivors had governments with revolutionary and nationalistic legitimacy, with a powerful official party, a tradition of resistance against U.S. political demands, and leaders who retained a significant, if shrinking, social base.[7]

Looking back at the elongated "decade of democratization" from the 1970s through the 1980s, four clusters of international causes can be identified to explain that phenomenon: economic factors, imperial factors, ideological factors, and domino factors.[8]

---

and Latin America, but some experts argue that other countries in Africa and Asia should be added. I lack the expertise or information to judge many Asian or African cases. Scholars can also disagree on what dates the new democratic regime began (for example, in Chile, a case could be made for 1988, 1989, or 1990). There still exists a controversy over the definition of the political system in Nicaragua under the Sandinistas, so its democratization is listed both in 1984 and 1990. Huntington 1991; Pastor 1989; Diamond and Plattner 1993, especially the chapter on Africa by Richard Joseph, 307–20.

[7] Drake in Stallings and Kaufman 1989, 39–58; Drake and Silva 1986.

[8] Rustow 1990.

Economic Factors

PRIOR ECONOMIC GROWTH

Economic growth made civil society more complex, assertive, and costly to repress. Without reverting to "modernization" theory, it remains true historically that a certain minimal level of socioeconomic modernization has been useful for democratization, although it has not been a necessary or a sufficient condition. In a protracted, slow, conflictual, and asynchronous process, the worldwide dissemination of capitalism has nurtured urbanization, education, industrialization, specialization, and social heterogeneity. The spread of capitalism has spawned new social classes, particularly the bourgeoisie, the petty bourgeoisie, and the proletariat. When those groups have demanded greater political participation, the result has been either severe repression, gradual democratization, or, in rare cases, social revolution.[9]

Pressures from emerging social strata to be taken into account were very notable in the first half of the twentieth century in many South American countries and in the 1970s in the Central American republics. In nearly all of Latin America, economic growth in the seventies augmented desires for Western-style consumption, for an improved standard of living, and for democracy in the eighties. Eventually, economic successes stimulated parallel desires for economic and political liberalism.[10]

NEW TECHNOLOGIES

At the same time, the development of new technologies facilitated the expansion of capitalism, the private sector, individualism, and democratic possibilities. While citizens became harder to police and control, the state lost power. Modern means of communication almost instantaneously brought information about successful economic models and democratization to consumers around the globe, raising expectations and mobilizations. This lightning learning was aided by the proliferation of cable television, especially the Cable News Network (CNN). Another liberating new technology was the personal computer, which delivered more power to individuals and less to the state. Fax machines also permitted more rapid and individual communication among and

[9] Johnson (1958); Klarén and Bossert (1986).

[10] Diamond, Linz, and Lipset 1988; Seligson in Malloy and Seligson 1987, 3–14; Cardoso in Stepan 1989, 299–326; Stephens 1989; Rueschemeyer, Stephens, and Stephens 1992; Arat 1988; Urrutia 1991.

within countries. In addition, the democratic opposition was helped by new campaign techniques from more advanced countries, such as polls and focus groups.[11]

INTERNATIONAL DEPRESSION AND DEBT CRISIS

Often in the past, fundamental changes in political systems have occurred as reactions to crises in the international economy. Although economic factors have provoked transformations of political regimes, they have rarely determined the new political direction. For example, during the Great Depression at the start of the 1930s, many strong leaders with new coalitions and programs took power. But these politicians and their projects were very diverse, including Adolf Hitler and National Socialism in Germany, Getúlio Vargas and the New State in Brazil, and Franklin Roosevelt and the New Deal in the United States. In such dramatic changes, usually the new government is the opposite of the previous administration, whether it was democratic or authoritarian, leftist or rightist. In Latin America, the debt crisis of 1930 toppled many democracies, while the debt crisis of 1982 mainly damaged dictatorships.[12]

As in the past, the recent inundation of regime changes was accompanied by economic crises. The petroleum shock and the world recession during 1973–1974 undercut several political regimes, especially those in oil-importing countries. Particularly shaken were the governments in Portugal, Greece, Spain, the Philippines, Brazil, Uruguay, and Chile. The second petroleum shock in 1979 also stunned several governments. At the same time, difficulties with foreign debts began to appear, notoriously in Peru.[13]

In the democratic tsunami, the first more general economic jolt was the international recession in 1981, partly caused by anti-inflationary policies in the United States. As U.S. interest rates rose, the foreign debt crisis took hold in 1982. Battered by that financial disaster, Latin America became weaker and more vulnerable to foreign pressure to convert to economic and political liberalism. Discontent with existing governments rose.[14]

The debt crisis facilitated democratization in four ways. First, it destroyed the image of economic efficiency cultivated by authoritarian

[11] Huntington 1991, 45, 61–72, 101–2; Skidmore 1993.

[12] Gourevitch 1986, 1978; Rosenau 1969; Gilpin 1987; Pridham in Pridham 1991, 1–30.

[13] Stallings in Fagen 1979, 217–53; Pridham (1984), especially the chapters by Pridham, 1–29, and Tovias, 158–71; Huntington 1991, 51.

[14] Fishlow in Stepan 1989, 83–119; Bacha y Malan in Stepan 1989, 120–42; Ekiert 1991; Stallings 1987; Kuczynski 1988; Kahler 1986; Roett in Hartlyn, Schoultz, and Varas 1992, 131–51; Smith 1991, 615, 632.

governments, leaving them with little legitimacy. Second, the financial debacle provoked massive protests against autocratic rule, with denunciations coming from many in the middle and upper classes as well as from workers. Third, such difficult circumstances reduced the desire of some dictators to continue governing. Fourth, the sudden scarcity of resources diminished the possibility of the authoritarians being replaced by a populist or leftist leader of a large, activist, progressive state aligned with an aggressive working class. This diminution of leftist, redistributive threats dispelled the long-standing fears of democracy harbored by right-wing groups.[15]

GLOBALIZATION AND NEOLIBERALISM

With the globalization of competitive capitalism and of neoliberal, free-market models in the 1980s, working-class organizations lost strength in most of the world. The internationalization of investment and production left trade unions with few economic or political allies. Consequently, the likelihood of populist or leftist governments shrank, as did efforts to redistribute income and power. With less to fear now from workers and reformers, business executives and military officers became more willing to accept formal democracies.[16]

Although debilitated, U.S. unions pressed harder than ever for democratic rights for their counterparts in Latin America. North American unionists promoted that cause principally through the American Institute for Free Labor Development. Their campaign had more impact than in the past for three reasons: The right-wing dictatorships and neoliberalism had sapped Latin American unions and increased their need for external assistance; the winding down of the cold war had doomed communist alternatives; and U.S. trade unionists had acquired a greater stake in improving conditions for Latin American workers so that U.S. capitalists would not be lured abroad by weak unions and low wages. U.S. labor leaders denounced the repression of unions and wages in underdeveloped countries as illegal unfair trade practices.[17]

In Latin America, neoliberalism and privatization—while exacting cruel social costs—multiplied the number of supporters of private property and capitalism. Meanwhile, enthusiasm for populism or socialism shriveled. A central objective of nationalistic socialism and populism had been to use the state to control capital, but that was no longer a

[15] Frieden 1991; Huntington 1991, 45.
[16] Roxborough in Stallings and Kaufman 1989, 91–108; Frieden 1991, 152–53; Gourevitch 1986, 224, 227.
[17] Buchanan in Lowenthal 1991, 296–328; Romualdi 1967; Spalding, Jr. 1977; MacLeod 1993.

very viable strategy in the face of the globalization of economic competition. More limited, constrained democracies became more acceptable to capitalists. According to partisans of neoliberalism, the reduction of the state, the invigoration of the private sector, the expansion of property ownership, and the reliance on market mechanisms comported with classic theories of the economic prerequisites for a liberal political system. Allegedly, individualism would now dominate both the economic and political marketplaces.[18]

The 1982–1983 recession fortified the democratic opposition in most of Latin America. From 1984 onward, worldwide economic recuperation generated an international consensus in favor of combining liberal economics and politics. By the early nineties, Latin America was growing, some countries quite rapidly, thus facilitating democratic consolidation.

International economic agents—such as the International Monetary Fund and the World Bank—reinforced the neoliberal consensus. They even strayed beyond economics to make some gestures in favor of democracy. The same pitch came from U.S. economic institutions, such as the Agency for International Development. Whereas the principal source of foreign loans in the 1970s was private banks, that role in the 1980s was taken over by public agencies, adding more weight to their pronouncements.

For Latin Americans, the possibilities of entering into free-trade agreements, especially with the United States, solidified their propensity to wed economic and political liberalism. Washington preferred to negotiate such accords with democratic governments. However, for special geopolitical reasons, it signed the first agreement in Latin America with Mexico, whose mixed political system contained significant authoritarian elements.[19]

Imperial Factors

Besides economics, other forces (strategic, geopolitical, diplomatic, and so on) emanating from the Great Powers also undermined dictatorships, fortified their opponents, and encouraged liberalization. During the second half of the 1980s, four of the most powerful entities in the world were in favor of democratization: the United States, Western Europe, the Soviet Union, and the Vatican. With the influence of Washington on the capitalists and the armed forces and that of the papacy on the Ro-

[18] Hachette and Lüders 1992.
[19] Stallings 1993; Stallings in Haggard and Kaufman 1992, 41–88; Nelson and Eglington 1992.

man Catholic Church, the three Latin American groups historically most favorable to authoritarianism were being pushed toward democracy.

THE IMPACT OF THE UNITED STATES AND WESTERN EUROPE

Without being ethnocentric, it is worth noting that the democratic tsunami most influenced countries that were close to the West in their geographic and strategic locations, their histories, their cultures, their languages, their religions, their societies, and their economies. These countries were more susceptible to currents flowing from the United States and Western Europe. Partly for that reason, democratization had more success in southern Europe, Latin America, and Eastern Europe than in Africa, the Middle East, or Asia.[20]

In the long run, perhaps the most important influence of the United States and Western Europe was their roles as successful economic, political, and cultural models. Their success aroused discontent and envy among those oppressed and tempted the oppressors to emulate their model. Naturally, the United States carried more weight in Latin America, and Western Europe in the rest of Europe. The North Americans had the most clout with the two Latin American groups traditionally most powerful, conservative, and authoritarian: the military and the capitalists. For example, the Pentagon sent officers to convince their Latin American counterparts to take seriously the new U.S. policy in favor of democracy. In similar fashion, Washington reversed an attempted "self-coup" by President Jorge Serrano of Guatemala in 1993 mainly by communicating its displeasure to the armed forces and the business elites.[21]

In Latin America, direct pressure from the United States and, to a lesser degree, from Western Europe had a positive, although discreet, impact on democratization. These concrete actions intensified the general dissemination of international signals and incentives favorable to democracy. Although any one nudge rarely evoked much response, the cumulative effect of many forms of prodding helped the democratizers.

Instruments used by the United States to foment democracy stirred up opposition to dictators. These included: pronouncements by officials in Washington and in U.S. embassies; annual reports by the State Department on human rights in every country in the world; reports carried by international media outlets; interchanges between universities and intel-

[20] However, several Asian countries joined the democratic camp, at least nominally (Di Palma 1990, esp. 183–200; Huntington 1991, 85–87).
[21] Whitehead in O'Donnell, Schmitter, and Whitehead 1986, 3–46; Tovias in Pridham 1991, 175–94; Sidjanski in Pridham 1991, 195–211; Pridham in Pridham 1991, 212–45.

lectuals; programs of economic and social assistance—often to new social movements and to democratic activists—from the Agency for International Development and the Inter American Foundation; technical
and publicitary aid from the National Foundation for Democracy, established in 1984; finances for the Center for Electoral Promotion and
Assistance, operating out of Costa Rica and helping many countries
improve voting procedures, such as by registering voters for the 1988
Chilean plebiscite; committees to observe elections; and economic pressures. Other mechanisms, such as suspension of military aid or invasion
by U.S. armed forces, also raised a tyrant's costs of not liberalizing.[22]

The most recent official U.S. promotion of democracy began with
Congressional Democrats and the election of President Jimmy Carter in
1976. The State Department inaugurated its annual publication on the
status of human rights in foreign countries in 1977; the U.S. government
was supposed to take those conditions into account in its allocation of
military assistance abroad. Although exhortations for democracy did not
produce major successes immediately, they did help democratization stay
on track in Ecuador and Peru, and they contributed to the preservation of
electoral democracy in the Dominican Republic.

At the same time, Carter's initiatives created space for human-rights
movements under authoritarian regimes. Some future leaders of democratization escaped from jail, torture, and death partly because of U.S.
pressure. By promoting the concept of human rights around the globe,
Carter undermined the legitimacy of dictators. In the final analysis, his
policies had their maximum impact in the long run, sowing seeds for
transitions that came later.[23]

In his first administration (1981–1985), President Ronald Reagan
privileged the crusade against communism over the campaign for democracy. Consequently, his administration warmed up to previously
scorned right-wing dictators. Then his initial policy changed for three
key reasons: the need to criticize rightist as well as leftist dictators in
order to justify U.S. intervention in Central America and the escalating
conflict with the USSR; the desire to respond to idealism in U.S. public
opinion; and the necessity to recognize the international torrent of democratization. In his second administration (1985–1989), Reagan gave
more support to democratic transitions.[24]

Since the human-rights policy had become a consensus between Democrats and Republicans, Presidents George Bush (1989–1993) and Bill

[22] Carothers 1991, 203–10, 226–36; Fossedal 1989, 71–77; Muravchik 1991, 182–83,
204; Huntington 1991, 93–94.

[23] Schoultz 1981; Carter 1982; Muravchik 1986; Nelson and Eglington 1992; Lowenthal 1990; Fossedal 1989, 60–64; Huntington 1991, 91–100.

[24] Carothers 1991; Muravchik 1991, 4; MacEwan 1988; Blasier in Malloy and Seligson
1987, 219–34; Malloy in Malloy and Seligson 1987, 235–58.

TABLE 5.1
Relationship between Latin American Regime Type and U.S. Foreign Policy

Period	Dominant Regime Type in Latin America	Dominant U.S. Foreign Policy toward Democracy
1920s	Democracy	Positive
1930s	Dictatorship	Neutral
1945–1948	Democracy	Positive
1948–1954	Dictatorship	Neutral/Negative
1958–1963	Democracy	Positive
1964–1976	Dictatorship	Neutral/Negative
1984–1993	Democracy	Positive

Clinton (1993–1997) continued promoting democracy, especially in Europe, Russia, and Latin America. They did so most dramatically with the use of force in Panama and Haiti. Following the collapse of the Soviet Union, the United States could support democracy in the hemisphere without worrying primarily about communism. However, that was not a universal or uniform policy, as Washington maintained fairly normal—albeit strained—relations with autocratic regimes in Asia, the Middle East, and Africa.

Historically, there has been a superficial correlation between political systems in Latin America and foreign policies of the United States. During democratic eras in the region, the United States has been prone to support democracy. Table 5.1 shows this relationship from when the United States became the hegemonic power in most of the hemisphere after the First World War. The connection between cause and effect in this table is unclear. It could be that the foreign policy of the United States in favor of democracy promoted democratization in Latin America, or it could be that the arrival of democracy in Latin America promoted support for it in the foreign policy of the United States. Normally, it seems that there has been reciprocal action between changes in Latin America and in U.S. policy. For example in the 1980s, the first democratizations helped convince the White House to stop coddling dictators; thereafter, the new U.S. policy in favor of democracy facilitated the ouster of other tyrants.[25]

[25] Table 5.1 should be used with care. One problem is the debatable designations of certain regimes as democratic or dictatorial, especially in the Caribbean basin. Another problem is the dicey definition of U.S. policy as favoring democrats or dictators. For example, the State Department has usually justified all U.S. policies in Latin America as intended to foment democracy, even in interventions against the reasonably democratic governments of Jacobo Arbenz in Guatemala, Salvador Allende in Chile, and Daniel Ortega in Nicaragua.

In this century, Western Europe has had much less influence in Latin America, although its shadow has been growing in the last fifteen years. At the same time, Western Europe has been increasingly emphasizing its preference for democracy. Its main impact has been in southern and Eastern Europe, where democratic credentials became necessary to join the European Community, thus creating economic incentives for democratization. The moderation of the democratic left in Western Europe also impressed its neighbors and its counterparts in Latin America, as well as dictators leery of leftists. In 1982, the defeat of Argentina in the Malvinas/Falklands War by Great Britain, with support from the United States, shattered an authoritarian regime, galvanized its opponents, engendered disorder, and began the return to democracy in the Southern Cone.[26]

CHANGES IN THE SOVIET UNION AND EASTERN EUROPE

The dramatic changes in the Soviet bloc not only freed numerous countries but also made democratization more tolerable to right-wing despots elsewhere. The beginning of the reforms of Mikhail Gorbachev in 1985 and the subsequent termination of the cold war dampened ideological conflicts in Latin America and most of the world. The communist model and its Cuban version lost credibility. This left Latin America's orthodox communist parties with no program and authoritarian right-wingers without that enemy to justify military rule. Since the majority of the Latin American transitions occurred before the complete disintegration of the Soviet empire in 1989–1990, however, this factor helped mainly with the consolidation of democratic systems.[27]

NONECONOMIC INTERNATIONAL ORGANIZATIONS

Many noneconomic groups joined the great powers in advocating democracy. Multinational public institutions such as the Organization of American States and the United Nations placed more emphasis on fostering and preserving human rights and democracy. At the same time, many private, nongovernmental organizations (NGOs) such as Amnesty International joined the democratic chorus. Examples of such transnational actors included defenders of human rights, churches, academic associations, professional organizations, and trade unions. They pro-

---

[26] Pridham in Pridham 1991, 212–45; Huntington 1991, 87–89.

[27] Muñoz 1992; Angell in Bethell 1995; Cavarozzi in Hartlyn, Schoultz, and Varas 1992, 101–27, Carr and Ellner 1993; Castañeda 1993; Jowitt 1992, 255–63; Szoboszlai 1992; Plattner in Diamond and Plattner 1993, 26–38; Di Palma in Diamond and Plattner 1993, 257–67; Ekiert 1991, 285–89.

moted civic organizations that were independent from the state and capable of dissidence. Calls for change also came from international coalitions of political parties, especially Christian democrats, socialists, and communists. All these groups isolated the dictator and heartened his or her adversaries.[28]

Ideological Factors

LIBERALISM

Among many elites and intellectuals in numerous countries, an international consensus developed around representative democracy and neoliberal economics. From Washington and London, Reaganism and Thatcherism helped resurrect and spread the gospels of political and economic liberalism. This ideological offensive—especially the arguments favoring democracy—was propelled by visits of First World intellectuals to poorer countries with authoritarian regimes, trips by intellectuals from the democratic opposition in those countries to the United States and Europe, foreign financial and moral support for democratic intellectuals under dictatorships, and participation of those opposition intellectuals in struggles for democratization. The North American and British campaigns in favor of liberalism had an exceptional impact in the Western Hemisphere. Although Latin America contained many partisans of authoritarianism, it also maintained an authentic and significant liberal tradition that was resuscitated in the 1980s.[29]

The neoliberal crusade nurtured the creation of a somewhat more democratic Latin American right wing, thereby stripping away supporters of dictatorship. Rightist politicians espousing liberty in politics as well as economics—whether sincerely or not—included León Febres Cordero in Ecuador, Fernando Collor de Mello in Brazil, Alfredo Cristiani in El Salvador, Mario Vargas Llosa in Peru, and the Party of National Action in Mexico. Some of these movements had strong ties to the business sector.[30]

HUMAN RIGHTS

Beginning in the 1970s, the universalization of the concept of human rights gradually delegitimized many authoritarian regimes. Dictators lost the capacity to avoid foreign investigations and accusations by hid-

---

[28] Pridham in Pridham 1991, 239–42; Muravchik 1991, 218–19.

[29] Muravchik 1991, 195–97; Puryear 1992; Puryear 1994; Lowenthal 1990.

[30] Espinal in Hartlyn, Schoultz, and Varas 1992, 86–100.

ing behind national sovereignty. Former domestic issues of repression became international concerns.

In parts of the world, the gross violation of human and democratic rights became unacceptable, almost like the repudiation of slavery in the nineteenth century. The pronouncements of Carter, the accords of Helsinki, the celebration of the twenty-fifth anniversary of the Universal Declaration of Human Rights, and the democratic conversion of the second Reagan administration accelerated this process. The blossoming of an international network of human rights activists helped the champions of democracy.[31]

Linked to the crusade for human rights was the international campaign in favor of women's liberation. Feminism brought more Latin American women into human-rights organizations, into committees seeking accountings for torture and murder by the dictatorships (for example, the Mothers of the Plaza de Mayo in Argentina), into new social movements, and into associations calling for women's rights. They created demands that were very difficult to repress or meet and thus pulled away some of the despot's traditional backers. Females played an important role in the establishment of democracies that promised to pay more attention to their needs.[32]

RELIGION

It may be significant that democratization has been less common in countries dominated by non-Christian religions. The majority of the democratizations in the tsunami took place in the heavily Catholic countries of Latin America and Europe. In the history of the Americas, the Roman Catholic Church had been one of the bastions of conservative and authoritarian governments. It switched to more reformist and democratic positions through Vatican II in 1963–1965 and the Second Congress of Latin American Bishops in Medellín, Colombia, in 1968.

Some of the Latin American dictators in the 1970s tried to invoke traditional Catholicism to consecrate their regimes, but they experienced little success. Instead, key sectors of the church gave succor to the opposition and coaxed devout dictators toward liberalization. Although never monolithic, the church became a transnational ally of democracy and social reform.[33]

---

[31] More research is needed on the causes of the transnationalization of human-rights expectations. For some of the arguments, see Kirkpatrick in Gettleman, et al. 1981, 15–38; Schoultz 1981; Carothers 1991; Frohmann 1993; Huntington 1991, 89–91.

[32] Jaquette 1989; Valenzuela in Drake and Jaksic 1991, 161–87.

[33] Swatos 1995; Lernoux 1989; Smith 1982; Carter 1991; Cava in Stepan 1989, 143–67; Bruneau 1982; Mainwaring 1986; Mainwaring and Wilde 1989; Sigmund 1990; Le-

Standing on the shoulders of Max Weber, some observers have argued that the democratic tsunami was due, in part, to the propagation of Protestantism. This faith grew rapidly in Latin America from the 1960s to the 1990s. In several countries, it proved especially attractive to members of the military and the urban poor. Some converts exhibited an increased commitment to individualism, capitalism, and democracy, making them harder for dictators to control. Others, however, evidenced political apathy, opposed leftist reformers, and accepted authoritarian governments. In light of these contradictions, it will require much more research to establish a coherent, compelling connection between Protestantism and democracy in Latin America.[34]

Domino Factors

A puzzling domino effect occurred from the late 1970s to the beginning of the 1990s in Latin America and Eastern Europe. After the tumble of each dictatorship, the collapse of the next authoritarian regime became more likely. Although there was no doubt that an international cycle of political contagion was taking place, there were few satisfactory explanations for this contamination.

Why did democratization spread like wildfire in Latin America? One answer is that most of the dominos were buffeted at the same time by the international forces already discussed in this chapter. A second factor behind the ripple effect is that the new democracies supported similar transformations in their neighbors. They felt safer that way since democracies are less likely to attack other democracies. They even started engaging in collective action to promote and prop up democracies in their region so that each new democracy had more international allies. Meanwhile, dictatorships became increasingly isolated and illegitimate. Another key is that modern means of international communication rapidly delivered news and lessons around the globe.

An additional response to the domino question is that both democratic and undemocratic actors learned political lessons from other countries in transition. Their education made duplication of the process in their own nation more probable. In the experiences of their neighbors, they saw the political possibilities, the effective strategies and tactics, the costs and benefits of changes, and the international reactions.

---

vine 1979, 1992; Mainwaring, O'Donnell, and Valenzuela in Mainwaring, O'Donnell, and Valenzuela 1992, 1–16; Huntington 1991, 45, 72–85; Ekiert 1991, 306–7.

[34] Huntington 1991, 72–76; Diamond and Plattner 1993, x, xv; Lipset in Diamond and Plattner 1993, 134–37; Martin 1990; Stoll 1990; Willems 1967.

Proponents of democracy observed the virtues of that political system in and of itself, and they redoubled their efforts to replicate their neighbors' privileges. In Latin America, the authoritarian forces learned from each toppling domino that a transition to an elected government did not necessarily usher in communism, populism, economic disaster, social chaos, destruction of the military, or the reduction of national security. For many despots, the risks and costs of authoritarianism soon surpassed those of democratization.[35]

The Chilean Case

To show how this global interpretation might be applied to a particular case, we will impose this scheme on the Chilean experience. International factors will be highlighted, perhaps even exaggerated.

At the beginning of the 1980s, the authoritarian regime of General Augusto Pinochet looked invincible. Pinochet enjoyed several advantages: a stable and growing economy; a new authoritarian constitution supposedly approved by two-thirds of the voters in the 1980 plebiscite; new institutions and regulations to continue his domination until 1990 and perhaps on to 1997 and beyond; social tranquillity maintained by repression of the working class and satisfaction of the middle and upper strata; solid support from the armed forces, the business executives, and many segments of the middle sectors; an oppressed, divided, demoralized, and impotent opposition; neighbors with very similar dictatorships; and right-wing governments in Washington and London who sympathized with authoritarian regimes that opposed communism and embraced neoliberal capitalism.

In short, order prevailed, and the opposition was feeble. Under such conditions, no autocrat would be likely to liberalize. For the dictator, there were no incentives for liberalization, whose costs might well exceed those of the status quo. In 1981, hardly anyone would have predicted a takeover by Pinochet's opponents by the end of the decade. What changed to bring about his defeat and exit?

Imported from the United States in the mid-seventies by the so-called Chicago Boys, Pinochet's neoliberal economic model strengthened the capitalists and weakened the working class and unions. Market-oriented reforms undercut the classic base of the left. Therefore, the entre-

---

[35] Przeworski 1991, 3–4; Diamond and Linz in Diamond, Linz, and Lipset 1988, 47–48; Huntington 1991, 100–106; Di Palma 1990, 14–26.

preneurs and the armed forces became less fearful of democracy by the late eighties.[36]

Although the formal transition to democracy began in 1988, the informal and invisible transition started six years earlier. Pinochet's omnipotence was shaken first by the economic crisis of 1981–1982, partly caused by the U.S. recession. Aggravated by the foreign-debt burden, this disaster of the free-market model ignited massive social protests from 1983 to 1985. In turn, those street demonstrations motivated the democratic political parties to reemerge with new leaders, ideologies, and strategies. Pinochet's initial reaction was to pummel the opposition, but then he began to liberalize. Little by little, he permitted more press freedom, more political party activities, more repatriation of exiles, and other openings.[37]

Gaining traction in 1985, the resurgence of the Chilean economy was fueled by three international factors: falling prices for petroleum, rising prices for copper, and declining interest rates. Following the catastrophe between 1981 and 1984, economic recuperation gradually stimulated a consensus on the neoliberal economic model in Chile and in most of the countries of the hemisphere. The international popularity of economic and political liberalism fostered an understanding between the right-wing government and the center-left opposition in Chile, although the government was more dedicated to the liberal model of economics and the opposition to the liberal model of politics. This confluence paved the way for a transition to democracy without severe conflicts over the economic system. Although the opposition's Concertation for Democracy lambasted the inequitable distribution of income, it wanted to avoid populism and inflation after having observed the calamitous recent experiments in Peru, Argentina, and Brazil.[38]

In part, the increasingly moderate opposition parties changed their programs and practices as a result of lessons learned overseas, especially by exiles. From other transitions, they perceived the necessity of multiparty cooperation. From the examples of the Philippines, Uruguay, and Brazil, they adopted the approach of defeating the dictator through his own system.

With the support of foreign foundations, Chilean intellectuals survived and developed fresh ideas and concepts, partly through interchange with foreign scholars. Exceptionally important was the conver-

[36] Campero in Drake and Jaksic 1991, 128–60; Angell in Drake and Jaksic 1991, 188–210.

[37] Garretón in O'Donnell, Schmitter, and Whitehead 1986, 95–122; Stallings in Stallings and Kaufman 1989, 181–200; Drake and Jaksic 1991.

[38] Silva in Drake and Jaksic 1991, 98–127.

sion of socialist intellectuals and politicians to ideas less revolutionary and more democratic; this transformation derived from their bitter experience of failure and exile, from dialogue with political thinkers in other countries, from the example of moderate socialist parties in Europe, from the reforms of Gorbachev, and from their own redefinition of socialism and democracy. The participation of Chilean intellectuals in the country's democratic parties, in the campaign against Pinochet, and in the government of Patricio Aylwin contributed mightily to redemocratization.[39]

At the same time, many of these changes in Chile's political parties were supported by the United States, Europe, foreign foundations, the Catholic Church, international party organizations, and democratic neighbors. Under Pinochet, domestic questions acquired international dimensions, especially issues concerning human rights, democracy, and the economic model. The Chilean democratic forces tapped into a global network of activists in favor of democracy and human rights. Meanwhile, almost no foreign group expressed its solidarity with the authoritarian camp.[40]

From 1984 on, the United States campaigned in favor of democracy in Chile. That campaign formed part of Washington's revived prodemocratic foreign policy and was driven by its desire to avert a Nicaraguan-style revolution in Chile and its response to the revitalization of the democratic movement in Chile. Although never intense, U.S. pressure grew steadily as the 1988 plebiscite approached. North American unions backed the anti-Pinochet efforts of Chilean unions. From the United States, the National Foundation for Democracy and the National Democratic Institute encouraged the unity of the Concertation parties, the mobilization of the electorate, and the "No" campaign in the plebiscite on Pinochet's continuation. Particularly notable was U.S. action on the eve of the voting, when the State Department denounced any intention by the dictatorship to cancel or annul the election. The arrival of international delegations to observe the referendum also helped the democratic coalition.[41]

The crumbling of the Soviet and Eastern European regimes had an important impact in Chile because of the strength of its Marxist parties and of the anticommunism of the Pinochet regime. As a result, the Communist Party of Chile lost significance, Pinochet's attempt to resuscitate the electorate's fear of Marxism did not bear fruit, his supporters and the United States overcame their dread of the Chilean left, and

[39] Garretón in Drake and Jaksic 1991, 211–50; Puryear 1994.
[40] Portales in Drake and Jaksic 1991, 251–75; Muñoz 1986.
[41] Drake and Valenzuela 1989, 18–36; Buchanan in Lowenthal 1991, 306–7; Fossedal 1989, 72–77; Muravchik 1991, 209–10; Portales in Drake and Jaksic 1991, 251–75.

a firm alliance was solidified between the socialists and the Christian Democrats. Following the transition from Pinochet, the enormous changes in Russia and Eastern Europe contributed even more to the consolidation of Chilean democracy.

The climax of redemocratization in Chile was the 1988 referendum to prolong or terminate Pinochet's rule. The expansion of the concept that human rights and democracy were transnational questions could be seen in the evolution of Pinochet's plebiscites. In the elections controlled by him in 1978 and 1980, Pinochet could denounce and exclude foreign critics as an insulting intrusion in domestic affairs. In 1988, it was futile to invoke nationalism to prohibit the arrival of foreign observers to verify the cleanliness of the plebiscite.

The honesty of the plebiscite was also protected by the Roman Catholic Church and the Concertation. The leaders of the opposition deployed fax machines and computers and adopted tactics practiced abroad to monitor crucial elections. Aided by a publicity and polling campaign planned partly with a U.S. firm, the democrats won the battle of public opinion.

The opposition prevailed even among women voters, on whose traditional conservatism Pinochet had counted. Some Chilean women called for "democracy in the nation and in the household," and females surprised Pinochet by supplying a majority of their votes to his opponents in the plebiscite. The "No" triumphed by 55 percent to 43 percent. After an equally strong Concertation victory in the 1989 presidential and congressional elections, President Patricio Aylwin of the Christian Democrats installed the revived democracy in 1990.

Pinochet and his backers accepted democratization because the benefits outweighed the costs by the end of the 1980s. The foreseeable costs of maintaining the dictatorship probably would have included massive social and political disorder, class conflict, economic disruptions, radicalization of the left, draconian repression, escalating violence, divisions within the authoritarian camp, and international ostracism. By contrast, the return to civilian rule pacified dissident social sectors, encouraged compromises between capital and labor, preserved the neoliberal economic model, moderated the political parties, isolated the few remaining revolutionary leftists, installed a stable and gradualist democratic system, turned power over to an acceptable centrist civilian coalition, maintained a conservative judiciary, enhanced national security, and attracted international acclaim and investment.

At the same time, Pinochet suffered little. He retained command of the army and the right to be a senator for life, prevented any retribution for human-rights abuses, preserved the commanders and professionalism and unity and budget of the armed forces, and forced his successors to operate within his restrictive constitution, which included unelected right-wing senators, a voting system biased toward the right, military oversight through a national-security council, and other authoritarian features. The only significant perquisite Pinochet lost was some personal power. The rest of the authoritarian coalition was willing to sacrifice that asset in order to obtain the benefits of limited redemocratization.

Would this victory by the Chilean opposition have been possible without the international changes from 1982 to 1990? Of course, but it might have been more difficult and less probable. It is impossible to know, but a different combination of international ingredients might have produced or facilitated a different outcome.

To conjure up a counterfactual history, it is necessary to begin by eliminating the economic collapse and debt crisis of 1982. Let us suppose that foreign financing and prosperity, instead of crashing, continued until 1990. Therefore, social protests never exploded, and the political parties remained dormant and divided. There was no international proliferation of cable television, personal computers, or fax machines. International economic agents claimed neutrality as to regime types. No free-trade movement developed to integrate Latin America more completely with the hegemonic United States.

Meanwhile, suppose there was no global wave of democratization. Classic liberalism did not experience a renaissance. Imagine that Carter's government did not promote human rights. In turn, the Reagan administration maintained cordial relations with authoritarian regimes. U.S. unions remained captives of the cold war and opposed leftist organizations south of the border.

At the same time, Western Europe continued its traditional indifference to domestic political squabbles in Latin America. International organizations soft-pedaled human rights and democracy. Foreign foundations and scholars withdrew from the inhospitable atmosphere in Latin America. No worldwide campaign for women's rights took off. The Catholic Church never veered in a reformist direction, never criticized dictatorships, and never sheltered the democratic opposition. Protestantism did not flourish in Latin America. Neither the cold war nor the Soviet Union's grip on Eastern Europe came to an end.[42]

In this alternative history, Pinochet reached the 1988 plebiscite with over a decade of order and prosperity, with his neoliberal and anticommunist doctrines intact, and with the support of the United States, England, and Chile's dictatorial neighbors. With these advantages, he retained enthusiastic backing from the capitalists, the middle sectors, the rural population, the women, and the military. No powerful interna-

---

[42] Sheahan in Lowenthal 1991, 346–47.

tional or national forces disturbed his regime or tugged it in a democratic direction.

In the counterfactual world of 1988, Pinochet tightly controlled the entire electoral process and prohibited foreign interference. Against an anachronistic, fragmented, brutalized, and depressed opposition, he easily won 7 percent more of the votes to obtain a majority in the plebiscite. As a result, Pinochet continued in power for at least eight more years.

Conclusion

It may well be that this essay exaggerates the importance of international factors. Many times, the key to political changes is the interaction between external and internal forces. The international conjuncture can offer opportunities, such as loans, market niches, or support for democracy, but there is no guarantee that a country will be able to take advantage of these openings. Every nation has to construct its own history, in relation with some structures, conditions, and tendencies beyond its control.

Whatever the global currents in an historical epoch, democratization in a particular country will still depend ultimately on the intelligence and courage of its own political actors. It will also depend on the choices of the dictators. Short of armed revolution, the opposition must take the tyrant's preferences into account. They must convince him that repression is costly and that liberalization is beneficial to him and his programmatic objectives.[43]

If the central argument of this chapter about the importance of the global or regional context has some validity, then the international climate in the future may do extensive damage to democratic regimes. The external environment can contain not only opportunities but also threats, risks, and perils, such as economic depressions, wars, and anti-democratic ideologies. In the past, some authoritarian governments have been able to resist democratic tides. The challenge now is to construct and consolidate democratic systems that can survive hostile international storms in the future.[44]

---

[43] Whitehead in O'Donnell, Schmitter, and Whitehead 1986, 3–46.
[44] Hakim and Lowenthal in Diamond and Plattner 1993, 293–306.

6

The Political Economy
of Authoritarian Withdrawals

STEPHAN HAGGARD AND ROBERT R. KAUFMAN

A MYRIAD of factors have contributed to the trend away from authoritarian rule in the last two decades. International diplomatic pressures, the end of the cold war, the "contagion effect" of democratic transitions in neighboring countries, and socioeconomic changes associated with long-term economic development all played some role in the dramatic political transitions that have occurred since the 1970s. In this chapter, however, we focus on a factor that has not received the attention it deserves in the literature on democratic transitions: the severe economic shocks that struck many developing countries during the 1980s.[1]

There are a number of reasons why short-run economic conditions warrant closer attention. Economic crisis does not, by itself, appear to be either a necessary or sufficient condition for authoritarian withdrawal; some authoritarian governments survived crises and others relinquished power in good times. Nonetheless, the withdrawal of authoritarian leaders was correlated with severe economic crisis in a large number of developing countries. This was particularly true in Latin America, Africa, and Eastern Europe, where the shocks of the 1980s were especially profound. It is plausible that economic deterioration affected the balance of power between regime and opposition in these cases, thus increasing the incentives for authoritarian rulers to exit.

A second reason to examine the impact of economic crisis is that it appeared to affect the terms on which authoritarian governments withdrew. Authoritarian governments that avoided crisis or adjusted effectively not only were better positioned to resist pressures to leave office but also maintained greater control over the timing and conditions of their exit when they did choose to withdraw. Since the terms of authoritarian withdrawal have strongly influenced the institutional characteristics of incoming democratic governments, it is important to explore the

---

This chapter draws on chapter 1 of Haggard and Kaufman 1995.

[1] Typical of analyses stressing the primacy of purely political processes is O'Donnell, Schmitter, and Whitehead 1986.

reasons why some regimes were more vulnerable than others to the political pressures generated by economic shocks.

We offer two sets of arguments. First, economic crises have the potential to undermine the "authoritarian bargains" forged between rulers and key constituents. Crises expose rulers to private-sector defection and to opposition social movements "from below." The resulting political isolation makes it more difficult to rule and reduces the capacity of incumbents to extricate themselves from office on favorable terms. Where such crises are avoided or effectively managed, by contrast, authoritarian leaders are more likely to retain support from key social groups and within the government itself. This in turn allows them to negotiate the new democratic institutional framework in a fashion more likely to maintain their prerogatives, favor the chances of their political allies, and restrict the freedom of maneuver of incoming democratic oppositions.

These observations naturally raise the question of why some authoritarian governments are able to avoid or effectively manage crises while others are not. Institutional features of authoritarian regimes are significant in this regard, playing a crucial intervening role between economic crises and authoritarian withdrawals. Military authoritarian regimes generally lack organizational structures for recruiting leaders, adjudicating conflicts within the elites, and mobilizing broader political support; for this reason, they are more vulnerable to crises and generally have shorter life spans than governments ruled by dominant parties. Only in a handful of cases where power was highly concentrated did military regimes overcome these institutional disabilities.

Unlike military regimes, dominant-party governments typically possess sophisticated institutional mechanisms of political and social control, including over the military itself. Economic performance in dominant-party systems varies widely, but control of a dominant party enhances the capacity of rulers to prolong their stay in power through a combination of repression, cooptation, and limited political reform.

We examine these propositions in several steps. In the first section, we survey the way economic factors, including both the level of development and short-run performance, affect the stability of authoritarian regimes. In the second section, we provide an empirical overview of recent transitions, distinguishing those that occurred during or following economic crises from those that took place in good times.

We focus particular attention on the middle-income countries of Latin America and Asia, where the "third wave" of democratization gained its initial momentum: Argentina, Brazil, Chile, Peru, Mexico, and Uruguay in Latin America and Korea, Taiwan, the Philippines, Thailand, and Turkey in Asia. Comparisons among these countries are

facilitated by some broad but important commonalities: substantial dif-
ferentiation between business elites and political-military organizations;
relatively large private industrial sectors; sizable middle and working
classes; and significant ties to the international economy. Transitions in
the dominant-party socialist regimes of Eastern Europe appear comparable in some ways and are discussed at various points. However, more
systematic comparisons are limited by the distinctiveness of their command economies and by the overwhelming role of Soviet decisions in
their transitions.

In the last section, we outline the institutional factors that made military and dominant-party regimes more or less vulnerable to economic
crisis. We close by outlining the implications of our findings for politics
in new democracies.

Economic Development and the Stability of Authoritarian Regimes

The Lipset Hypothesis

Virtually all theoretical discussion of the effect of economic factors on
regime type has focused on the proposal raised over thirty years ago by
Seymour Martin Lipset: that a high level of development is a precondi-
tion for the emergence and maintenance of democratic rule (1959).
Notwithstanding the controversy it has generated, there are both theoretical and empirical reasons why the Lipset hypothesis is plausible (for
a review of these hypotheses, see Hadenius 1992, 77–82). As Robert
Dahl has suggested, the diffusion of organizational resources associated
with a complex, developed economy expands the range of groups capable of influencing politics. "A modern dynamic pluralist society dis-
perses power, influence, authority and control away from any single
center toward a variety of individuals, groups, associations and organizations" (Dahl 1989, 252). Such developments, in turn, increase first
the costs of repression relative to those of toleration and thus the
chances that authoritarian rulers will acquiesce to pressures for political
liberalization and democratic reform when they arise.

Empirically, the correlation initially observed by Lipset between measures of economic development and democracy has remained one of the
strongest findings in political science (for comprehensive reviews of the
literature and presentation of new empirical findings, see Hadenius
1992, Diamond 1992, and Helliwell 1994). With some important exceptions such as India, very poor countries tend to be authoritarian;
rich countries are overwhelmingly democratic.

There is, however, wide variation in regime type among middle-income countries that are neither very rich nor very poor. Samuel Huntington has suggested that such middle-income countries occupy a "zone of transition or choice, in which traditional forms of rule become increasingly difficult to maintain and new types of political institutions are required to aggregate the demands of an increasingly complex society" (1991, 201). As he points out, the recent wave of democratic transitions has occurred primarily among these middle-income countries.

But prior to the recent wave of democratic transitions, many of these same transitional countries spawned new forms of authoritarian rule. The well-known work of Guillermo O'Donnell found that bureaucratic-authoritarian installations occurred in the most developed Latin American countries, not the least (1973). In a recent cross-national study, Lipset, Seong, and Torres found an "N-curve" relationship between authoritarianism and economic development. The probability of nondemocratic regimes increased with development in a middle range of countries (per capita income between $2,346 and $5,000 in 1980) but decreased with development among lower and upper-income countries.[2]

In short, the relationship between level of development and regime type seems indeterminate among middle-income countries, which have been characterized by both authoritarian and democratic rule. A certain threshold of national income may constitute an important condition for democratic rule, but the level of economic development tells us little about why democratic transitions occur when they do.

Economics and Politics: The Equation in the Short Run

An alternative hypothesis is that the stability of authoritarian regimes depends both on the overall level of development and on economic conditions in the short run.[3] Authoritarian regimes vary according to which segments of the population are given preference, but all are responsive to the economic interests and demands of at least some sectors of their societies. Inclusionary authoritarian regimes such as Peru's initially mobilized mass support from above. Some authoritarian regimes, such as those in Central America and Africa, are based on highly personalistic ties between rulers and traditional social elites, ethnic groups, or clients. Bureaucratic-authoritarian regimes have been more typical of middle-income developing countries. Such regimes are based on an alliance between the military and technocrats, an economic reform program, and

[2] Lipset, Seong, and Torres 1991; Diamond 1992.
[3] See also Londregan and Poole 1990.

support from some portions of the modern private sector, both domestic and foreign.

Whatever the nature of the underlying authoritarian bargains, poor economic performance—whether the result of external shocks, bad policy, or both—means a reduction in the resources available to political elites for sustaining bases of support. The effort to control inflation or to undertake structural reforms in response to crisis can further weaken the government's hand. Stabilization of inflation and balance-of-payments adjustment typically involve policies that reduce aggregate income in the short run. Though these stabilization measures are likely to be the most difficult politically, structural-adjustment measures also have distributional consequences that governments are typically unable to fully offset through compensatory measures. Moreover, a number of structural-adjustment measures, such as trade liberalization, imply the withdrawal of rents from powerful and privileged groups.

In some cases, authoritarian rulers may be able to weather economic distress by forcing the costs of adjustment onto excluded groups. However, there are significant constraints in attempting to do so. Authoritarian governments cannot appeal to broad principles of democratic legitimation. Coercion is also costly and generally either ineffective or counterproductive in securing the confidence of the private sector. To survive, such governments must sustain some base of support; in this sense, they are accountable even if that accountability is not always institutionalized and is focused on a relatively narrow range of social interests.

For nonsocialist developing countries, we can construct a simple model of the effects of economic crisis by tracing the interests and likely political responses of three sets of political and economic actors: private-sector business groups; middle-class and "popular sector" organizations; and the elites that control the state and the instruments of coercion.

First, deteriorating economic performance disrupts the authoritarian bargains that rulers typically forge with segments of the private sector. The specific bases of business support depend, of course, on the structure of the economy, the resources available to specific groups, and the political project of the government. Authoritarian regimes have rested on a wide variety of coalitional foundations, including agro-export elites, import-substituting industrialists (in most Latin American countries), and export-oriented manufacturing firms (in East Asian countries including Korea and Taiwan). Yet in all mixed economies, business elites are pivotal actors because they control both existing assets and the flow of investment that is crucial to continued growth. Even where authoritarian governments restrict the formal political access of such groups, political leaders nonetheless seek their cooperation and tacit support.

This cooperation can be secured in at least three ways: by promising protection against perceived threats to private property; by pursuing development strategies that privilege certain sectors; and by providing more particular favors or rents. Economic crisis and corresponding pressures for policy adjustment weaken the ability of the government to deliver on all three fronts and thus encourage a reassessment of the overall political bargain.

The initial reactions of the private sector to poor economic performance typically focus on changes in specific policies or government personnel. But if private-sector actors believe that authoritarian governments are unwilling or unable to change policies detrimental to their individual and collective interests—in short, if they lose confidence—business can quickly recalculate the costs associated with democratization; this is particularly likely where there are opportunities to ally with moderate oppositions. On purely self-interested grounds, crises can push business groups to view democracy as the system most likely to provide them with opportunities to defend their interests.

The defection of private-sector groups poses particularly serious challenges to incumbent regimes. Such groups are well placed to play organizational and financial roles within the opposition. But more important is the fact that loss of private-sector confidence confronts the government with bleak prospects for future investment and growth. It is possible to coerce individuals and even to seize their assets, but it is difficult to force them to invest.

Middle- and lower-income groups, by contrast, are more vulnerable to political repression. But authoritarian regimes have relied on material rewards to win support or deflect opposition from these groups as well, and an economic crisis clearly weakens the ability to do so. In a number of authoritarian countries, rulers bid actively for the allegiance of portions of the popular sector through public employment, large-scale public-works projects, and consumer subsidies. Even in harshly antilabor regimes, material payoffs have played an important role. In Korea, Taiwan, and Singapore, for example, the political control of labor was a component of export-led growth strategies. But this growth strategy also rested on investment in education and resulted in a steady improvement of living standards that bought the government the acquiescence, if not support, of some segments of the working class. Even in the Southern Cone countries of Latin America, arguably the most labor-repressive of all authoritarian regimes, governments used exchange-rate policy, partial indexation, and other forms of compensation to shore up workers' incomes.

The primary political weapon of mass-based groups and social movements in authoritarian settings is the mobilization of protest: strikes, street demonstrations, or, where opportunities exist, referenda and electoral campaigns. These actions are frequently directed at political objectives, but it would be misleading to interpret their strength as stemming from purely political causes. Such movements often have their origins in reaction to economic grievances: unemployment; inflation in the prices of staples, fuel, and transportation; and declining real wages.[4] More important, crisis conditions provide opportunities for the political leaders of the opposition to draw in new adherents by linking economic circumstances to the exclusionary nature of the political order.[5]

Most crucial to the survival of authoritarian regimes, finally, is the continuing loyalty of the politico-military elite itself: the heads of the armed forces, strategic segments of the state apparatus, or the individuals who control the machinery of the ruling party. We follow O'Donnell and Schmitter, Przeworski, and others in arguing that, except in cases of military defeat and foreign occupation, the proximate cause for the exit of authoritarian regimes can almost always be found in splits within this elite.[6] The crucial question is the extent to which economic conditions play a role in creating these divisions in the first place.

O'Donnell and Schmitter argue that the emergence of divisions between hard-liners and soft-liners reflects preferences and assessments of risk that are not systematically related to economic conditions.[7] Agencies or individuals involved in earlier acts of repression, for example, are more inclined to adopt a hard-line position against political liberalization than are officers who are less potentially exposed to future reprisals. Similarly, willingness to use force in response to protest may also reflect purely political assessments about the efficacy of coercion in de-

---

[4] This is not to suggest that all grievances are economic, particularly among middle-class groups. Because of their access to communications and organizational resources, white-collar groups, particularly within the liberal professions, play an especially important role in antigovernment protests. These groups do not always favor democracy, but arbitrary governmental authority can pose threats not only to their careers but to professional norms, such as the integrity of the law or of universities. Except during periods of intense polarization, they are thus inclined to press for constitutionalism. Their incorporation into popular democratic movements is often pivotal to the process of political transition, in part because it effects the government's calculus concerning the use of coercion.

[5] For a useful discussion of the way these mobilizations can be affected by the strength of the union movement and past relationships to the party and the incumbent regime, see Valenzuela 1989.

[6] See O'Donnell and Schmitter in O'Donnell, Schmitter, and Whitehead 1986, 15–17, and particularly Przeworski 1991, 51–94, on whose analysis we draw in the following paragraphs.

[7] O'Donnell and Schmitter 1986; Przeworski 1991.

terring the escalation of protest or about the possibilities of reaching agreement with a moderate opposition.

Even where economic crises are not the source of factional conflicts between hard-liners and soft-liners, however, they are likely to widen them. In the first instance, economic downturns affect the loyalty of the political and military elite directly by reducing the ability of the government to deliver material benefits. Like any other component of the public sector, military establishments are threatened by adjustment measures, such as devaluations (which increase the cost of foreign procurement), reductions of pay, and budget cuts.

Speaking more broadly, the defection of private sector groups and the widening of popular-sector protest are likely to deepen divisions over the costs of coercion and the risks that it will prove ineffective. It is precisely under such conditions that the splits within the regime begin to have strategic importance for the transition process. Soft-liners begin to calculate that the corporate interests of the ruling elite are best guarded by conciliation rather than further repression. Even when the objective is a "broadened dictatorship" rather than a transition to democratic rule, the division within the government between soft-liners and hard-line defenders of the status quo provides the opportunity for the opposition to press for broader political reforms.

Economic Crisis and Authoritarian Withdrawals: Empirical Patterns

The relevance of short-term economic performance to authoritarian withdrawals can be gauged in a preliminary way by a survey of twenty-seven democratic transitions that occurred between 1970 and 1990. Transitions are defined here as the first year of a competitively elected government; the two exceptions are Brazil, in which the opposition came to power through the electoral college, and Thailand, where the prime minister was selected by legislators, not all of whom had been elected. Table 6.1 compares economic performance with respect to both GDP growth and inflation in the period immediately prior to the transition—the transition year itself and the previous two years—against the economic record in the five-year period before that. Countries are ranked by the extent to which conditions deteriorated during the transitional years compared against the previous trend.

As table 6.1 shows, transitions occurred under a wide range of conditions, including relatively strong economic growth in some cases. Nevertheless, in a substantial majority of the cases, the years preceding the transition were marked by declining growth, increasing inflation, or

TABLE 6.1
Economic Performance Prior to Democratic Transitions

Country, Year	Avg. GDP Growth Transition Year and Two Previous years (A)	Avg. GDP Growth Five Previous years (B)	A − B
Honduras, 1982	−0.5	7.6	−8.1
Romania, 1990	−4.3	2.9	−7.2
Philippines, 1986	−3.2	3.9	−7.1
Ecuador, 1979	6.3	13.2	−6.9
Portugal, 1976	1.3	7.4	−5.9
Bolivia, 1982	−1.5	4.4	−6.6
Argentina, 1983	−3.2	2.4	−5.6
Uruguay, 1985	−2.4	2.0	−4.4
Hungary 1990	−2.3	1.8	−4.1
Spain, 1977	2.5	6.2	−3.7
Nicaragua, 1990	−4.6	−0.9	−3.7
Greece,1974	4.3	7.7	−3.4
Thailand, 1973	6.3	9.2	−2.9
Nigeria, 1979	2.6	5.3	−2.7
Senegal, 1978	0.1	2.5	−2.4
Thailand, 1983	5.8	7.8	−2.0
Argentina, 1973	3.2	4.4	−1.2
Poland, 1989	2.2	3.1	−0.9
Guatemala, 1986	0.0	0.6	−0.6
Peru, 1980	3.5	4.1	−0.6
Czechoslovakia, 1989	1.7	2.2	−0.5
Turkey, 1974	6.5	6.9	−0.4
Brazil, 1985	3.3	3.1	0.2
El Salvador, 1984	−0.9	−1.2	0.3
Turkey, 1983	4.3	3.0	1.3
Chile, 1990	6.3	3.9	2.4
Korea, 1988	11.7	8.5	3.2
Ghana, 1979	3.3	−1.9	5.2
Paraguay, 1989	5.7	0.1	5.6

(*cont.*)

both. Twenty-one of the twenty-seven countries experienced declining growth prior to the transition; among the remaining cases, long-term growth rates were very low in El Salvador and Ghana and had declined by historic standards in Brazil. Two-thirds of the transitions were also

TABLE 6.1 (*Continued*)

Country, Year	Avg. Inflation, Transition Year and Two Previous Years (A)	Avg. Inflation Five Previous Years (B)	A – B
Brazil, 1985	188.7	75.5	113.2
Poland, 1989	112.2	34.1	78.1
Bolivia, 1982	69.7	10.1	59.6
Ghana, 1979	81.3	26.4	54.9
Peru, 1980	61.2	24.3	36.9
Argentina, 1973	51.4	19.7	31.7
Portugal, 1976	22.2	7.7	14.5
Greece, 1974	15.6	2.1	13.5
Hungary, 1990	20.5	7.1	13.4
Uruguay, 1985	58.9	45.6	13.3
Guatemala, 1986	19.7	7.7	12.0
Philippines, 1986	24.7	13.8	10.9
Spain, 1977	18.8	9.9	8.9
Turkey, 1974	14.3	7.5	6.8
Thailand, 1973	6.9	2.5	4.4
Honduras, 1982	12.2	7.9	4.3
Paraguay, 1989	23.6	19.5	4.1
Romania, 1990	2.7	1.7	1.0
Nigeria, 1979	15.7	16.0	– 0.3
Czechoslovakia, 1989	0.5	1.9	– 1.4
El Salvador, 1984	12.2	14.4	– 2.2
Ecuador, 1979	11.7	14.1	– 2.4
Thailand, 1983	7.2	9.8	– 2.6
Korea, 1988	4.3	7.3	– 3.0
Chile, 1990	19.2	23.5	– 4.3
Argentina, 1983	204.4	211.2	– 6.8
Senegal, 1978	5.3	13.9	– 8.6
Turkey, 1983	32.9	51.7	– 18.8

Source: International Monetary Fund, *International Financial Statistics*, various issues. Comparable data for inflation in Nicaragua is not available.

preceded by increasing inflation. In Argentina's most recent transition (1983), inflation had declined somewhat relative to the earlier period, but it remained at extremely high levels by international standards; Turkey showed a similar pattern of reduced but nonetheless significant inflationary pressures.

Only in Korea, Chile, and Turkey did transitions occur during periods of high and rising rates of growth and declining rates of inflation. Thailand presents a somewhat ambiguous case, since growth slowed substantially in the early 1980s when compared to its previous pace. However, overall economic conditions remained highly favorable in Thailand throughout the 1980s. Growth rates were among the highest in the world and inflation moderated; for these reasons, we do not consider Thailand a crisis-induced transition. These four cases—Korea, Chile, Turkey, and Thailand—thus constitute anomalies for a purely economic theory of authoritarian withdrawal.

On the other hand, although yearly growth rates improved slightly in some other countries prior to transitions, in most instances they remained very low. Brazil, for example, experienced a brief economic upswing in the year prior to the transition, but this had been preceded by several years of very severe recession. Moreover, the outgoing regime had failed to confront a number of pressing adjustment issues, and inflation accelerated substantially prior to the change in regime; we therefore consider Brazil a crisis-induced transition.

The inferences that can be drawn from these data about the causal relationship between economic conditions and regime change are limited if we do not examine countries in which regimes survived severe economic shocks. There is surprisingly little cross-national statistical work on the economic determinants of regime change, however. One recent exception is a study by Mark Gasiorowski, which uses a pooled time-series design to explore the relationship between economic conditions, measured in terms of growth and inflation, and transitions to and from democracy.[8] Gasiorowski finds little effect of growth on democratization but argues that in the 1980s high inflation had a statistically significant effect on the probability that authoritarian regimes would move toward democracy.

To clarify theoretical expectations, it is useful to consider those regimes that did not democratize in response to economic crises. During the 1970s and 1980s, these survivors consisted mainly of authoritarian regimes in Africa and the Middle East and, until 1989, the communist regimes of Eastern Europe. The survival of authoritarianism in these regions was attributable in part to the continued backing of external patrons. Regimes in the more advanced Eastern European states collapsed quickly once Soviet support was withdrawn. Authoritarian regimes in poor countries have arguably been kept alive by the unwillingness of external donors to sever foreign aid, usually for strategic as well as humanitarian reasons. Important sources of political pressure on the

[8] Gasiorowski 1993.

poorer African countries in the early 1990s were the evaporation of a strategic justification for continued support and a greater willingness to link continued assistance to political reform.[9]

The failure of democracy to take root in poorer countries, however, also reflects structural conditions highlighted by Lipset in his original analysis. In particular, the capacities of rulers in very poor countries to prolong their dominations were facilitated by the relative weakness of organized interests. Highly dependent private sectors and geographically dispersed rural cultivators lacked the independence or organization to launch sustained protests in the face of declining economic conditions. In these societies, economic hardship was often associated with social violence, palace coups, and the deterioration of central control over population and territory.[10] But into the early 1990s, predatory personalist rulers were surprisingly adept at resisting reform and clinging to office through continued access to external aid, repression, and careful maintenance of select patronage relations, particularly in volatile urban centers.[11]

A plausible hypothesis that combines economic conditions in both the long and short run is that authoritarian regimes are more vulnerable to economic downturns in middle-income capitalist countries. In such societies, wealth holders are more sharply differentiated from the political elite. Social groups hold substantial and independent organizational and material resources that are crucial to regime stability. The middle and working classes are politically relevant, and there are lower barriers to collective action on the part of low-income urban groups. Countries fitting this description are also more likely to have prior histories of party politics, labor mobilization, and civic association. In both southern Europe and Latin America, these political traditions provided the basis for political mobilization during periods of crisis.

Variations in Responses: The Institutional Bases of Authoritarian Rule

Neither these socio-economic factors associated with level of development nor short-term economic conditions are fully able to explain the pattern of regime change, however. Four cases constitute anomalies to the pattern: Korea, Chile, Turkey, and Thailand. Moreover, we also find

[9] See Nelson and Eglington 1992.

[10] See Londregan and Poole 1990.

[11] For reviews of the constraints on democratization in Africa, see Jackson and Rosberg 1985, Diamond in Diamond, Linz, and Lipset 1988, 1–32, and Callaghy and Ravenhill 1993.

middle-income developing countries in which authoritarian rule proved durable in the face of economic shocks. In particular, one-party states outside of Eastern Europe showed surprising persistence and a substantial ability to control the pace of political liberalization. In Latin America, the Stroessner regime in Paraguay, based on an alliance between the military and the dominant Colorado Party, was not forced from power until 1990. Dominant parties continued to dominate the political landscape in the mid-1990s in Mexico, Taiwan, Indonesia, and Singapore, despite increasing opposition. One-party systems in Africa began to face more severe challenges in the early 1990s, in part as a result of declining external support. Nonetheless, single-party structures in countries such as Zambia contributed to the surprising longevity of authoritarian rule in the face of secular economic decline and severe external shocks.[12] In Eastern Europe, communist regimes survived the declining economic performance of the 1980s, and some, including Poland and Romania, weathered acute crises before finally being toppled by external developments.

These observations suggest that institutional differences among authoritarian regimes constitute an important intervening variable between external shocks and authoritarian withdrawal. In general, military regimes in middle-income capitalist countries appeared more vulnerable to economic shocks than their dominant-party counterparts. Severe economic difficulties played an important role in almost all of the transitions from military rule in Latin America. Military governments faced strong challenges from civil society yet lacked the institutional advantages associated with a strong party organization.

However, some military regimes were able either to avoid crisis or to weather social protest and engage in successful economic adjustments; these adjustments, in turn, served to prolong authoritarian rule and provide outgoing rulers with greater influence over the transition process. The differences between successful and unsuccessful regimes was partly fortuitous: Some rulers were simply more skilled than others in manipulating the rivalries within the opposition and the ruling coalition itself. But the more successful governments also appeared to share some common institutional features, particularly mechanisms that concentrated authority, reduced factionalism within the government, and increased the cohesion and decisiveness of both political and economic decision making. We turn now to a discussion of those military governments that proved vulnerable to crisis before discussing the military anomalies—Chile, Korea, Thailand, and Turkey—and the dominant-party cases.

---

[12] For a discussion of this factor in Africa during earlier decades, see Collier 1982. For a discussion of the current period, see Bratton and Van de Walle 1994.

TABLE 6.2
The Political Economy of Authoritarian Withdrawals

	No Economic Crisis	Economic Crisis
1. Political Challenges to the Regime	Primarily political demands for liberalization	Political demands overlap with: 1. Economically motivated mass protest 2. Defection of business elites 3. Internal division of military political elites over material benefits
2. Political Outcomes		
Military-dominant, low cohesion	Military-business-political coalition remains stable. Regime controls terms of transitions (Thailand)	Internal divisions raise cost of coercion. Government fails to control either elite defection or mass protest. Regime unable to adjust to crisis. Regime collapses, outgoing elites unable to influence structure of new regime. (Argentina, Bolivia, Brazil, Peru, Uruguay, the Philippines)
Military-dominant, high cohesion	Regime exerts strong control over terms of the transition (Chile 1990, Korea 1987, Turkey 1983)	Government adjusts to crisis, reasserts authority internally, represses opposition, regains business loyalty. Survives crisis, exerts control over terms of the transition. (Chile 1981–1982, Korea 1980)
Dominant party	Regime exerts strong control over terms of liberalization, transition ambiguous (Taiwan)	Government adjusts to crisis, exerts strong control over terms of liberalization, transition ambiguous. (Mexico)

Vulnerable Military Regimes

The military governments that had difficulty adjusting to economic shocks and attendant political challenges were characterized by uncertain or divided control over the bureaucracy and the main instruments of economic policy and by economic teams that were politically weak or internally divided. To a certain extent, these divisions reflected disagreements over the technical diagnosis of daunting economic problems. More typically, they reflected broader political, economic, and ideological conflicts within the military establishment itself, divisions that made the regime politically as well as economically vulnerable.

One important source of conflict lay in the division of labor between the military officers holding political office and those who remained in charge of military organization. The interests of these two groups were especially likely to diverge during periods of economic crisis, when the military as *government* faced unpopular policy choices that had consequences for the armed forces as an *institution*.[13] The most durable arrangement for managing such conflicts was a fusion of military and political authority in the head of state. But this pattern was approximated only in Chile and Korea among the countries considered here; we discuss those cases in more detail below.

In other cases, the military high command retained independence with regard to appointments and promotion, yet was excluded from day-to-day political decision making. This arrangement posed serious challenges to the government in power. Conflicts between military presidents and the military command contributed to the overthrow of Juan Velasco in Peru and Viola in Argentina. The Philippines constitutes a somewhat different case, since Marcos himself did not come from the military. However, the military split over the merits of Ferdinand Marcos's rule, and it was that split that proved fatal for the government.

One organizational mechanism for resolving tensions between the government and the military command was some form of collective rule—for example, through juntas or ruling councils. In Brazil and Uruguay, such arrangements arguably contributed to the maintenance of military cohesion and more orderly transfers of political authority. But collegial rule could not fully overcome a variety of other divisions, typically exacerbated by crises, that tended to emerge within military governments over time.[14]

[13] See Stepan 1971.

[14] In Argentina, the heads of the three branches of the armed forces were incorporated directly into a junta and a Legislative Advisory Council. But reciprocal veto powers made

In general, these conflicts were rooted in the expansion of military roles and the military's diversification into other specialized political, economic, or policy functions. These new roles provided officers opportunities to build independent organizational and political bases and weakened hierarchical lines of authority within the military chain of command. The resulting cleavages took a number of forms. In some cases, the autonomy of local commanders increased as a result of sustained internal war or drug-control operations; this was the case in Bolivia. Elsewhere, the involvement of officers in the management of state enterprises and other governmental agencies generated the potential for conflict, as well as the organizational base for alliances between officers and civilian groups opposing reform efforts; this pattern was visible in a number of Latin American and African countries.

Programmatic disagreements were most pronounced in the bureaucratic-authoritarian regimes, particularly in Latin America, that had come to office with quite explicit political and economic projects. Military factions opposing such projects typically had their own institutional bases of power in the armed forces or the state-enterprise sector and could count on powerful allies in the private sector or civilian political class as well. Within the Brazilian military, fierce factional struggles occurred throughout the 1960s and 1970s over how long to hold power, over on what terms, and over competing models of economic policy. In Argentina and Uruguay, opponents of the neoliberal policies of the mid-1970s had important bases of support in the planning and intelligence agencies and in the state-enterprise sector.[15]

These various divisions within the military elite made it more difficult for governments to provide consistent and coherent backing for the risky economic-policy adjustments required to establish credibility among important economic actors, including foreign creditors. As a result, the economic policy–making apparatus either fragmented into warring factions or cycled between teams with mutually inconsistent programs. These weaknesses, in turn, contributed to further decline in the credibility of the government with economic agents, further deepening the economic crisis and attendant political problems.

As in Latin America and the Philippines, extensive factionalism also pervaded the armed forces in Thailand; rapid and relatively successful

---

the government unwieldy and contributed to the fragmentation of the state apparatus. "As the guerilla threat was exterminated, internal splits reemerged over economic policy, political strategy, and the power and autonomy of the repressive apparatus," Ricci and Fitch in Goodman, Mendelson, and Rial 1990, 59.

[15] Ibid., 55–75. In Uruguay, military officials in control of the Banco de la Republica provided important sources of support for opposition to technocrats in the Finance Ministry. See Handelman in Handelman and Sanders 1981, 215–37.

economic adjustment in that country thus constitutes an anomaly. We attribute this exception to the fact that military factionalism was counterbalanced by other institutional features of the regime, including both a unifying monarchy and a cohesive technocratic elite that enjoyed substantial prestige and served to provide the military as a whole with important collective goods. The technocrats could not altogether prevent the military from making several important policy mistakes in the late 1970s, but the regime did avoid the severe macroeconomic disequilibriums that generated serious political difficulties in the crisis cases. As in the other noncrisis cases discussed below, this in turn permitted military-backed governments to exert considerable control over the pace of political reform. Despite an extensive political liberalization and gradual transition, the military never fully relinquished its role in the polity in the 1980s and launched another short-lived coup against the parliamentary system in 1991.

In all of the other factionalized military regimes, escalating economic crisis made the management of political pressures more difficult. Some military regimes sought to build support through controlled electoral openings. However, where government parties were weak, even controlled elections posed hazards for authoritarian rulers.[16] In the absence of dominant parties, such rulers were impelled to forge links to politicians or notables in order to orchestrate electoral victories; these politicians, in turn, were forced by electoral calculations to accommodate the opposition to at least some extent. In situations of economic crisis, opportunities for patronage declined, and such alliance-building efforts became more problematic, while the opportunities expanded for antiregime electoral oppositions to exploit economic grievances. This was particularly apparent in Brazil and the Philippines, where electoral contests crystallized opposition and served to weaken authoritarian rule.

Divisions within the government also affected the way economic elites weighed the risks of opening the political system to democratic oppositions. Where internal dissent was high, and particularly where that dissent centered to some extent on the conduct of economic policy, private-sector groups were more likely to lose faith in the capacity of the regime to manage crises. As a result, they were more inclined to support political reforms aimed at altering the system of representation.

Finally, cleavages within the elite expanded the opportunity for mass democratic oppositions by ultimately lowering the risks of antiregime protest. Of course, whenever interelite divisions arise, it is possible that hard-liners will gain the upper hand and pursue a repressive strategy.

[16] Perhaps the most consistent voice for this perspective is Bolivar Lamounier. See, for example, his essay in Stepan 1989.

However, such repression does not address the underlying economic problems such regimes face and may worsen them. Moreover, if some forces within the government dissent from the authoritarian status quo, they are likely to provide some encouragement for the opposition and may even form tacit alliances with it.[17] Under extreme conditions, repressing opposition initiatives may prove impossible because key portions of the military are unwilling to respond to orders to use force; this was most dramatically the case in the Philippines and East Germany.

Cohesive Military Regimes

Three military regimes present full or partial exceptions to the foregoing pattern of internal division; each was able to exert substantial influence over the timing and terms of democratic transition. Two of these, Chile and Korea, faced economic and political challenges in the early 1980s, and a third—Turkey—seized power in the midst of a deep economic, political, and social crisis. In all of these cases, governments weathered political challenges and did not leave power until they had made extensive adjustments in the economy and deep changes in the structure of the political system. In effect, these governments were able to create bases of support for the institutional and political changes they initiated during the authoritarian period.

The precise reasons for these exceptions hinge in part on case-specific factors, but in all three the capacity of the military establishment to contain divisions within its own ranks played a crucial role in the outcome. Three institutional factors worked to mitigate these divisions: the fusion of political and military authority; a greater specialization of military roles; and the length of time in power.

Of the countries considered here, Chile and Korea had by far the most cohesive military establishments. One characteristic of each case was the fusion of military and political authority in the head of state. This reduced the ambiguity about lines of authority, allowing the top political-military leader not only to control appointments and personnel decisions within the military but also to exercise dual control—through both military and civilian chains of command—over military personnel assigned to the government itself. This factor was crucial for the survival of the Pinochet regime in Chile. Even though Park Chung Hee and Chun Doo Hwan ruled nominally as civilians, both were military men whose power was buttressed by executive control over the military and a pervasive intelligence apparatus.

[17] Ramseyer and Rosenbluth have modeled the problem of oligarchic cohesion as a cartel. See Ramseyer and Rosenbluth 1995, chaps. 1 and 2.

A variety of factors also encouraged the insulation of corporate hier-archies and the maintenance of loyalty to the central command. In Chile, the governing responsibilities of the Chilean military expanded substantially under Pinochet. But ironically, the socialization of the mili-tary to a narrowly defined mission during several decades of democratic government resulted in strong obedience to the chain of command, which in turn facilitated Pinochet's control over the military establish-ment. In Korea, the threat from the north provided strong incentives for the maintenance of corporate unity within the armed forces. In the im-mediate wake of the Park assassination in 1979, a portion of the mili-tary elite was quickly able to reestablish internal discipline and to reas-sert its authority over the political system as a whole, surviving the worst economic difficulties the country had faced in twenty years.

In both cases, dependable support of the military establishment al-lowed the government both to crush political opposition and to provide unambiguous backing to coherent and powerful teams of economic technocrats. In Korea, Chun Doo Hwan gave unwavering support to his reform team. In Chile, Pinochet's support for the Chicago Boys is well known. Notwithstanding some important reshuffling of the policy makers during the shocks of the early 1980s, the two regimes' support for technocratic elites continued through the ends of their rules.

Turkey presents a more ambiguous institutional picture. Unlike either Chile or Korea, the military establishment there had been characterized by political factionalism and struggles over patronage; in this respect, it was closer to the "typical" Latin American military establishments than to Chile or Korea. As a result, the economic technocrats assembled un-der Turgot Özal had less extensive control over the bureaucracy, impor-tant segments of which were opposed to reform efforts; on some issues, the military itself proved recalcitrant. Turkey's economic adjustments, particularly with respect to fiscal policy and the state-owned enterprise sector, thus proved less far-reaching than those in Chile and Korea.

Unlike other military governments, however, internal division within the Turkish armed forces was held in check by the relatively limited tenure and purpose of the military intervention. During the escalating political crisis of 1979–1980, competing factions of military moderates and radicals drew together in the face of the paralysis of civilian govern-ment and near–civil war conditions. In exchange for the moderates' backing for intervention, radicals agreed to hold to a preannounced timetable for withdrawal. This unity of purpose almost certainly would have eroded had the military remained in power over a long period; this, in fact, had been the experience in comparable cases of "collegial" military government in Uruguay, Argentina, and Brazil. However, during the short period of military rule that ensued, the incoming government was able to sustain the institutional support necessary to undertake harshly repressive measures against opposition and to back important adjustment measures that had been initiated but had failed under the ousted democratic government.

Successful economic management did not insure the indefinite survival of these regimes. Even in good times, most rulers were eventually forced to respond in some measure to democratic forces based in the domestic working and middle classes and to foreign pressures, and in any case all had made public commitments to eventually withdraw from politics. However, in each of these regimes, as well as in Thailand, the capacity to engineer economic recoveries or sustain strong economic performance permitted incumbent elites to exert greater control over changes in the political rules of the game and the economic policy choices of successor governments. In short, the different transition paths we have outlined had important ramifications for the nature of their successor governments.

Political changes occurring under favorable economic conditions differed in at least three important ways from those that occurred during crisis.[18] First, transitions in good times were more likely to be characterized by the persistence or reconstruction of cooperative relations between the government and the private sector. In regimes unable to adjust to crisis, the defection of business groups from the ruling coalition left political and military authorities isolated vis-à-vis a broad but heterogeneous democratic opposition. Where economic crisis was avoided or managed successfully, relatively strong center-right blocs continued to play important roles on the political scene, with some capacity to veto departures from previous economic policies.

The regimes' successful adjustments or avoidance of crises also limited the roles played by middle-class and professional groups in populist antiauthoritarian coalitions. Where regimes had been unable to adjust, middle-class groups were more likely to join with the popular sector around distributive demands and political reform. In the noncrisis cases, middle-class groups sometimes joined mass movements for political democracy—as they did, for example, in Korea in mid-1987—but adopted more conservative positions on economic issues. This reinforced continuity in economic policy and tended to leave groups on the left more isolated.

Finally, even where rightist blocs accepted the necessity of democratization, successful economic performance increased their capacity to influence the rules of political competition, particularly those providing

---

[18] These propositions are explored in more detail in Haggard and Kaufman 1995, chap. 4.

guarantees for the interests of business and military elites and those regulating the entry of mass-based groups into the political process.

Dominant-party Regimes

Among the mixed-capitalist systems that are the subject of our analysis, dominant-party regimes appear substantially more resilient than their military counterparts.[19] If we scan the entire universe of such governments, this result does not appear to hinge on the capability to adjust to crisis; some of the worst-performing economies in the world have been in single-party regimes. Many of the Middle Eastern and African authoritarian regimes are dominant-party systems. The communist regimes of Europe proved increasingly incapable of engineering sustained growth but fell only after their external support collapsed. Among the middle-income capitalist economies that are the subject of this analysis, however, dominant-party regimes such as those in Mexico, Taiwan, and Indonesia have had more success both in initiating economic reforms and in constructing political coalitions to sustain them. These dominant-party regimes have also been more likely than their military counterparts to manage the longer-term political pressures that Lipset and others attribute to economic success. The dominant party provided rulers with a means to manage political reform and the opening of the economy without losing control of the political system.

Why would this be the case? Unlike military regimes, dominant-party authoritarian governments are characterized by a greater separation of political and coercive functions. This separation has several important implications. First, although dominant parties often become centers of bureaucratic privilege, they are more likely than military establishments to provide rulers with organizational means of controlling the state apparatus, including the military itself. Because the military establishment is less directly involved in ruling, it is less likely to be politicized, less prone to act as a source of centrifugal pressure on decision making, and less likely to mount coups.

Second, dominant parties provide an institutional mechanism for social and political control. Dominant parties are more effective than military organizations in coopting, controlling, and penetrating social groups such as unions or civic associations that can become the locus of opposition activity. Dominant parties are also useful in managing the elections that are surprising concomitants of many authoritarian governments. Compared to military rulers, political elites in Taiwan and

---

[19] We discuss dominant-party regimes at greater length in ibid., chap. 8.

Mexico were able to broaden the bases of their regimes without losing control over the political system; political change in both countries was tightly managed from the top. The existence of dominant parties also helps explain certain features of economic policies in the two countries. In Taiwan, as in the military cases that managed to avoid or survive crises, the dominance of the Kuomintang (KMT) guaranteed that the political opening would not produce significant change in the country's export-oriented development strategy. In Mexico, reforming political elites could draw on the organizational resources available through the PRI (Institutional Revolutionary Party) to initiate wide-ranging economic adjustments.

Both economic circumstances and political institutions help explain the controlled nature of the political transformation in the two countries. In Taiwan, successful economic performance and centralized control of the state allowed the KMT to maintain its hold on political power even while undertaking a gradual electoral opening. A reputation for competence in economic-policy making and a well-organized electoral machine allowed the KMT to secure the votes required to remain in office, despite the substantial disadvantages of being closely associated with an ethnic minority: the mainlanders who seized control of the island in 1949 following the defeat of the KMT in the Chinese civil war.

In Mexico, the economic recovery of the early 1990s provided the opportunity for a new round of political reforms aimed at modernizing the PRI and providing additional space for opposition groups. However, Mexico differed from Taiwan in the greater uncertainty surrounding its recovery. Unsure of whether they could prevail in more open contests with opposition parties, ruling elites in Mexico proved less willing than those in Taiwan to relinquish the institutional controls that were the basis both of economic adjustment and of their party's continued political dominance. The recurrence of economic crisis in December 1994 placed new pressure on the political system, both by providing new opportunities for opposition forces and by deepening centrifugal forces within the PRI itself. Nonetheless, the durability of the PRI in the face of the myriad economic challenges it has faced since 1982 remains a stunning testimony to the advantages provided by a coherent dominant-party apparatus.

Conclusion

In the puzzle of why authoritarian leaders willingly choose to relinquish authority and acquiesce in the establishment of democratic systems in which their political chances and even personal security are placed in jeopardy, economic circumstances constitute a plausible explanation. Crises increase the difficulty of holding on to power by leading to the defection of business supporters, increasing protest from below, and multiplying divisions within the ruling elite itself. These conditions not only make it more difficult to rule but also weaken the ability of incumbent authoritarian elites to negotiate the terms of their withdrawal. We would expect that authoritarian governments capable of avoiding or managing economic crises would face fewer political challenges and have greater leverage over the postauthoritarian order at the time when they do choose to withdraw.

While plausible, this economic analysis quickly raises the question of why a handful of authoritarian governments have escaped this logic and have proved more effective in managing the economy than others. The answer lies in the institutions of authoritarian rule: In divided military governments, crises further widen internal rifts, weaken the capacity to conduct coherent economic policy, and ultimately reduce the ability to manage political challenges. Those militaries able to overcome such divisions and dominant-party authoritarian systems proved more resilient.

Our analysis can also be extended to speculate on the future of democratic rule in those countries that have recently undergone transitions.[20] Though democratic governments can arguably draw on a reservoir of legitimacy that authoritarian regimes lack, new democracies may also be vulnerable to economic crises in the absence of cohesive parties and party systems. Countries with constitutional settlements that lead to highly fragmented and polarized party systems are likely to face greater difficulties in managing their economies than countries characterized by more cohesive parties and party systems. Such fragmented governments may prove vulnerable to a troublesome concentration of executive authority in the face of crises or even to authoritarian "solutions."

[20] See ibid., chaps. 5, 9, and 10.

7

When You Wish upon the Stars

WHY THE GENERALS (AND ADMIRALS) SAY YES TO LATIN AMERICAN "TRANSITIONS" TO CIVILIAN GOVERNMENT

BRIAN LOVEMAN

MILITARY GOVERNMENTS and presidents have been common in Latin America since the early nineteenth century. Just as common have been transitions to civilian administrations. Military coups continued to punctuate Latin American politics in the twentieth century.[1] Between 1920 and 1960, military coups occurred in every Latin American country except Mexico and Uruguay, and Uruguay suffered irregular regime changes with police and military participation in 1933–1934 and 1942.[2]

Latin Americans have experienced military regimes of varying ferocity and efficacy, and likewise with civilian governments. Repression of regime opponents has occurred routinely in most of the region; both military and civilian governments have used police and military forces to intimidate and eliminate their adversaries.

In most of Latin America, periodic military rule is a part of the political heritage and an imminent contingency in the present, if certain relatively well-known circumstances conspire to "call for" military inter-

---

[1] Wiarda (1979) suggests that "the coup in Latin America becomes something of the functional equivalent of elections in North America. Leaders are recruited and selected, alternative programs weighed, coalitions built, public opinion consulted, new governments formed, etc. . . . Both the electoral and nonelectoral routes to power carry some (but not total legitimacy)" (39). Edwin Lieuwen (1961) calculates 115 successful coups in Latin America and many times that number of unsuccessful rebellions, barracks uprisings (*cuartelazos*), and abortive coups up to World War I. Warren Dean (1970) provides data suggesting that the incidence of coups, despite periodicity, with evident peaks (1820s, 1840s, 1850s, 1870s, 1910–1915, early 1930s, late 1940s, and into the 1960s), has been relatively constant. Dean noted a correlation between coups cycles and international economic fluctuations.

[2] The number of successful military coups between 1920 and 1960 were: Argentina (7); Chile (2); Cuba (4); Venezuela (4); Costa Rica (1); Panama (3); Brazil (5); Colombia (2); Ecuador (9); Peru (4); Bolivia (9); Paraguay (7); El Salvador (6); Nicaragua (1); Dominican Republic (4); Honduras (2); Guatemala (6); Haiti (5). After José Nun in Lowenthal and Fitch 1986, 60.

vention. Sometimes military coups oust civilians, other times incumbent military governments. Popular beliefs, expectations, and experiences do not preclude military rule nor military mediation of policy making; the historical weight of institutions, political culture, and the recent past ("path dependence") make military coups and authoritarian government thinkable and make institutionalizing democracy in the region difficult.[3] J. Samuel Fitch puts this more emphatically: "In most Latin American countries the military coup d'état is an integral part of the political system, rather than an aberrant event."[4]

From 1978 to 1993, transitions from military to civilian governments have occurred in eleven Latin American nations.[5] These government changes have inspired euphoria among policy makers and academics over the supposed surge of democratization. They also generated a spate of studies on the timing, sequencing, types, and consequences of "transitions from authoritarian rule."[6]

Central to this literature are debates about the implications of prior liberalization, both political and economic vis-à-vis diverse sequences of economic liberalization followed by political liberalization, perhaps followed by democratization.[7] Such debates rarely assess the evolved con-

---

[3] "Path dependence" is used here in the sense that particular patterns of institutional development facilitate or impede later historical paths. For example, Barrington Moore, Jr. (1966) argued that the way commercial agriculture developed in various countries facilitated or impeded the development of democracy. In contrast, Brian Downing emphasizes the importance of Europe's medieval parliamentary institutions (representative assemblies, town charters, local government) and how these are affected by military modernization. "Warfare in parts of early modern Europe led to military modernization using domestic resources, and that was at least as important for authoritarian political outcomes as labor-repressive agricultural systems and a weak commercial impulse" (1992, 239). In the case of Latin America, the fusion of military and civilian authority and the salvational mission of the military-church alliance from the conquest to the eighteenth century made military participation in politics and administration the norm rather than an aberration. The Bourbon reforms after the 1760s further reinforced this tradition, frequently fusing military and civil authority for purposes of maintaining internal order and everyday administration. In this sense, from the conquest to the end of the colonial period, military institutions became guardians of ideological purity and state security.

[4] J. Samuel Fitch in Lowenthal and Fitch 1986, 151.

[5] Ecuador (1979); Peru (1980); Honduras and Bolivia (1982); Argentina (1983); El Salvador and Uruguay (1984); Brazil (1985); Guatemala (1986); Chile (1990); and Paraguay (1993).

[6] Among the most well known of these studies are O'Donnell, Schmitter, and Whitehead 1986; Malloy and Seligson 1987; Welch 1987; Maniruzzaman 1987; and Stepan 1988. Dankart Rustow (1970) set the stage for much of this literature. For review essays on this topic, see Gillespie 1987 and Stephens 1990.

[7] Robert Kaufman in O'Donnell, Schmitter, and Whitehead 1986; Adam Prezworski in O'Donnell, Schmitter, and Whitehead 1986; Welch 1987.

stitutional-institutional legacy of Latin American democracy prior to the 1959 Cuban Revolution that inspired the counterrevolutionary, antipolitical military regimes that took power beginning with the 1964 Brazilian coup.[8] Nor do they ask whether there is any reason to suppose that the liberalizing trends of the 1980s will be more permanent than previous episodes of liberalization in Latin America.

Underlying most of these studies is the assumption that military extrication from direct rule implies significant changes in Latin American institutions and politics. Most ask how and why military governments give way to civilian governments or, even more optimistically, why authoritarianism gives way to democratization. Although some of the studies note that such transitions have occurred in the past and ask if the most recent wave of transitions differs from previous movements from authoritarian to elected governments, almost none note the persistence of antidemocratic political institutions and practices or ask whether the transitions in certain ways reinforce and further legitimize these authoritarian foundations of Latin American politics.

"Democratic" Waves, Cycles, and Illusions

Many writers have commented on the apparently cyclical waves of authoritarian and fairly elected democratic governments in Latin America in the twentieth century. In 1954, twelve of twenty-one Latin American republics had military chief executives; in 1961, only one did (Paraguay). Over two-thirds of Latin Americans lived under military regimes in 1978; in 1993, military rule persisted only in Haiti.[9] From 1940 to 1988, without judging the fairness, competitiveness, or political context of elections for chief executives, "the number of elected governments increased after 1945, decreased after 1954, increased rather dramatically from 1956 to 1959, decreased slowly until 1972 and increased steadily after 1982."[10]

[8] See Loveman and Davies 1989.

[9] See Mitchell Seligson in Malloy and Seligson 1987; Remmer 1985; Blakemore 1986; Boström 1989, 3–19; Huntington 1991; Danopoulos 1988; Welch 1992, 323–42; Maniruzzman 1987; and Stepan 1988.

[10] Boström 1989, 7. On the other hand, illegal and unscheduled changes in governments—including coups, assassinations, "resignations," etc.—followed no apparent pattern: Venezuela (1950); Bolivia and Panama (1951); Bolivia and Cuba (1952); Colombia (1953); Brazil, Guatemala, Honduras, and Paraguay (1954); Argentina, Brazil, and Paraguay (1955); Haiti, Honduras, and Nicaragua (1956); Colombia and Guatemala (1957); Venezuela (1958); Cuba (1959); El Salvador (1960); Dominican Republic, Ecuador, Venezuela (unsuccessful), and El Salvador (1961); Argentina, Dominican Republic, Venezuela

Significant variations existed, of course, in the extent of the armed forces' institutional involvement in these episodes of military rule. In some cases, coups followed by long-term personalist rule (Anastasia Somoza in Nicaragua, Rafael Trujillo in the Dominican Republic, Fulgencio Batista in Cuba, Alfredo Stroessner in Paraguay) involved the armed forces in repression, corruption, and regime maintenance but not in routine policy making or the creation of a new political system. In other cases, key administrative posts, the public administration, and public enterprises (ranging from military industries, airports, ports, and steel factories, to import-export firms, fishing, oil, and other state enterprises) were more thoroughly colonized by military officers. This occurred in Guatemala as early as the 1930s and in El Salvador after 1948. It also became important for a time in Peru after 1968, in Chile after 1973, in Brazil and Argentina from the mid-1960s to the 1980s. It persists in Ecuador, Honduras, and Guatemala to varying degrees in the 1990s.[11]

This variation in the armed forces' stake in the state certainly influences the consequences of restoring civilian government but never precludes it, even in military rhetoric. Eventually, the pendulum swings back; the armed forces, apparently, return to the barracks. This is expected by the Latin American military. Officers seek to protect the fatherland against civilian betrayal and bungling in their role as guardians of the nation's permanent interests; they do not view themselves, except in this guardianship role, as surrogates for popular sovereignty. Neither military lore and doctrine nor any modern political ideology provide the basis for permanently substituting the armed forces for the people as sovereigns. This means that Latin American military officers and juntas always expect, eventually, to restore civilian government.

These swings between military governments and elected civilian governments both illuminate and disguise the nature of Latin American politics and of the armed forces' role in Latin American political systems. They imply, however, little about democratization on any dimension except the occurrence of elections, whether in the 1920s, 1950s, or 1990s. Several features of these swings, followed by elections and (sometimes) constitutional reform are salient. First, before 1964 few military governments (as opposed to military officers) survived in power very long, attempted to consolidate formally strict military rule, or elaborated a political rationale for a permanent military regime. Unlike the

---

(unsuccessful), and Peru (1962); Dominican Republic, Ecuador, Guatemala, Argentina (unsuccessful), and Honduras (1963); Bolivia and Brazil (1964); Dominican Republic (1965); and Ecuador (1966).

[11] Loveman 1994.

one-party dominant (PRI) Mexican authoritarian regime after 1940, or the unsuccessful efforts by El Salvadoran military officers to emulate it with a military-controlled political party, or similar efforts by General Omar Torrijos in Panama (1969–1978, with the 1972 succession constitution that legitimated his coup), Latin American military officers generally overtly adhere to the legitimating rhetoric, if not the spirit, of representative democracy as the proper sort of regime—eventually. They always favor transition, when it is safe, feasible, and appropriate.

The apparent waves or cycles of authoritarian and democratic government have coincided with international political, economic, and ideological trends and their interplay with domestic conditions (wars, depressions, the rise of fascism, then communism and the cold war). They have little to do with gradual movement toward democracy or the reverse movement toward institutionalized dictatorship. Indeed, no particular outcome predominated after the 1950s wave nor the changes in the 1960s. They merely reflect flurries of direct military intervention to manage externally and internally induced crises, to adjust or reshape the political system. In particular, this holds for the civilian regimes of the 1920s, the spate of temporary liberalizations following World War II and the collapse of the Depression dictatorships (1945–1948), and the returns to civilian rule in the late 1950s and early 1960s. Thus, the transitions in Peru (1956), Venezuela (1958), Colombia (1958), and Cuba (1959) led in quite different directions: repeated coups in Peru; long-term civilian government in Venezuela; pacted and limited democracy in Colombia;[12] socialism in Cuba. In the early to mid-1960s, Honduras (1963), Bolivia (1964), and Argentina (1966) experienced coups that again gave way to civilian governments, however briefly, by 1971.

Second, elections, plebiscites, and even constitutional conventions are used by military, civilian authoritarian, and more "democratic" regimes to legitimate themselves internally and internationally. (This use of elections, of course, is not limited to Latin America.) In this sense, they are useful instruments in regime stabilization and transition precisely because both civilian and military sectors accord legitimacy to elections and plebiscites for choosing leaders and making important political decisions. Military officers generally share this premise with their civilian counterparts because they acquired similar civic education before their

---

[12] In 1958, after years of ferocious violence that left thousands dead, Colombia's two major political parties, conservatives and liberals, agreed on "power sharing" in a "National Front." This pacted alternation of the presidency and sharing of other government offices lasted until 1974. See Daniel Pecaut in Bergquist, Peñaranda, and Sánchez 1992, 217–39. Pecaut begins his discussion by observing: "For more than thirty years now Colombia has preserved a limited democratic regime."

military socialization, and in Latin America military education usually reaffirms the importance of elections and popular sovereignty.

Such electoral events, however, may or may not be part of democratization or even democratic selection of chief executives and popular representatives or of democratic governance—notwithstanding the trend toward expanding the electorate by adding women, illiterates, and younger voters. In most instances, such elections serve important symbolic functions but are not essentially devices for expressing social choice regarding public policy or even particular candidates.

Latin Americans have substituted special elections, plebiscites, and new constitutions (succession constitutions) for routine elections since independence.[13] Both military and civilian leaders have recognized the sacramental character of "electoral blessings," whether the elections were routine, special, or plebiscitary. This has also been true historically for United States foreign-policy makers as they sought to stabilize Latin American regimes. Thus chapter 14 of the United States Marine Corps' 1940 *Small Wars Manual* was called "Supervision of Elections," a key Marine Corps function until World War II. As the manual suggests:

> The Government of the United States has supervised the presidential or congressional elections of neighboring republics on 12 different occasions. . . .
>
> The supervision of elections is perhaps the most effective peaceful means of exerting an impartial influence upon the turbulent affairs of sovereign states. Such supervision frequently plays a prominent role in the diplomatic endeavors that are so closely associated with small war activities.
>
> . . . It is well to consider the internal conditions that make the electoral supervision necessary. The electoral laws, the economic conditions, and the educational problems of the country concerned will often be found to be factors. The Electoral Mission can actually institute few permanent electoral reforms during the limited time that it is present in the country. It can, however, demonstrate a method of conducting elections that may serve as a model to the citizens for future elections. A free, fair, and impartial election cannot be held in a country torn by civil strife. Before such an election can be held, the individual must be made to feel safe in his everyday life. The presence of United States military and naval forces is often necessary to furnish this guarantee.[14]

The *Small Wars Manual* further recognizes that "in some countries, it is an established custom during electoral periods to arrest numerous citizens of the party, not in power, for old offenses, for charges of minor infringement of law . . . and upon charges that have absolutely no foun-

---

[13] Succession constitutions are constitutions adopted in constitutional conventions or plebiscites to legitimize new regimes after irregular government successions.

[14] *United States Marine Corps Small Wars Manual* 1987.

dation whatsoever," as such citizens are "automatically disenfranchised." Likewise the *Manual* warns against the evils of government
distribution of alcoholic beverages to voters, the use of public-works
projects to influence the vote, and government manipulation of the mass
media.[15] Notwithstanding these laudable precautions, such supervised
elections, or elections orchestrated by authoritarian regimes to buttress
their position or to provide a "soft landing" via extrication, rarely indicate that democracy has arrived (except in the eyes of some foreign
observers) and never preclude future military coups or veto over government policy.

Even if elected governments, some competition, and expanded electorates were weak indications of democracy (meaning an elected president, universal suffrage, an opposition obtaining at least 30 percent of
the vote, and 20 percent of the population voting), before 1950 in all
Latin America only Uruguay (with the exception of Venezuela from
1947 to 1948) met these criteria. By 1960, only seven countries (Argentina, Bolivia, Colombia, Costa Rica, Peru, Uruguay, and Venezuela) met
these criteria—hardly a wave of democratization, even by these weak
standards. (Peru and Bolivia experienced coups in the early 1960s.)
From 1960 to 1984, the number of countries meeting these criteria
never exceeded seven, though countries joined and fell from the list. In
1985, however, the number jumped to twelve, then to thirteen (1986–
1987), and back to twelve (1988).[16] In this sense, there was a unique
wave of electoral competition and participation in Latin America in the
1980s, even if it was not accompanied by more profound democratization of politics and society. Indeed, beginning in 1978 until the early
1990s, Latin America witnessed an electoral orgy.[17] (See appendix 1.)

Third, no modern political ideology, not even fascism and other vari-
ants of corporatism, provides a legitimating myth that supports permanent military rule. Latin American military officers themselves, imbued
with Hispanic, European (particularly French and German), and U.S.
professional and ideological norms as a result of years of military socialization and foreign training missions, share the fundamental premises of nineteenth- and twentieth-century Western political doctrine: a
world composed of sovereign nation-states, with national sovereignty
expressed in some sort of popularly elected representative government.[18]
While the armed forces' interpretations of these basic premises have
antiliberal, antipolitical, and antidemocratic spins, their interpretations

[15] Ibid., chap. 14, 5–9.
[16] Boström 1989, 12–17.
[17] See *Sistemas Electorales y Representación Política en LatinoAmerica* 1986; Cerda-
Cruz, Rial, and Zovatto 1992.
[18] On the role of European military missions in Latin America see Nunn 1983.

are not justification for permanent, direct military rule. The military also recognizes that, over time, governance without legitimacy becomes more costly to their institutions and to their countries. As Alain Rouquié comments, "A permanent system of military rule is almost a contradiction in terms. The army cannot govern directly and durably without ceasing to be an army."[19] To protect the fundamental long-term integrity of military institutions, officers must say yes to restoring civilian rule.

How, then, to understand the repeated military coups and the so-called transitions from authoritarian to democratic regimes in Latin America? Why do military leaders permit, sponsor, and accept transition to civilian governments? What do the military governments demand as conditions for transition? Has Latin America been "going democratic" since 1978?

The Whys and Whens of Military Coups

Despite the frequency of military coups in twentieth-century Latin America, professional military officers in most of the region detest politics, engage in governance reluctantly, and extricate themselves institutionally from direct political rule without regret once the armed forces' corporate interests safely allow disengagement. (This is not always true, of course, for individual officers who become enamored of power and establish personalist dictatorships rather than military governments.) Military officers routinely blame civilian government corruption, incompetence, tolerance of subversion, inability to maintain order, and generalized socioeconomic breakdown for precipitating military coups. The armed forces' view is that circumstances force them to intervene to protect and defend the fatherland's permanent national interests against internal subversion and decay, disorder, economic collapse, and foreign intrigues.[20]

[19] Alain Rouquié in O'Donnell, Schmitter, and Whitehead 1986, 111.

[20] See Loveman and Davies 1989, 194–303 for speeches and declarations by officers justifying military coups in this manner. Thus, Argentine General Leopoldo Fortunato Galtieri declared in 1980, "It was necessary for the Argentine Army and the other armed security and police forces to come together to eradicate that scourge [terrorism] and to reestablish order and security" (201–2); Bolivian General Hugo Banzer Suárez declared in 1971 that "the agents of anarchy and extremism were preparing to take the country by storm in order to place it at the service of interests foreign to the fatherland and to destroy our institutions and cultural heritage" (216); Brazilian General Ernesto Geisel told his military comrades in 1976 that "it was the armed forces which confronted and fought the subversive movements. These movements, which aimed at the destruction of our nation, had, to a great extent, been inspired from abroad" (233).

Significantly, there is a high correlation between military rhetoric justifying coups and the circumstances extant when coups occur. Coups are preceded by economic crisis, public disorder, political polarization, and perceived threats to the military. They occur when military officers believe a crisis exists that civilians cannot resolve, when civilians call on the military to resolve political conflicts (for example, executive-legislative stalemates or highly polarized situations that threaten internal order), and when officers are convinced that only their action will "save the fatherland" and not incidentally protect their own historical and institutional prerogatives.[21] In short, military officers rarely invent reasons for a coup. Reasons exist that predictably, if not deterministically, provoke coups. Key civilian groups, sometimes even a majority of the population, support the coups when they occur. The military genuinely believes that its coups are a legitimate last resort, given the prevailing circumstances.

The Latin American armed forces generally recognize the great risks intervention entails for their institutions and their own careers and, therefore, despise the civilian venality and ineptitude that requires them to risk direct political rule. They claim a constitutional and supraconstitutional mission as guardians of national security and sovereignty. They retain a residual sovereignty in the name of the nation and its people that obligates them to prevent governments, elected or not, from sacrificing the nation's permanent interests to short-term political exigencies. Preventing governments from forgetting, neglecting, or attacking the permanent national interests is the armed forces' duty as "the carnal, concrete, living expression of the *patria*, whose mission is the defense of unity, of integrity, and of honor, as well as of everything essential and permanent in the country."[22] Their mission "transcends governments, groups, and persons, where the principle of National Security predominates over all others."[23] Fulfilling this mission is a last resort, not the armed forces' permanent aspiration.

This salvational and guardianship mission clearly justified the coups in Argentina in 1966 and 1976, in Brazil in 1964, in Chile and Uruguay in 1973, in Peru in 1968, in Bolivia in 1971, and in Ecuador prior to 1978. It was also present in Honduras and Guatemala in the 1960s and 1970s. The resulting military governments—whether juntas, as in Chile after 1973 and Peru after 1968 or civil-military coalitions with hybrid government institutions (such as popularly elected legislatures or even civilian presidents combined with new institutions such as national-

[21] See Fitch in Lowenthal and Fitch 1986, 26–55; Dean 1970.

[22] "*El Ser Militar*," in *El Soldado*, no. 94 (Jan.–Feb. 1984), cited in Perelli in Goodman, Mendelson, and Rial 1990, 97.

[23] Gallardo and Ocampo 1992.

security councils under military tutelage) as in Brazil after 1964 and
Uruguay after 1973—are not expressions of the military institutions'
desire to rule directely and permanently, though individual ambitious
officers may enjoy the role of sovereign. Rather, they are transitory
devices for restoring order, cleansing the political system, or even re-
designing government and society to prevent the recurrence of similar
breakdowns, always with a view to the eventual restoration of civilian
administrations.

Obviously, not all authoritarian regimes are military, and not all military officers come to power through coups. Mexican politics has been
noncompetitive, dominated by a single party (PRI) that manipulates
elections and has seriously constrained opposition since the 1930s.
Since the 1960s, Cuba has hardly been democratic, but just as clearly it
is not a military regime (though the internal role of the military and
secret police has been important). This was also the case for the Sandi-
nista government in Nicaragua (1979–1990). Such revolutionary regimes appeal to a different sort of legitimating myth and create distinc-
tive political and administrative institutions from those associated with
most military governments.

The same is true for military officers who come to power through
elections, however "free and fair," or through designation by legislative
or constituent assemblies. Argentine Colonel Juan Perón (ruled 1946–
1955), whose government was not particularly democratic, used elections, a vague populist ideology (*Justicialismo*), an official political
party, and a mobilization strategy that distinguished it from governments that come to power through coups. The Peruvian military government after 1968 also resorted to populist rhetoric to justify its efforts
to "reconstruct" Peruvian politics.[24] Nevertheless, when military officers
come to power through coups, eventual transition to civilian government is as predictable as the possibility of subsequent coups.

Military governments, like all governments, are fallible. They miscalculate, overreact, underreact, and, more generally, experience both
successes and failures in policy implementation. They vary in their abilities to bequeath redesigned political institutions to their nations, in their
efficacies as economic managers, and in their capacities to orchestrate
the inevitable transition back to civilian government. The Uruguayan
military misjudged their ability to convince voters to accept their proposed constitution in 1980; the Argentine junta committed political sui-
cide with the Malvinas War against Britain; General Pinochet overesti-
mated his ability to win the 1988 plebiscite that would have perpetuated

[24] See "Manifesto of the Revolutionary Government of Peru, 1969" in Loveman and
Davies 1989, 250–52.

his government until 1997. These leaders were caught in their own traps; their own rules led to unfavorable outcomes. In all these cases, however, the military leaders assumed from the outset that eventually a transition would occur. In this sense, military extrication from direct political rule is not a puzzle to be solved. What needs to be explained are the immediate reasons for transition, the modes of transition, and the long-term consequences of military regimes, including their progressively more chilling effect on real democratization in Latin America.

Why Do Military Leaders Sponsor, Permit, or Accept Transition to Civilian Government?

This question has two easy, universal answers and many complex, conjunctural, idiographic ones. The easy answers are that the military has achieved its objectives or that it has failed so miserably that transition cannot be avoided. In the first case, political (re)stabilization has occurred, civilian allies no longer "need" the overt military presence, and therefore prefer return to "normal" government, civilian (especially populist and leftist) opposition has been so weakened that it does not represent a credible threat to the patria, and continued direct exercise of power is unnecessary, even onerous.[25] Under these conditions, the military demands or seeks assurances against retribution for the coup, against its actions in government (for example, corruption, violation of civil rights, torture, and murder), and for guarantees for the military institutions (maintenance or enhancement of prerogatives such as some budget autonomy, control over "internal" affairs such as military education, promotions, retirements, and social-security funds). They leave office reminding civilians that serious misbehavior risks a return of military rule. In the second case, either external or internal failures, or some combination, have eroded the military's credibility and undermined its ability to rule. Obvious examples are the Argentine junta's disastrous war against Britain (1982) and the Uruguayan government's loss in the 1980 constitutional plebiscite.

Whether extrication occurs after victory or defeat certainly influences the timing and mode of transition and the military's relative position in the political system after transition. In either case, however, extrication is attractive to military officers because the longer the military retains direct control, the more difficult it is to maintain key institutional values. Militaries in power are subject to erosion of hierarchy, diffusion of roles and functions, factionalization, corruption, loss of prestige and

[25] See Eduardo Silva and Guillermo Campero in Drake and Jaksic 1991, 98–127, 128–58.

public support, and responsibility for the unavoidable failure of some social and economic policies. They also see a gradual increase in the powers of the intelligence services and "special" units that conflicts with the usual professional and organizational norms of the armed forces. This annoys, even angers, most professional officers. Military officers give great importance to internal cohesion, verticality of command, and procedure. The longer they remain in government, the harder it is to sustain these against political pressures (for example, promotion of officers for political reasons or retirement of officers who prefer more technical/professional missions and a rapid "return to the barracks"). Perhaps most important, the heroic moment (the salvational coup) blurs; the daily routine and the complexity of governance prevails. This is neither the armed forces' forte nor their legitimating mission. The constant domestic and international accusations of human-rights abuses and repression disturb most officers (since the "dirty work" is typically performed by small specialized units, and officers are genuinely concerned about the honor and prestige of military institutions). Extrication in some acceptable fashion is their preference, as long as the honor and prerogatives of their institutions can be assured.

While extrication always involves uncertainty, and civilians can never be entirely trusted to keep their side of any bargain, the risk is reduced significantly through planned, phased withdrawal, institutional constraints on incoming civilian governments, and the lingering effect of repression during the military regime's tenure. As Karen Remmer aptly puts it, "Shifts in the direction of moderation and pragmatism are less a cause of democratic transition than a consequence of authoritarianism."[26]

Usually this is possible. Most transitions to civilian rule are planned. Rules are made for transferring government to civilians in new constitutions (for example, Chile, 1980), informal "pacts" (Uruguay, 1984), or incremental changes in electoral, party, and constitutional norms (Brazil, 1979–1985). In many cases, all these techniques are used. When officers fail to devise such planned exits, unplanned transitions occur (Argentina, 1983–1984), but even these involve negotiations and efforts to soften the impact on military institutions. That this is the case is clear in military writing and in interviews conducted by scholars and journalists with military officers in the region. Stepan reports that in Brazil the bulk of the military as institution made a "Dahlian calculation": "The more the costs of suppression exceed the costs of toleration, the greater the chance for a competitive regime."[27] The key amendment necessary here is that the military calculated the costs to the military institutions

---

[26] Remmer 1991a, 202.
[27] Stepan 1988, 66–67.

and then to Brazil and allowed transition to civilian government after assuring themselves of protection against retribution and veto power over certain policies in the incoming administration.

Similar calculations took place in Ecuador, Peru, Bolivia, Honduras, El Salvador, Uruguay, Guatemala, and even Chile.[28] The exception to this pattern after 1978 was Argentina (1982–1983) in which military defeat in a war with Britain destroyed the credibility of the junta and the armed forces, constituting more a breakdown of the regime than extrication.[29] Even in the Argentine case, the military attempted, although not very successfully, to orchestrate disengagement rather than suffer an inglorious, disorganized retreat. And even in Argentina, the military ultimately intended to withdraw from direct rule. The particulars of each case vary considerably. Both domestic and international factors affect the timing, character, and relative success of the military in protecting their institutions and retaining policy influence in the successive civilian governments. But, ultimately, all military governments say yes to transition. But can we then say that when they do so, Latin America is going democratic?

What Does the Military Demand as Conditions for Transition?

What the military seeks in transitions are certain institutional guarantees and, to the extent possible, to fix the subsequent rules of the game, including a formal constitutional and statutory role for the armed forces in the new regime. Each instance of military intervention reestablishes the credibility of future interventions, further restrains civilian leaders, further embeds in Latin American politics, for civilians and the military, the legitimacy and eventuality of the armed forces' tutelary and guardianship role. Greater levels of repression predictably make successor civilian regimes more moderate, "prudent," and cautious. The eventuality of subsequent coups becomes both a formal and informal element in the Latin American political system, more salient in some (Bolivia, Ecuador,

[28] On Ecuador, see Isaacs 1993; on the Peruvian transition and new constitution, see Ballestros 1993, 15–28; on Bolivia, see *Bolivia: Neoliberalismo y Derechos Humanos* 1988; on Honduras, see Amnesty International 1988; on El Salvador, see Walter and Williams 1993 and Munck 1993; on Uruguay, see "Texto de Acuerdo Entre las Fuerzas Armadas e Políticos en que Se Acuerda el Nuevo Proceso Democrático," in Alfonso 1989 (483–86), Rial 1990, Weinstein 1988, Howard Handelman in Drake and Silva 1986 (201–14), and Gillespie 1991; on Guatemala, see Yurita in Goodman, Mendelson, and Rial 1990 (75–90) and Morales 1989 (the ex-defense minister of Guatemala also confirmed in a personal interview that such calculations took place); on Chile, see Loveman 1991.

[29] Pion-Berlin 1989.

Argentina, Guatemala, Peru) prior to 1964 than others (Chile, Uruguay, Colombia) but never absent.

In some cases, civilian government was rare before the 1880s (Peru, Bolivia, Guatemala). In others, civilians usually occupied the presidency (Colombia, Chile, Costa Rica). In no cases were the armed forces without influence; by the mid-1920s, military governments had at one time or another taken control, short-term or long-term, everywhere in the region. After 1964, systematic state terrorism, torture, repression of opposition political forces, and pervasive brutality made all too clear the consequences of effective populist or leftist challenges to the fundamental institutions of the patria. This recent path followed by many Latin Americans was the immediate prologue to so-called democratization in the 1980s and 1990s.

Once the decision is made to extricate themselves from direct political rule, military leaders seek to reduce uncertainty, protect their institutions and careers, and provide for political stability. Above all else, military leaders aim to prevent retribution. Generally, they succeed. Since 1978, with the notable exception of military leaders in Argentina and selected, notorious cases in Chile, El Salvador, and Bolivia (usually involving pressure from the United States), the military involved in the coups and subsequent human-rights abuses (torture, murder, disappearances) have been amnestied (or self-amnestied). In addition, in most instances guarantees were given concerning military budgets, retention (or enhancement) of institutional prerogatives, and continuation of the military role in national defense, security, and other policy making.

From Ecuador and Peru to Brazil, Uruguay, Chile, and the countries of Central America, the outgoing military regimes conditioned the post-1978 transitions on conserving their own institutional and political roles. Only in Argentina, as a result of the Malvinas debacle, did they fail to protect themselves. However, attempted coups against Presidents Raúl Alfonsín and Carlos Menem brought new laws extending immunity from prosecution to most officers and soldiers and, with Menem, amnesties even for the junta leaders (1992–1993). (Nevertheless, significant downsizing and budget reductions indicated that in Argentina the costs of "unplanned" transition after regime breakdown were significant for the armed forces.)

In general, the military regimes exacted impunity and maintenance of most institutional prerogatives as the price for transition. The legacy of fear they left and the periodic threats of new coups if civilians failed to be prudent usually impeded the civilian governments from reneging on their promises or seriously undermining the military's position in the years after transition.[30]

[30] See McSherry 1992.

Is Latin America Going Democratic?

Obviously, the answer to this question depends on what is meant by "democracy." So much has been written about democracy, what it is and is not, what its minimal (procedural) features are, and what its more extensive socioeconomic implications might be that only the barest discussion is provided here as a benchmark for considering the post-1978 Latin American cases.[31] This benchmark will allow both clearer perspective on the cyclic versus linear democratization in Latin America on certain dimensions and on the enduring impediments to real democratization on others (unaffected by waves, cycles, gradual modernization, and progress). The latter certainly include the historical and institutional role of the military in Latin American politics.

The most common English rendering of the Greek word from which the modern concept of democracy derives is "government by the people." This vague notion implies nothing about how the people should govern, which people should govern, and what limits, if any, should exist on this government. Many different forms of government relying on majoritarian principles and various systems in which majoritarian principles are modified by more or less severe limits on incumbent governments all claim to be democracies. They vary in political architecture (confederal, federal, centralist), in provisions for local and regional government and administration, in party and electoral systems, in the extent of media freedom, in the role of religious, labor, and other secondary associations, and in legal treatment of political opposition.[32]

Despite such variation, certain procedural norms have come to be identified with democracy in its representative version: alternation in government office as the result of free, fair, periodic elections; broad public contestation (without repression of opponents) both for electoral purposes and in discussing public policy; freedom of mass media and access to it by regime opponents and supporters; generalized respect for civil liberties and rights and the rule of law; some provisions for government accountability (especially if it exceeds its authority); and the possibility that those elected may routinely exercise their authority within

---

[31] The discussion that follows coincides in the main with Dahl 1982; Lijphart 1984; and Schmitter and Karl 1991.

[32] While this is not the place to consider these issues, the legal capacity of citizens to organize themselves to solve problems apart from or in collaboration with government is an essential component of democracy. Democracy, in the sense of "self-governance," rather than "state governance," requires much more elaborate specification than this minimalist definition of democracy. State-centric, centralized models that allow election of central government officials and require formal government "recognition" for efforts at self-government or that stifle local and regional government autonomy also impede democratization in a deeper sense than discussed here.

specified legal limits. This version of democracy, or more appropriately, constitutional democracy, is incompatible with unconstrained majoritarian rule by temporarily dominant coalitions and elected governments. It presumes stipulated constraints on government authority and the possibility of remedy if government officials, whether civilian or military, abuse their authority.

The particular methods of achieving these basic conditions may vary greatly (for example, regarding representation, multimember legislative districts and proportional representation versus single-member districts with winner-take-all provisions or, in the case of legislative excesses, judicial review by regular courts versus specialized constitutional tribunals). Likewise, access to and influence over policy makers may vary sharply among groups of voters. Nonetheless, taken together, these are the core attributes of democracy. They may be achieved partially, more fully, or virtually completely. However, they are somewhat independent of one another. Electoral participation, for example, may expand without stronger guarantees of civil rights and liberties, freer mass media, or broader political competition. They may also be reversed or lost entirely. Rankings of countries on scales of democracy and democratization abound; a nation's score changes from year to year and decade to decade. Democratization is not automatic, either in cyclical or linear fashion, nor are elements of democratization necessarily permanent.[33]

Elected governments per se imply little about democracy. The symbolic character of elections may confer temporary or even longer-term legitimacy or its veneer, but elections provide no other evidence of democracy or democratization. Napoleon Bonaparte's plebiscitary machinations and those of dictators in Latin America since Argentine *caudillo* Juan Manuel de Rosas orchestrated a house-by-house, verbal "yes-no" vote on his exercise of "extraordinary powers" in the early nineteenth century demonstrate the importance of proper acknowledgement of popular sovereignty in the political creed that replaced monarchy.[34] Such electoral circuses and more modern "demonstration elections" are essentially staged public-relations devices, indispensable democratic sacraments administered by the priests (domestic or foreign) of transition.[35]

[33] For examples of efforts to operationalize these dimensions of democracy and rank nations see Vanhanen 1990; Kenneth A. Bollen in Inkeles 1991, 3–20; and Michael Coppedge and Wolfgang H. Reinicke in Inkeles 1991, 47–68.

[34] Juan Manuel de Rosas was made constitutional dictator in a plebiscite in Buenos Aires in 1835. Verbal votes given to an official who went house-to-house gave Rosas a 9,716 to 4 victory, thus demonstrating the great popular support for his assumption of "the sum total of public authority." See Loveman 1993, 279.

[35] See Herman and Brodhead 1984; Hermet and Rose 1978.

Latin American leaders have resorted to these sacramental rituals since independence. In the early twentieth century, the United States was so firmly committed to political stabilization through elections in the Caribbean and Central America and used the Marine Corps so frequently to supervise such elections that it was made an official Marine mission—a precedent for the legitimating missions of the Organization of American States and United Nations "observers" in Central America, Chile, and elsewhere in the 1980s and 1990s.[36]

Thus, Samuel Huntington's definition of "a twentieth-century system as democratic to the extent that its most powerful collective decision makers are selected through fair, honest, and periodic elections in which candidates freely compete for votes and in which virtually all the adult population is eligible to vote" is an important starting point for democratization but only a starting point. (Despite its limitations on this dimension, the 1980s definitely represent a breakthrough in Latin American politics.) It neglects most of the crucial aspects of democracy, even the extent to which particular groups or parties are excluded from electoral competition and the media is chilled, so long as the candidates who do participate may "freely compete for votes" and most adults may cast ballots.[37] Also unmentioned is the fact that in most Latin American countries voting (for those eligible) is compulsory, though the extent of enforcement and penalties for abstention vary considerably (see table 7.3). This requirement means that it is often difficult to express dissatisfaction or simply avoid electoral participation through abstention. High turnouts impress foreign observers, particularly the United States media, but the meaning of such turnouts is often lost on those unaware that abstention entails monetary fines, prevents voters from obtaining government services and employment, and sometimes much worse.

Even if elections and inclusionary suffrage are keys to democratization, Huntington's emphasis on waves of democratization is somewhat misplaced. The number of presidential elections in Latin America has not varied substantially from decade to decade from 1851 to 1990 (between thirty-five and forty-five per decade), with the exception of a precipitous drop from 1971 to 1980, which saw only fourteen, a return to the levels of 1841–1851. This roughly corresponds to the post-1964 era of the military authoritarian regimes initiated with the 1964 Brazilian coup. In the five years from 1981 to 1986, the wave of presidential elections reached twenty-one, recuperating to traditional levels.[38]

[36] See Drake and Silva 1986.
[37] Huntington 1991, 5–9.
[38] Enrique C. Ochoa in Wilkie and Lorey 1987, 904, table 3423.

TABLE 7.1
Latin American Presidential Elections, by Decade, 1840–1986

Decade	Number of Elections
1841–1850	12
1851–1860	39
1861–1870	35
1871–1880	45
1881–1890	40
1891–1900	42
1901–1910	40
1911–1920	45
1921–1930	41
1931–1940	43
1941–1950	38
1951–1960	38
1961–1970	35[a]
1971–1980	14[a]
1981–1986	21[a]

[a]Does not include Brazilian elections from 1964 to1984 because presidents were chosen by Congress.
Source: Enrique Ochoa, in *Statistical Abstract of Latin America 25*, table 3424, p. 904.

The two most important formal limitations on electoral participation in Latin America, gender and literacy, have been addressed gradually since the mid-nineteenth century and particularly since World War II, but with no noticeable waves or cycles of voter incorporation unless 1946 to 1980 is viewed as a continuous wave. Likewise, enfranchisement of younger voters between sixteen and eighteen is not entirely a recent phenomenon, though it has significantly increased the size of some electorates after the 1970s (table 7.3). By the early 1990s, eighteen-year-olds voted everywhere except Bolivia (where voting is permitted at eighteen only if married); sixteen-year-olds voted in Nicaragua and Cuba. In the Dominican Republic, anyone who is or has been married obtains the suffrage, even if below the voting age of eighteen. Literacy requirements had been abolished, although in some cases where voting was otherwise mandatory, it was optional *(facultativo)* for illiterates (Brazil, Ecuador) and for those over sixty (Argentina, Brazil, Peru). In the case of female suffrage, one country enfranchised females in the 1920s, three in the 1930s, five in the 1940s, six in the 1950s, and two in the 1960s. In some cases, female voting was made discretionary, in contrast to mandatory voting for males. In other cases, the voting age for women varied from that of men or even varied according to marital status. These discriminatory provisions generally disappeared by the 1990s.

TABLE 7.2
Female Suffrage in Latin America

Country	Year First Enfranchised	Females First Vote in Presidential Election
Ecuador	1929[a]	1940
Brazil	1932	1945
Uruguay	1932	1938
Cuba	1934[b]	1940
El Salvador	1939[c]	1950
Dominican Republic	1942	?
Panama	1946	1948
Venezuela	1947[d]	1947
Argentina	1947	1951
Chile	1949	1952
Costa Rica	1949	1953
Bolivia	1952	1956
Mexico	1953	1958
Colombia	1954	1958
Peru	1955	1956
Nicaragua	1955	1957
Honduras	1956[e]	1957
Paraguay	1961	1963
Guatemala	1965[f]	1966

Source: After Boström, 1989, 11, with addition of Cuba.
Notes: [a] Facultative until 1967, voting mandatory for literate men.
[b] By decree of revolutionary government but not implemented when U.S. failure to recognize government leads to its fall.
[c] Vote is facultative, twenty-five if married, thirty if single. Men vote at eighteen, made compulsory in 1886.
[d] Able to vote in local elections as of 1945.
[e] Granted the vote in 1954 but facultative instead of mandatory.
[f] Literate women enfranchised in 1945.

By the end of the 1950s, in only seven Latin American countries did voters comprise 20 percent of the population, hardly a wave on this dimension of participation, despite the temporary predominance of civilian governments. However, greatly expanded electorates from the 1970s to the 1990s means that the current transition (1978–1994) from military to civilian governments is associated with much more inclusionary eligibility rules and voter participation.[39] This *is* an important departure from the past for Latin American politics but, to reiterate, not one that necessarily democratizes other aspects of the political systems.

More inclusionary voting rules little affected the other dimensions of

[39] See Boström 1989, 13–15.

TABLE 7.3
Evolution of Voting Age and Literacy Requirements in Latin America, as of 1993

Country	End Literacy Requirement	Voting Age	Year Established	Mandatory
Argentina	1912	18	1863	yes[a]
Bolivia	1952	18	1952	yes[b]
Brazil	1988	16	1988[c]	yes[d,e]
Chile	1970	18	1970	yes
Colombia	1936	18	1975	no
Costa Rica	1913	18	1971	yes
Cuba	1901	16	1976	yes
Dominican Republic	1865	18	1865[f]	yes
Ecuador	1978	18	1978	yes[d]
El Salvador	1883	18	1886[g]	yes
Guatemala	1945	18	1945	yes[d]
Honduras	1894	18	1924	yes[h]
Mexico	1857	18	1973	yes
Nicaragua	1893; 1948[i]	16	1984	no[j]
Panama	1904	18	1972	yes
Paraguay	1870	18	1870	yes
Peru	1979	18	1979	yes[a,k]
Uruguay	1918	18	1934	yes[h]
Venezuela	1946	18	1958[l]	yes

Notes: [a]Aged eighteen to seventy; optional if older. [b]Vote rose from 120,000 in 1951 to 958,000 in 1956, after illiterates given the vote. [c]Optional for those aged sixteen to eighteen. [d]Optional for illiterates. [e]Optional for ages sixteen to eighteen and over seventy. [f]1869–1873 raised to twenty-one; after 1873, again eighteen. [g]As of 1883, twenty-one or any age if married; as of 1886, married or eighteen. [h]Optional for women. [i]Age increased to twenty-onw for unmarried illiterates in 1939; age reduced in 1948 to eighteen if married or literate. [j]Registration mandatory, voting optional. [k]Optional for illiterates [l]First made eighteen in 1946, raised to twenty-one from 1951 to 1958.

democratization, including the extent to which elections themselves could be characterized as "fair, free, and competitive." In most cases, the fundamental character of Latin American political systems remained unchanged: They are regimes founded on the notion of protected democracy rather than liberal democracy.

Protected Democracy

The transitions from military to civilian regimes in Latin America since 1978 have reaffirmed the political victories of the antipopulist, counter-

TABLE 7.4

Constitutional Suffrage Requirements in Latin America, as of 1993

Country	Voting Age	Other Provisions	Constitutional Article(s)
Argentina	18	none	14
Bolivia	21	18, if married	41
Brazil	18	mandatory until age 60; optional for illiterates and those aged 16–18; active-duty conscripts may not vote.	14
Chile	18	mandatory; active-duty military and police su-pervise elections	14 18
Colombia	18	active-duty military may not vote	40
Costa Rica	18	mandatory	95
Cuba	16	active-duty military may vote	132, 134
Dominican Republic	18	younger if ever married	13
El Salvador	18	mandatory	71–73
Guatemala	18	separate election law; active-duty military may not vote	147 248
Honduras	18	mandatory	36, 40
Mexico	18	mandatory	34
Nicaragua	16	registration mandatory	47
Panama	18	mandatory	125, 129
Paraguay	18	mandatory	118, 120 152
Peru	18	mandatory until age 60	65
Uruguay	18	mandatory	74, 77, 80
Venezuela	18	mandatory	110

revolutionary civil-military coalitions that took power in many Latin American nations from the 1964 Brazilian coup until the Argentine coup of 1976. These regimes gradually consolidated an updated version of Latin American protected democracy.

Protected democracy is not a new concept. It was anticipated by Tocqueville who, referring to the French Revolution, wrote that when the state, personified by public officials, presumes a directive and moral mission rather than the more humble task of representation and stewardship,

It is not the people who predominate . . . but those who know what is good
for the people, a happy distinction which allows men to act in the name of
nations without consulting them and to claim their gratitude while their rights
are being trampled underfoot. . . . It is a discovery of modern days that there
are such things as legitimate tyranny and holy injustice, provided they are
exercised in the name of the people.[40]

Exercise of government authority by those claiming to implement a tele-
ological project or historical mission or to impose a virtually sacred
common good or to defend the "permanent interests of the nation" is
incompatible with democratic politics. This political model, reminiscent
of the guardians' in Plato's *Republic*, is inherently antidemocratic. This
is true for authoritarian systems of diverse ideological and religious per-
suasions. General Pinochet's Chile required that education "be imbued
with common spirit, identified with national values, with the Christian
cultural tradition, and with the historical project of the Chilean nation."[41] Fidel Castro's revolutionary Cuba expects that "our teachers
must be an example of socialist morality; they must resolutely oppose
any deviation from the new set of values created by the revolution."[42]

Protected democracy institutionalizes vigilance of permanent values
in vanguard parties, religious institutions, monarchs, or other guardians. In Latin America, this has often meant the armed forces. This
feature of Latin American politics took hold in the nineteenth century
and has been consistently reaffirmed, despite so-called waves of democratization. Illustrative is the clause in Peru's 1856 constitution that obligates the armed forces to disobey the government if it violates the constitution or the laws. According to ex-military officer and leading
authority on the Peruvian military, Víctor Villanueva,

This meant accepting, implicitly, that apart from the suffrage, sovereignty re-
sided in the army rather than in the people. The latter had the right to elect
governments, and the army the duty of ousting them when it [the army] determined that they violated the constitution.[43]

Latin American protected democracy developed several characteristic
features in the nineteenth century that have been reinforced in the twentieth century in law and practice. First, Latin American constitutions
typically assign a broad internal and external mission to the armed
forces. This mission includes domestic law enforcement, upholding the
constitution, protecting the honor, sovereignty, and territorial integrity

---

[40] Tocqueville 1835, 1:416–17).
[41] Decreto de Educación, 1892, Nov. 21, 1973.
[42] Fidel Castro, quoted in *Granma Weekly Review*, July 19, 1981.
[43] Villanueva 1973, 66–67.

of the nation, and sometimes a number of other political tasks, ranging from insuring proper presidential succession to economic development. This constitutional mission (supplemented or interpreted in "organic laws") makes the armed forces virtually a fourth branch of government. The military does not intervene in politics; it carries out its constitutional and statutory mission.[44]

Article 208 of the 1967 Bolivian constitution is illustrative; it is broader than some and narrower than others in its definition of the military's mission:

> The armed forces have as their fundamental mission defending and conserving national independence, the stability and security of the Republic, and national honor and sovereignty; to assure the rule of the Constitution, guarantee the stability of the legally elected government, and cooperate in the integral development of the country.

This constitutional language justifies military coups for numerous reasons. It is a permanent rationale for protected democracy. Similar conceptions informed the military coups after 1964 in Latin America. Thus, the Chilean armed forces "intervened institutionally, according to the juridical option that any political corps has to depose an illegitimate government . . . assuming a role, in itself just and opportune, to achieve the salvation of the nation's traditions and its permanent values."[45] Importantly, ex-president Eduardo Frei, accepting this basic premise for protected democracy, added: "The military has saved Chile. . . . [They] were called on by the people and fulfilled their legal duty. . . . If a people has been so weakened and harassed [acosado] that it cannot rebel, . . . then the Army substitutes its arms and does the work."[46] Protected democracy is not a concept imposed by the armed forces on Latin American nations. It is a design for government and political culture that has evolved since 1810 in which the military is assigned a guardianship role. This constitutional design is incompatible with limited government; it provides a permanent rationale for unconstrained exercise of government authority to confront "emergencies" and defeat "enemies, subversives, and heretics." It legitimizes—indeed, makes obligatory—internal wars against citizens that threaten the institutional order and the nation's permanent interests.

Protected democracy buttresses the constitutional mission of the armed forces with constitutional provisions for regimes of exception as basic elements of political design. Regimes of exception (suspension of

---

[44] For details on the historical background of these provisions, see Loveman 1993; for the 1978 to 1993 period, see Loveman 1994.

[45] Johnson 1987, 16–17.

[46] Cited in ibid., 91–92.

civil liberties and rights, delegation of extraordinary powers to presidents, army officers, and other public officials, and other emergency measures) permit virtual constitutional dictatorship. They have been used in Latin America since the first nineteenth-century constitutions; only two of 103 constitutions adopted by 1900 failed to include such provisions. The most well known regime of exception is the "state of siege," which in its original version permitted suspension of all constitutional provisions in favor of executive emergency powers. First adopted in Chile in 1833, this type of exceptional regime was incorporated into many Latin American constitutions and was widely used to repress and intimidate internal opposition. In many so-called democratic regimes, civil liberties and rights have been suspended, and governments have ruled by decree for years or even decades (for example, Colombia from 1958 to 1974). In supposedly democratic Colombia, from 1965 until 1987 civilians accused of crimes during states of siege were assigned to military jurisdiction, with loss of civil liberties and rights, even to the writ of habeas corpus.[47]

From 1950 to 1960, there were over one hundred occasions of the declaration or extension of a state of siege in Latin America—a period prior to the Cuban Revolution, the rise of guerrilla movements and counterrevolutionary military regimes, and without external war or armed invasion.[48] In most of Latin America, regimes of exception have routinely been imposed to confront student demonstrations, strikes, land occupations, and other political protests. They are so embedded in Latin American political life that they have become hegemonic premises, carrying over to all the post-1978 constitutions adopted as part of the transitions from military rule. The post-1964 military regimes used the traditional regimes of exception, added new ones in some cases, and insisted on still others in transition constitutions. These regimes of exception have been used in Bolivia, Ecuador, El Salvador, Guatemala, Peru, and Argentina since transition to civilian rule.

Several other features of Latin American protected democracy include security legislation (laws on internal security, antiterrorism laws, public-order laws) criminalizing certain types of political opposition and further expanding military functions and jurisdiction; proscription of political parties and other groups and movements with "foreign," "exotic," or antirepublican ideologies;[49] restrictions on the mass media justified by

[47] D. Juan Carlos Palou Trías, in *Posición Constitucional de las Fuerzas Armadas en Iberoamérica y en España* 1992, 57–70.

[48] Karst and Rosenn 1975, 223.

[49] For example, the 1965 Honduran constitution prohibited "the formation, inscription, and functioning of political parties that proclaimed or practiced doctrines contrary to the democratic spirit of the Honduran people" (article 39); the 1950 Nicaraguan constitution

"national security" concerns; criminal codes with special provisions for political crimes and "crimes against the internal security of the state"; military jurisdiction over civilians for stipulated crimes (for example, terrorism, attacks on military officers, crimes against internal security); restriction or full exclusion of civilian courts' jurisdiction over military personnel (for example, in cases of alleged kidnapping, torture, or murder "while in service"); formal corporate representation for the armed forces in policy making (for example, in congress, the judiciary, executive agencies, public administration, and public enterprises); partial budget autonomy and guaranteed minimal budgets from designated sources (for example, percentages of export revenues, special taxes, off-the-books enterprises unsupervised by the legislature); and broad constitutional and statutory autonomy over "professional" and "internal matters," such as military education, tenure of service commanders, promotions, reassignments, retirements, and pensions.

The particular form such antidemocratic provisions take varies from country to country. Together, however, these interwoven strands in the political fabric of protected democracy impede elected officials from governing, erode civil liberties and rights, chill the media, constrain effective political contestation and opposition, and ultimately threaten the polity with a legitimate coup if circumstances so justify. So long as these basic features of Latin American politics remain, no transition from military to civilian governments, whether by election, constitutional convention, or divine intervention will allow an affirmative answer to the question "Is Latin America going democratic?" The civilian governments installed since 1978 have, with variations, induced some political liberalization, but they have also reaffirmed the fundamental elements of protected democracy. Real democratization requires dismantling the basic features of protected democracy and military guardianship.

(reformed in 1955) prohibited the formation and activities of communist parties and "those that sustain similar doctrines, and any other party [connected] to international organizations"; and, prior to 1975, Costa Rica prohibited parties that "in their programs, ideologies, actions, or international connections, tend to destroy the foundations of democratic organization in Costa Rica" (1949 constitution, article 98). Similar provisions or legislation were enacted at various times in other countries (for example, proscription on Peronismo in Argentina, and on communists in Chile, Guatemala, Brazil, and Paraguay).

Appendix 1

LATIN AMERICAN ELECTIONS, 1978–1989

Country	Election Type	Date	Purpose/ President-elect
Chile	plebiscite	April 1, 1978	affirm government action
Ecuador	plebiscite	Jan. 15, 1978	approve new constitution
Costa Rica	general	Feb. 5, 1978	Rodrigo Carazo
Paraguay	general	Feb. 12, 1978	Alfredo Stroessner
Colombia	parliament regional/local	Feb. 26, 1978	
Guatemala	general	Mar. 5, 1978	Romeo Lucas
El Salvador	parliament	Mar. 12, 1978	
Colombia	presidential	June 4, 1978	Julio Turbay
Perú	constituent assembly	June 18, 1978	
Bolivia	general	July 9, 1978	(annulled)
Ecuador	presidential (first round)	July 16, 1978	
Panama	parliament	Aug. 6, 1978	
Brazil	parliament state assemblies	Nov. 15, 1978	
Venezuela	general	Dec. 3, 1978	Luis Herrera
Ecuador	presidential (second round); deputies, provincial	Apr. 24, 1979	Jaime Roldós
Bolivia	general	July 1, 1979	Hernán Siles (doesn't take office until 1982)
Mexico	parliament	July 1, 1979	
Colombia	regional/local	Mar. 9, 1980	

Country	Election Type	Date	Purpose/ President-elect
Honduras	constituent assembly	Apr. 24, 1980	
Peru	general	May 18, 1980	Fernando Belaúnde
Bolivia	general	June 29, 1980	Hernán Siles (but General Luis Meza governs)
Chile	plebiscite	Sept. 11, 1980	new constitution
Peru	municipal (general)	Nov. 23, 1980	
Uruguay	plebiscite	Nov. 30, 1980	new constitution (rejected)
Peru	municipal (complimentary)	Nov. 8, 1981	
Honduras	general	Nov. 29, 1981	Roberto Suazo
Costa Rica	general	Feb. 7, 1982	Luis A. Monge
Guatemala	general	Mar. 7, 1982	Aníbal Guevara (annulled; military junta appoints General Ríos Montt)
Colombia	parliament regional/local	Mar. 14, 1982	
El Salvador	constituent assembly	Mar. 28, 1982	
Dominican Republic	general	May 16, 1982	Salvador J. Blanco
Colombia	presidential	May 30, 1982	Belisario Betancourt
Mexico	general	July 4, 1982	Miguel de la Madrid
Brazil	parliament state governors state assemblies local	Nov. 15, 1982	
Paraguay	general	Feb. 6, 1983	Alfredo Stroessner
Argentina	general	Oct. 30, 1983	Raúl Alfonsín (ends term six months early)

Country	Election Type	Date	Purpose/President-elect
Peru	municipal	Nov. 13, 1983	
Venezuela	general	Dec. 4, 1983	Jaime Lusinchi
Ecuador	presidential (first round); national deputies provincial	Jan. 29, 1984	
Colombia	regional	Mar. 11 1984	
El Salvador	presidential (first round)	Mar. 25, 1984	
Panama	general	May 6, 1984	Nicolás Ardito (resigns 1985)
Guatemala	constituent assembly	June 10, 1984	
Nicaragua	presidential; constituent assembly	Nov. 4, 1984	Daniel Ortega
Uruguay	general	Nov. 25, 1984	
El Salvador	parliament; municipal	Mar. 31, 1985	
Peru	general	Apr. 14, 1985	Alán García
Mexico	parliament	July 7, 1985	
Bolivia	general/local	July 14, 1985	Víctor Paz Estenssoro (elected by Congress)
Guatemala	general (first round) general (second round)	Nov. 3, 1985 Dec. 8, 1985	Vinicio Cerezo
Argentina	parliament (partial)	Nov. 3, 1985	
Peru	municipal (complimentary)	Nov. 10, 1985	
Brazil	prefectural	Nov. 15, 1985	
Honduras	general	Nov. 24, 1985	José Azcona
Costa Rica	general	Feb. 2, 1986	Oscar Arias
Colombia	parliament regional/local	Mar. 9, 1986	

Country	Election Type	Date	Purpose/ President-elect
Dominican Republic	general	May 16, 1986	Joaquín Balaguer
Colombia	presidential	May 25, 1986	Virgilio Barco
Ecuador	plebiscite	June 1, 1986	on role of "independents" in elections
Ecuador	regional/local	June 4, 1986	
Peru	municipal	Nov. 9, 1986	
Brazil	parliamentary state assemblies governorships	Nov. 15, 1986	
Haiti	constitutional referendum	Mar. 29, 1987	new constitution
Argentina	parliament (partial)	Sept. 6, 1987	
Haiti	general	Nov. 29, 1987	suspended
Bolivia	municipal	Dec. 6, 1987	
Ecuador	general (first round);	Jan. 31, 1988	
	presidential (second round)	May 8, 1988	Rodrigo Borja
Paraguay	presidential	Feb. 14, 1988	Alfredo Stroessner (ousted Feb. 3, 1989, by coup)
Colombia	regional/local assemblies	Mar. 13 1988	
El Salvador	parliament/ local	Mar. 20, 1988	
Guatemala	municipal	Apr. 24, 1988	
Mexico	general	July 6, 1988	Carlos Salinas
Chile	plebiscite	Oct. 5, 1988	on continuation in power of General Augusto Pinochet
Brazil	prefectural municipal	Nov. 15, 1988	
Venezuela	general	Dec. 4, 1988	Carlos A. Pérez (removed from office by congress, 1993)

Country	Election Type	Date	Purpose/ President-elect
El Salvador	presidential	Mar. 19, 1989	Alfredo Cristiani
Uruguay	plebiscite	Apr. 16, 1989	amnesty for human-rights violations by military
Paraguay	general	May 1, 1989	General Andrés Rodríguez
Bolivia	general	May 7, 1989	Jaime Paz (elected by congress)
Panama	general	May 7, 1989	Annulled
Argentina	general	May 14, 1989	Carlos Menem (takes office six months early)
Chile	plebiscite	July 30, 1989	constitutional reforms
Peru	municipal	Nov. 12, 1989	
Brazil	presidential (first round); presidential (second round)	Nov. 15, 1989 Dec. 17, 1989	Fernando Collorde Mello (impeached for corruption)
Honduras	general	Nov. 26, 1989	Rafael Callejas
Uruguay	general; plebiscite	Nov. 26 1989	Luis A. Lacalle
Bolivia	municipal	Dec. 3, 1989	
Venezuela	municipal; state governors	Dec. 3, 1989	
Chile	general	Dec. 14, 1989	Patricio Aylwin (four-year term)
Costa Rica	general	Feb. 4, 1990	Rafael Calderón
Nicaragua	general	Feb. 25, 1990	Violeta Barrios de Chamorro
Colombia	parliament regional/local	Mar. 11, 1990	
Peru	general (first round); presidential (second round)	Apr. 8, 1990 June 10, 1990	Alberto Fujimori

Country	Election Type	Date	Purpose/ President-elect
Dominican Republic	general	May 16, 1990	Joaquín Balaguer
Colombia	presidential	May 27, 1990	César Gavira
Ecuador	provincial/ local	June 17, 1990	
Brazil	parliamentary state assemblies state governors	Oct. 3, 1990	
Guatemala	general (first round)	Nov. 11, 1990	
Brazil	governors (first round)	Nov. 15, 1990	
Colombia	constituent assembly, plebiscite	Dec. 9, 1990	new constitution
Argentina	constituent (new province)	Dec. 9, 1990	
Haiti	general	Dec. 16, 1990	
Guatemala	presidential (second round)	Jan. 6, 1991	Jorge Serrano (leaves office after "autogolpe" and attempt to close Congress, 1993)
Panama	parliament (partial)	Jan. 27, 1991	
El Salvador	parliament/ local	Mar. 10, 1991	
Paraguay	municipal	May 26, 1991	
Argentina	deputies/ governors	Aug. 11, 1991 Sept. 8, 1991 Oct. 27, 1991	
Mexico	parliament	Aug. 18, 1991	
Peru	municipal (partial)	Aug. 18, 1991	
Colombia	parliament/ governors	Oct. 27, 1991	
Bolivia	municipal	Dec. 1, 1991	

Source: Cerdas-Cruz, Rial, and Zovatto 1992, appendix 1.

8

Political Structure and Economic Liberalization

CONDITIONS AND CASES FROM THE DEVELOPING WORLD

WILLIAM B. HELLER, PHILIP KEEFER,
AND MATHEW D. MCCUBBINS

LIBERALIZATION has become the orthodoxy of economic development. In pursuit of deregulation, privatization, and free trade, an increasing number of countries have taken a leap of faith from government planning of the economy to the invisible hand of the marketplace. Many countries, such as Chile, have successfully liberalized and now experience high rates of growth and development. Others' attempts at liberalization have yielded little more than chaos, with economic and political disruption. Given the potential rewards and the obvious risks, it is natural to ask under what conditions we might expect to see liberalization, both attempted and successful.

Scholars have sought to answer this question by suggesting a link between economic crises such as debt crises, inflation or declining income, and policy change. Although there is some support for this hypothesis, there are numerous counterexamples. Many countries have reformed, for example, even though they were not suffering a crisis (e.g., Japan), while other countries have failed to reform despite persistent economic crises (e.g., Senegal). Economic crisis may indeed be a factor that affects economic policies directed at liberalization, but it is neither necessary nor sufficient to bring about economic reform.

We are interested here in defining necessary and sufficient conditions for reform. Liberalization will come only when made possible by the confluence of three necessary conditions. First, liberalization will not be attempted unless the political leaders consider reform desirable. This requires a change in the interests or incentives of the leadership so that reform becomes attractive relative to the status quo of government

An earlier version of this paper was presented at the annual meeting of the Public Choice Society and Economic Science Association, Houston, Texas, April 12–14. We thank Scott Basinger, Greg Bovitz, Vin Brandt, John Carey, Paul Drake, Dan Kaufman, Christopher Nevitt, Sunita Parikh, Mike Thies, Jeff Weldon, and a lively audience in Houston for their valuable input.

ownership and planning. This could come about in a number of ways, including changes in the leadership itself, changes in the leadership's support coalition, or changes in the value of the status quo to the leadership. Note that we leave the definition of "desirable" open; reform might be desirable for ideological reasons, but it also could be useful in denying issues to political opponents. The key to the desirability of reform is that it depends on the known, inferred, or imputed preferences of the reformer and not on objective standards. In economic terms, reform is desirable if it leads to an expected benefit for the reformer that is greater than the expected benefit from doing nothing. Second, for reform to occur, policy makers must believe that they can identify plausible alternatives that correspond to their preferences. Third, liberalization will not occur unless policy makers who favor reform control the political resources to enact and implement the policy change. This requires that reformers both play a role in agenda setting and control the institutional means to legislate and execute policy. In other words, reformers have to control all the key institutions from the outset or, failing that, they must replace or form coalitions with those who have the institutional (or possibly organizational) wherewithal to block reform.

Liberalizing reform will occur only if these three conditions are met. The conditions are necessary since it is difficult to conceive of anybody undertaking to proposing reform in the absence of the first two conditions (that is, positive expected benefits), and it seems clear that reform will succeed only if the third condition holds. The conditions are sufficient in that they require no additional circumstances to make reform occur. It is possible to break the conditions into more detail (e.g., the power of unions to mobilize street demonstrations and the propensity of politicians to care), which we will do to some extent in discussing individual cases below, but these three conditions as stated are necessary and sufficient for liberalizing reform.

Institutional structure sets the context for political decision making and reform. Although there exists no straightforward relationship between institutions and outcomes—such as "authoritarian countries can reform while democracies cannot"—institutions do create incentives for political leaders and thus shape and constrain their actions. In different contexts, institutions might make reform more feasible or might hinder it. Institutional structure can stack the deck in favor of reform and provide incentives for the leadership to enact liberalizing policies.

While the three necessary conditions may seem obvious, the existing literature on policy reform does not systematically explore them and their relation to reform. However, we cannot begin to understand when events such as coups, elections, or economic upheavals will lead to liberalization until we understand these political foundations for moving to more liberal policy. Here, we look at the three conditions, particularly the first and third, comprehensively. In the following section, we describe these conditions further. We then demonstrate the importance of these conditions with an analysis of the recent histories of economic liberalization (or lack thereof) in seven cases: Chile, South Korea, Mexico, India, Turkey, the Philippines, and China. These cases run the gamut from established democracies to democratizing (or recently democratized) political systems to an authoritarian regime. Although these brief case studies are too few to constitute a test of the necessity or sufficiency of the three conditions, they clearly illustrate the fundamental importance of political structure to reform outcomes.

Conditions for Reform

Traditionally, the dichotomy between strong and weak states forms the basis for the analysis of economic reform. In Huntington's classic formulation, for example, economic growth in the absence of strong state leadership is likely to lead to political chaos (Huntington 1968). In this view, the social unrest caused by economic reform requires a relatively insulated state, which can impose short-term costs on the society in pursuit of long-run benefits. As many, including Huntington himself, have noted, however, this prediction rarely seems accurate, for democratic states also have the highest level of economic development (see, e.g., Lipset 1959; Dahl 1971, 62–80; Huntington 1984,).

We believe explanations of liberalization based on concepts of strong and weak states and on liberal and illiberal political traditions are insufficient to explain why governments ever choose to liberalize or why some succeed where others fail. It is not necessarily true that strong governments adopt liberal economic policies, nor is it the case that political liberalization is inextricably linked with weak governments. A more fruitful approach to the analysis of reform considers directly the incentives of policy makers and their capacity to implement policies that correspond to their preferences.

We see the fundamental source of both illiberal policies and pro-liberal reform as political. Illiberal policies—even inefficient, costly ones—tend to survive for political reasons (Bates 1988a, 1988b). Politicians care about how policy affects their bases of support. That is, they care about outcomes—the distribution of income, wealth, or political power in society—and not about policy per se. Politics, rather than economic efficiency, determines winners and losers when politicians have interests in benefiting their constituents. The politically charged issues, such as the incidence of benefits and losses from policy change, thus become vitally important. Indeed, the expected incidence of benefits and costs will be critical to the decision of whether to liberalize or not.

A government will institute policy change if and only if three conditions hold: a potentially decisive group within the government prefers some plausible alternative to the status quo; the same decisive group within the government can obtain sufficient knowledge to formulate an appropriate policy to yield the desired outcome; and this decisive group can both legislate and implement policy changes to obtain the desired outcome and expects to remain decisive after the reform.[1]

The essence of these three conditions is that the government must want to change policy, must know how to change policy to produce desired outcomes, and must have the ability to change policy. We discuss these three conditions in turn.

Condition 1: The Desirability of Reform

Policy makers' political preferences determine whether reform is desirable. Although individuals' personal and ideological interests are difficult if not impossible to discern, we can identify the institutional factors that structure decision makers' motivations. In democratic systems, officeholders' tenure in power depends on whether they maintain their constituents' favor. Electoral laws affect policy makers' preferences by shaping and reinforcing leaders' reliance on their constituents' support (Mayhew 1974; Carey and Shugart 1995).[2] Therefore, the interests of the socioeconomic coalition supporting the political leadership in part determines the desirability of reform relative to the status quo.

Particular policies distribute benefits and costs—such as who pays the tax bills, who receives government-sanctioned monopoly rights, and so on—among members of society. Reform tends to redistribute these benefits and costs. The political risks of reform, however, threaten to devalue the benefits of liberalization and magnify its costs. Thus, for political leaders to choose to reform their economies, the net expected utility from the proposed policy change—the risk-weighted benefits minus the risk-weighted costs—must exceed the expected net value of retaining the illiberal status quo. Since officeholders remain in office only with the "permission" of their supporters, we presume that they have the incen-

[1] For a similar argument and discussion of cases related to public-enterprise reform, see World Bank 1995.

[2] The logic behind this assumption comes from Mayhew's portrayal of elected politicians as goal-oriented, reelection-seeking actors.

tive to make policy to benefit their constituents. Therefore, we expect to
see liberal reforms only if constituents who support the government
stand to enjoy a net gain from liberalization.

Government ownership and regulation of the means of production,
however, secures the benefits of production for certain constituents—for
example, the military, labor, or the landed elite. What circumstances
might lead to a change in the calculus of benefits and costs? Four types
of circumstances are sufficient to alter the relative values of the status
quo and reform. First (and most obviously), an altogether new leadership will face different benefits and costs from individual policies; different leaders represent differing constituencies, whose interests are expected to vary. If the new leadership's core constituents are likely to
benefit from privatization—particularly if the new leaders have been
selected because of a promise to privatize—then the impetus for reform
may be sufficient to fulfill our first condition. If we define regime change
narrowly as the passage of government control from one political party
to another, the connection with reform is clear as long as the parties
appeal to different constituencies. For example, until recently, a change
in control of government in Britain from Conservative to Labor (or vice
versa) has carried with it clear, predictable implications for government
policy (see, e.g., Butler and Stokes 1976, Moodie 1971, 30–32). In general, a change in leadership should be a clear indicator of a shift in the
desirability of reform.

Second, even if the individuals in power do not change, coalition realignments—a change in the government's base of support—can provide a motive for reform. As long as political leaders care about maintaining their hold on power, changes in their supporters' preferences
will induce them to alter their policy stances.[3] They may do so in order
to create new bases of support more amenable to their own preferences
or in response to a change in the institutions that structure their incentives. For example, an electoral change that requires broadening coalitions could lead to significantly different patterns of constituency preferences. Constituency changes or electoral realignments therefore might
indicate a sufficient change in leaders' preferences to make reform desirable.

The two previous sufficient circumstances stem from changes in the
government's support coalition. Two more possibilities consist of changes
in the value of the status quo itself. First, the value of the status quo
may be altered due to an external change in the economic environment,
such as a debt crisis, runaway inflation, or a recession. If the set of

[3] For an excellent discussion of office seeking as a motivation for politicians, see Laver
and Schofield 1990, 39–60.

policies in place maintains the economic dire straits or hinders the economy's ability to heal itself, then the net value of reform will increase greatly.

Predicting the magnitude of a crisis needed to produce a given reform is not a simple task, however. A crisis that affects resources available to the government may vary in the degree to which it stimulates reform depending on such factors as demographic pressures, technological change (see, e.g., North 1981), the availability of foreign aid, the overall state of the government's economic policies, and so on. In addition, a number of political or procedural factors can affect the size of the drain and how much it constrains the government—from legally mandated accounting practices, for example, to the political salience of budget shortfalls (see, e.g., Alt and Lowry 1994; Cox and McCubbins 1991; Fiorina 1992). The Latin American debt crisis of 1982 is one clear example of a widely perceived change in resource constraints. The crisis sounded the death knell for import-substitution industrialization in many Latin American countries. Nevertheless, while leading to reform in Mexico, it marked the beginning of eight years of steadily deteriorating economic performance and policy in Peru. Elsewhere, foreign aid softened the blow of economic crisis, and therefore economic pressures failed to motivate reform efforts. Thus, a macroeconomic crisis may indicate a change in the desirability of reform, but—contrary to common belief—it is not in itself sufficient to guarantee reform.

Finally, the value of the status quo may change "internally" due to the accumulated effects of the leadership's own decisions. State ownership of enterprises often diminishes the enterprise's capital stock as the government expropriates the enterprise's cash flow, depreciating its assets. Hence, a utility, for example, may become nonproductive due to insufficient reinvestment. In this way, a purely internal change—rather than a macroeconomic crisis—as policies accumulate over time may devalue the status quo policy. In this example, privatization may be an attractive alternative to reinvestment. In the broader set of cases, liberalization in general may be seen as an attractive solution to a devalued status quo, even if the ruling coalition remains constant.

We recognize that the assertion that reform will occur only if leaders want reform may sound almost tautological. However, our emphasis on the leaders accentuates that the existence of a crisis itself does not necessarily imply that a reform will occur; further, the interests of and changes in the leaders' socioeconomic coalition determine whether reforms are desirable. In case studies, then, we should be able to identify for every reform program clear cases of either leadership change, coalition realignment, or economic factors that make reform relatively attractive compared to the status quo. Figure 8.1 summarizes this asser-

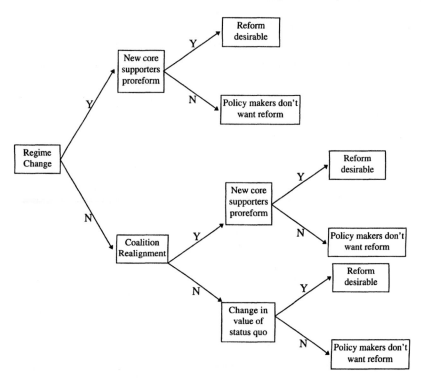

Figure 8.1 Why Do Some Governments Liberalize and Others Do Not? (Condition 1)

tion. However, these occurrences are each sufficient only to fulfill the necessary condition of desirability. Where reform does not follow liberalization-favoring changes in the coalition or in the value of the status quo, some other necessary condition has not been fulfilled. Therefore, knowledge of reform policies and the political feasibility of reform limits the degree to which desired reform actually occurs.

Condition 2: Knowledge

The second condition for reform is that leaders must have the political and technical knowledge of how to accomplish their policy objectives. Knowledge is important for two reasons: first, no leader will propose policy change without the belief that the change will lead to better outcomes; second, policies designed in the absence of sufficient knowledge might lead to unintended consequences. For our purposes, we assume that this second condition is met in most cases. Governments have myr-iad resources to draw on in this respect, such as educated elites, infor-mation-gathering agencies, technology transfer, and third parties that can offer specialized expertise to decision makers.

Condition 3: The Feasibility of Reform

Reform will take place only if the policy makers who want reform have the means to enact policy change. This is the essence of the third neces-sary condition. Which policy makers have the means to institute or block policy change is again a question of political structure: the rules that define who sets the agenda and who has authority to veto or amend the agenda setter's proposals (Lijphart 1984; Carey 1993, 1994; Grofman and Lijphart 1986; McNollgast 1992). First, agenda setters are those actors who possess the authority to propose policy change. For example, in the United States, the House of Representatives and the Senate share agenda power.[4] In most parliamentary systems, the agenda is controlled by the prime minister or various cabinet ministers. Second, "veto gates" consist of institutional hurdles that must be crossed for a proposal to become legislation. Veto players are defined as those actors who control veto gates. The preferences of veto players must be taken into account by strategic agenda setters, as their veto power may consist of the ability to block legislation outright (presidents, second legislative chambers, partners in a multiparty coalition government, and legislative committees often have this power), or they may have other, weaker means to amend, postpone, or oblige other actors to negotiate with them on policy. Veto players' authority might be circumscribed as in the United States, where a presidential veto can be overridden by a two-thirds vote in both congressional chambers, but it can also be absolute.

The nature and number of veto gates and veto players are influenced by both electoral and governing institutions. The number of veto players can vary from one (in the hypothetical case of an absolute dicta-tor or a single party majority in a unicameral parliament) to many (as in multiparty coalition governments; see Tsebelis 1995). Table 8.1 shows some general types of electoral rules and some of their effects. A pro-portional-representation system, for example, tends to lead to multi-

---

[4] The agenda power that is commonly attributed to the U.S. president goes only so far as making proposals. However, on most policy—and certainly with respect to the bud-get—Congress is free to ignore any proposals the president (or anyone else outside Con-gress) may make. Agenda-setting power is not only the authority to make proposals but also the authority to ensure that decision-making bodies consider them.

TABLE 8.1
Electoral rules and Their policy effects

Electoral system	Election	Candidate Selection	Effect on Party System	Effect on the Likelihood of Policy Change
Proportional Representation	Candidate-centered: open list, single-member district, non-transferable vote	Local committees or party leaders National party congress National party leaders	Proportional-representation rules do not in themselves lead to more or less parties, but they do make it easier for smaller parties to win legislative seats	More localization leads to more particularistic policy benefits to constituents. Politicians may have to cut deals across constituencies, which makes changing policy difficult due to bargaining costs. The greater the number of parties, the more likely that policy enactment requires coalition bargaining across parties. Each party in the governing coalition is a veto player, making its policy more difficult to enact.
Plurality	Party centered: closed list—or, as in Britain, "decisive" elections (Strom 1990) and strong party discipline	Primary (open or closed)	Plurality election rules tend toward the formation of a two-party system.	The more candidates compete on grounds other than party label—for example, intraparty primaries and the single, nontransferable vote—the more politicians will seek to claim credit for particularistic policy. There corresponds a reduction in party discipline.

party legislatures and governing coalitions and thus often increases the number of parties able to block policy.

Vetoes may also be created by such constitutionally defined institutions as bicameral legislatures, federalism, or presidentialism. Table 8.2 provides a categorization of the effects that different political institu-

TABLE 8.2
Institutional Rules and Policy Authority

Institution	Structure	Agenda Authority	Consequences
Government Structure	Presidential	Proposal power: propose legislation? decree power? Veto power: package or line item? absolute or circumscribed?	The more expansive the president's powers, the more he or she is likely to prevail in getting his own policy passed. A reformist president with the power to propose legislation is much more likely to be able to carry out reform than a president with only a package veto. Of course, it is very difficult to reform against the wishes of a powerful president.
	Parliamentary	Can parliamentary backbenchers propose or amend legislation? Degree of cabinet control over legislative process?	The power of the cabinet vis-à-vis the parliament tends to be an artifact of electoral rules and coalitional makeup more than constitutional institutions. Some such institutions do play a role in strengthening the government's hand, however, by giving the government special agenda powers (Huber 1992; Heller 1995).
Legislative Structure	Unicameral legislature		Due to the additional veto gate of the second legislative chamber, reform is more difficult than a unicameral system. The flip side of this, of course, is that it also is more difficult to change policy once it is in place. Increased numbers of vetos over policy—particularly if they have diverse interests—may lead to inflation, higher taxes, increased deficits, and fewer resources available for in-

TABLE 8.2 (*Continued*)

Institution	Structure	Agenda Authority	Consequences
	Bicameral legislature	Do chambers have coequal powers? Do both possess veto powers?	vestment (McCubbins 1991a, 1991b; Alt and Lowry 1994; Cox and McCubbins 1991; Fiorina 1992).
Federalism	Unitary state	How dependent are local authorities on the central government?	The existence of multiple tiers in policy making makes implementation more difficult unless policies enjoy widespread support. Reform policies often may be weak, as politicians focus on local constituencies in creating particularistic policies.
	Federal state	Do regional governments have access to their own resources?	
Judiciary	Independent	Can courts set their own agenda?	The existence of an independent judiciary (where the U.S. Supreme Court qualifies as quite independent, and Stalinist courts and sixteenth-century England's Star Chamber rank as quite subservient) may enable reform-minded politicians to lock their preferences into legislation and guard against it being undermined in the implementation stage (McCubbins, Noll, and Weingast 1987, 1989; McNollgast 1992).
	Subservient	Are courts dependent on politicians or elections for their influence?	

tions have on the number and nature of veto players. The division of policy authority among various actors—and even among tiers of government—may increase bargaining costs and reduce effective bargaining space. Requiring the agreement of additional players implies, all else equal, a greater diversity of interests and hence greater disagreement over changes to the status quo. Therefore, increasing the number of veto players is likely to reduce the likelihood of reform, but it should also make policies more sustainable, as they will be more difficult to alter in the future. Rules also determine the autonomy of different institutions in policy making. Certain bodies may have the authority to veto only certain types of policy. For example, the German upper house (*Bundesrat*) possesses a veto over policy affecting the states (*Länder*) but not over national policies. Therefore the lower house (*Bundestag*) is autonomous in making national policies but not policies that impact the states directly.[5] Furthermore, the degree of independence of the judiciary, as well as the sphere within which they can make or review policies, is defined largely by formal rules and may—as in the case of France (Stone 1992)—provide another potential veto gate over policy. In general, rules of procedure are used to determine winners and losers in policy making. Combined with the constraints of constitutional structure, we may determine a great deal about the feasibility of reform by investigating who holds what veto gates and within what spheres of policy those vetoes are legitimate.

Figure 8.2 summarizes the influence of institutions on reform possibilities. To enact reforms, reformers must control the agenda sufficiently to make proposals. If reformers do control the agenda, they must further control the veto gates necessary to legislate changes to policy. If those conditions are met, the next question is whether they have the economic and political capital to pay the costs that reform might necessitate in popularity as well as in tangible side payments to the reform's potential opponents. These payments may have to be made to potential coalition partners in order to gain the approval of all veto players. Gaining compromise among coalition partners is made more difficult when there are numerous preferable alternatives or multidimensional issues, either of which may increase bargaining costs and may entail time-consuming negotiations. Consider, for example, the problem of building a coalition to rationalize telephone or electric rates. In order to gain the support of rural consumers, whose rates might be dramatically increased, reformers may need to change banking laws (to cheapen

[5] Some scholars (e.g., Lijphart 1984) believe there are systematic connections between a federal state, with the upper house both having a veto and representing the states directly, and an independent judiciary to enforce the "federal bargain" (e.g., Bednar, Eskridge, and Ferejohn 1994).

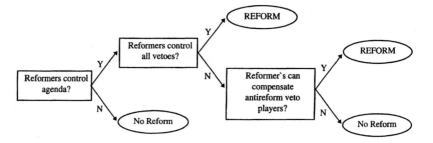

Figure 8.2 Will Reform Succeed? And to What Degree? (Condition 2)

money), create farm or mining subsidies, and so forth to create offsetting benefits for those consumers. This increases the range of policies over which policy makers must agree, made necessary by the need to build a coalition in favor of reform. Bargaining costs are exacerbated in coalition governments where different coalition partners hold different ministries, each with veto power over policy changes within their jurisdictions (Laver and Shepsle 1990). Figure 8.2 demonstrates that neither preferences nor institutions alone can account for why and when policy reforms are enacted. The coincidence of both, however, will fulfill two of the necessary conditions for change.

The success of policy reform depends crucially on whether supporters believe in the long-term viability of the government's reform promises. In order to build support for reform, policy makers must be in a position to both overcome opposition and convince their constituents who stand to benefit from the reform to support the proposal. The latter is unlikely to occur unless supporters believe that the new policy will be implemented and sustained. If governments undertake reform for economic reasons, they must convince investors—a further group whose support, although not in the coalition, might prove necessary for the reform's success—of the reform's long term viability as well. In the absence of credible government commitment, investors hesitate to commit capital to investments whose rate of return may vary with political and policy shifts. Investors in privatizing industries are unlikely to make investments that face political risk unless they can be guaranteed either a sufficiently high rate of return to compensate them or a veto or voice in the decision-making process (see, e.g., chap. 4, above).

The long-term feasibility of reform may be tenuous to the extent that reforms are passed by fragile coalitions or in the face of significant opposition. Even if a decisive group can initiate reform, it might not remain decisive long enough to implement reform. Anticipation of changes in electoral results, within a party, or within a governing coalition may forestall reform even when it is desirable and feasible in the short term. To undertake or persist in reform in light of this requires the government to account for the riskiness of a reform proposition.

Cases

When our three necessary and sufficient conditions for reform hold, then policy will change. If those with the political authority to promulgate reform have no desire to do so, then we expect to see no policy change. If some veto players prefer the status quo to reform, then we expect to observe either no attempts to change policy (if policy makers anticipate failure and decide not to bother) or only attempts that are stymied.

The case studies that follow do not constitute a test of the necessity and sufficiency of our three conditions. The sample size is too small to allow for rejection of counterfactual hypotheses. However, we believe the cases are diverse enough to provide a persuasive picture of both necessity and sufficiency. All of our cases involve some form of liberalization, ranging from deregulation of the private sector to the privatization of public enterprises. We narrow the field of possible choices by looking only at developing countries because we assume that their resources are tight and therefore that the conflicts over and the effects of reform are likely to be more pronounced and easily identified. Moreover, the policy debates regarding liberalization have potentially the greatest implications for these countries since liberalization in general marks a more substantial departure from previous policies than in developed countries. We also present cases of relatively successful reforms as well as unsuccessful ones. Finally, there is what we see as a dangerous tendency to affirm that successful economic liberalization can best be achieved by authoritarian governments. Hence, we present some cases where political liberalization and a concomitant openness to policy conflict was already either in place (as in India) or part of the political debate.

We studied seven countries: Chile, China, India, South Korea, Mexico, the Philippines, and Turkey. Of this sample, Chile's liberalization efforts have met with the most success. Korea also has been quite successful, and reforms in the Philippines appear to be gaining steam. Mexico's ambitious liberalization plans have been marginally successful, while India and Turkey have made little headway. In China, the "marketization" of many of that country's state enterprises has proceeded with little apparent liberalization at all.[6]

---

[6] Whether marketization without liberalization signals that the policy has been successful or unsuccessful depends entirely on one's perspective. While it is clear that liberalizers

Chile

The success of economic reform in Chile seems consistent with the conventional wisdom that dictators may reform more easily than democracies, as Chile reformed under the iron hand of Augusto Pinochet. Dictators, as sole veto players, are seemingly unconstrained by institutional checks and can thus set policy as they like. An examination of Chile with respect to the conditions for reform, however, suggests that the reforms are sustainable "despite" the recent transition to democracy.

Until the early 1970s, Chile provided a shining example of democratic politics in Latin America. Elections were regular and respectable, and state involvement in the economy was limited. In 1970, Salvador Allende was elected president with a scant plurality of one-third of the votes cast. Allende, who campaigned on a socialist platform, proceeded to nationalize a large number of firms or simply "intervene" by bringing them under direct state control without formal state ownership. From November 1970 to March 1972, the Chilean state increased the number of firms in which the state owned a controlling interest from 43 to 164 (Oppenheim 1993, 63). More than half the increase can be accounted for by firms in which the state owned more than 99 percent interest. Allende's policy preferences, extreme though they seemed, were consistent with those of his constituents: nonagricultural working-class voters, who were more likely to gain from nationalization, favored him by a wide margin over his two competitors from the center and the right.

In 1973, Pinochet took power in a coup. During his tenure in power, the state reduced its role in the economy significantly. A program of liberalizing reforms occurred throughout Pinochet's regime (1973–1989), but two major periods of reform took place in 1974, following the coup, and in 1985, after a debt crisis and recession. Both periods of reform activity are consistent with our model's predictions regarding the desirability of reform. In the first case, following the 1973 coup, a leadership change occurred, and with it a new constituency rooted in the upper and middle classes became represented by the political leadership (see Valenzuela 1978, table 15).[7] In the second case, the debt crisis significantly reduced the value of the status quo to the government. Perhaps out of fear of a socialist resurgence, the Pinochet government reasserted a policy of economic liberalization. The creation of a vibrant,

---

should be unhappy with the progress of Chinese reforms, we suspect that the reformers themselves are getting just the results that they wanted. We should note in this context that our model addresses the question of whether reforms will be implemented, not the efficacy of those reforms.

[7] However, there exist no electoral results from the 1970s to confirm this assertion.

capitalist economy was seen as the surest way to prevent the forces that elected Allende from again realizing their ambitions for the Chilean economy (Drake 1993; Corbo, Lüders, and Spiller 1995).

As a solidly ensconced dictator with the essentially complete loyalty of the military and a well-deserved reputation for suppressing dissent, Pinochet was in a position to implement whatever reforms he saw fit. In other words, the Pinochet government easily fulfilled our third necessary condition for reform, in that no institutional or social barriers appear to have inhibited the reform's feasibility in either period.[8]

An outstanding fact of the Chilean case is the government's emphasis on sustainability. Pinochet understood that preventing nationalization and intervention in the economy by subsequent governments would be difficult. In part, the 1980 constitution was an attempt to address this problem. The actions taken conform with our prior argument regarding feasibility, in that the 1980 constitution placed additional veto players in the way of subsequent policy change. For example, the electoral laws adopted gave excessive representation to sparsely populated rural areas. The electoral formula used to elect members of the Chamber of Deputies (proportional representation in two-member districts, with votes totaled according to the d'Hondt counting method; Caviedes 1991) provides the second-strongest party in a district a good chance at equal representation with the first-strongest party.[9] Smaller parties that can muster just over one-third of the district vote can compete and win seats even in districts where the larger party commands an overwhelming (but smaller than two-thirds) majority. Due to this rule, Pinochet's allies remain disproportionately strong in the Chamber of Deputies. Beyond the electoral rules, constitutional rules governing selection to Chile's upper house are designed to ensure overrepresentation of the natural allies of Pinochet's policies. The constitution specifies that membership of the upper house will be augmented by up to eight appointed senators—the *designados*—and by an indeterminate number of "life senators," an honor bestowed on those who have occupied the presidency for at least six years (1980 constitution, article 45). Given the legislative and electoral institutions now in place, Pinochet's supporters control at least

[8] As for the second condition, while in most cases we choose simply to assume that leaders can get the necessary expertise and information somewhere if they want it, the Chilean case is worthy of note in this regard. In Chile, Pinochet was able to draw on the expertise of the much-maligned Chicago Boys—young, American-educated economists who advised Chile's policy makers or made policy themselves (Frieden 1991, 155; Piñera 1994, 227).

[9] Many observers think of Chile's small-district d'Hondt system as distinct from proportional representation altogether. They see it, rather, as a "binomial majoritarian system" (Godoy Arcaya 1994, 303)

one veto gate in the policy-making process. According to our earlier prognosis, any reform that does not benefit Pinochet's constituents is not feasible. Hence, it would be very difficult for a later government to reverse the liberalization policies enacted under Pinochet's rule.

Pinochet's institutional reforms have succeeded to date. The electoral law–induced parity in the Chamber of Deputies militates against any party or coalition having a strong majority in the lower house, and the senatorial appointments made by Pinochet before leaving office have denied the governing Concertation for Democracy—a coalition of seven parties dominated by the Christian Democrats (DC)—a majority in the Senate. As shown in table 8.3, the Concertation won majorities of the elected seats in the Senate in 1989 and 1993 but ended up with only 47 and 46 percent of seats because of the designados. The Christian Demo-

TABLE 8.3
Chile: Votes and Seats, 1989 and 1993

Party	Election: December 1993			Election: December 1989	
	Popular Vote (Percent)[†]	Percent Senate Seats	Percent Chamber Seats	Percent Senate Seats	Percent Chamber Seats
Christian Democrats[c]	27.0	27	31	28	33
Socialist Party[c]	12.0	11	13	9	15
Party for Democracy	12.0	4	13	2	6
Radial Party[c]	3.0	2	2	7	5
Social Democrats[c‡]	0	0	0	2	0
Other[c]	1	0	1	0	0
Communist Party[L]	5.0	0	0	0	2
Independent[L]	5	0	0	0	0
Other[L]	—	0	0	0	0
Renovación Nacional[R]	16	24	24	28	27
Unión Democrática Independiente	12	7	13	4	12
Center Center Union	3	2	2	0	0
Independent[R]	5	4	3	1	2
Total	100	81*	100	81*	100

Notes: [c]member of Concertation; [L]member of left opposition to Concertation; [R]member of right opposition to Concertation; [†]popular vote figures for 1989 elections not available; *percentages add up to less than 100 because the appointed senators are not counted. (There were forty-seven Senate seats in 1989, with nine designated senators, and forty-six seats and eight designated senators in 1993.)
Source: Compiled by Dan Kaufman.

crats have controlled the presidency since Pinochet stepped down, first through Patricio Aylwin (who took office with 55 percent of the popular vote in 1989) and now through Eduardo Frei (who garnered 58 percent of the popular vote in December 1993; see Auth 1994, 341).

The institutional reforms that accompanied the economic reforms allowed Pinochet's liberalization to succeed despite a change in power, but the current deadlock may break in the near future.[10] In 1997, certain designados are set to be replaced by four new appointees, who may shift the balance within the Senate toward the Concertation (Baldez-Carey and Carey 1997). However, despite the change in leadership and accompanying change in support coalition membership, the new government does not appear to significantly favor changes to the current liberal policy. The actions of the 1989 and 1993 governments do lend support to the idea that the existing reforms are secure. Prior to the 1989 elections, the Concertation sought to avoid conflict and promote consensus. Since then, the Concertation has accepted economic liberalization and the economic model promoted by Pinochet's regime (Godoy Arcaya 1994, 305). In essence, the Concertation represents a compromise wherein its more left-wing members have given up many of their traditional economic and political goals in favor of the center-right's version of capitalism and democracy (Drake 1993, 4).

The Chilean case is consistent with the model's predictions regarding both the desirability and the feasibility of reform. The 1973 and 1982 reforms were preceded by clear shifts that made policy change preferable to the status quo. Furthermore, Pinochet, as dictator, could feasibly implement his policy preferences and was additionally capable of reforming institutions to make reform sustainable. The institutional changes provide a key contribution to our ideas about how the structures of electoral representation and legislative procedure (i.e., veto gates) may sustain reform beyond the regime itself. Due to the success of the current policy in promoting growth and development, institutional and socioeconomic factors jointly maintained the liberal reforms, despite the change in power.

South Korea

The sobriquet of "miracle" has long been affixed to the stunning record of Korea's economic growth. It may also be applicable to the political

---

[10] Not all the institutional barriers to policy change are in the legislature. Pinochet managed to appoint many conservative justices and also made both the central bank and the military into bastions of conservative strength that are well shielded from political meddling.

reforms that led to the democratic transfers of power in 1988 and 1992. Following the adoption by plebiscite of a new constitution in 1987, President Chun Doo Hwan—who had seized power in a coup in the early eighties—was replaced by democratically elected General Roh Tae Woo. This new political configuration precipitated a series of economic reforms.

In the 1988 elections, Roh's Democratic Justice Party (DJP) failed to win an overall majority in the National Assembly. In 1990, the DJP merged with two rival parties to form the Democratic Liberal Party (DLP), which managed to hold onto a bare majority through the 1992 elections, albeit not without a fair amount of internecine strife. In December 1992, South Koreans elected Kim Young Sam, their first civilian president in over thirty years (see Rich and Johnson 1993). Table 8.4 summarizes election results in the newly democratic South Korea. As president, Kim undertook a number of surprising reforms. His policy reforms led to liberalization, while his procedural reforms allowed the liberalization to be sustained over strong opposition.

Government officials have traditionally determined access to credit, investment, and imports. Since his victory, Kim has taken dramatic steps to loosen many of these restrictions. In the face of stiff opposition, he partially opened rice markets, and Korea has opened 132 of the remaining 224 closed business sectors (though key sectors such as financial

TABLE 8.4
Distribution of Seats by Party, Korean National Assembly[a]

	Dec. 1987	Dec. 1992	May 1993	Jan. 1994
Democratic Justice Party[b]	125			
Reunification Democratic Party[b]	59			
New Democratic Republican Party[b]	35			
Peace and Democracy Party	70			
Democratic Liberal Party		149	167	172
Democratic Party		97	95	96
Unification National Party (United People's Party)		31	14	11
Other	10	22	23	20
Total	299	299	299	299

Notes: [a]The *CIA World Factbook* notes that the intraelection changes in party-seat shares "reflects the fluidity of the current situation where party members are constantly switching from one party to another (see http://www.econ.unihamburg.de/ciawfb/ks.htm)." [b]Merged into the Democratic Liberal Party in February 1990.

Source: Europa World Yearbook, 1991, 1609; *Europa World Yearbook, 1994,* 1734; *CIA World Factbook 1993; CIA World Factbook 1994.*

services, cable television, and cellular telecommunications remained closed). Legal reforms have moved parallel with changes in economic policy, three of which are particularly noteworthy. First, Kim acted to prohibit the establishment of bank accounts under fictitious names, "through which businesses had slipped money to politicians." Second, the government has conducted a popular, vigorous, anticorruption campaign (Flake 1994; see also Glain 1994), leading to the arrests of many high-ranking businessmen and the two previous presidents (including Roh Tae Woo). The third and most profound change has been the reform of administrative procedures (the Basic Law for Administrative Regulations and Civil Affairs). The new law abolishes administrative guidelines, notices, and regulations that lack legal basis. Moreover, the government is also now required to provide notice and allow comment on proposed rule making along the lines of the U.S. Administrative Procedure Act. By opening up administrative decision making to public scrutiny and public participation, government decisions are more predictable and transparent (*Economist Intelligence Unit Country Profile [EIU], 1992–93, Korea*). Since the opacity of government decision making has been a principal means by which government policy has favored some firms over others, particularly established firms over potential competitors, this law is a crucial link to a more competitive internal market.

The reforms were desirable to Kim principally because they broke the concentration of political power that supported his most dangerous opposition, the old core of the DJP. The administrative reforms allowed Kim to better control a bureaucracy composed entirely of structures and personnel built up under military and DJP governments. The popularity of the anticorruption measures further enhanced the reforms' political attractiveness, particularly since Kim's supporters were unlikely to be caught in the anticorruption net, having been excluded from power for decades.[11]

Reform also met the feasibility condition in that Kim was decisive on the issues for which he sought reforms. While, as table 8.4 shows, the party maintained only a scant majority in the National Assembly and former members of the DJP (the target of Kim's reforms) were presumably well placed to block reforms that they disliked, Kim was able to overcome their opposition, as the sheer popularity of such anticorrup-

---

[11] April 1996 parliamentary elections denied Kim Young Sam's DLP a legislative majority. The president remains a decisive player, due to his constitutional prerogatives, but this new development could "slow down policy making and economic reform" (Schuman 1996). At the same time, of course, the separation of powers and the presence of a key veto player (the president) who clearly favors the reforms already wrought means that the new parliament is unlikely to be able to roll back reforms, even should it want to.

tion measures made dissent difficult. Despite the costs that the policies imposed on former DJP members, serious resistance to the policy would have jeopardized their future at the polls. This absence of opposition allowed Kim to sustain the political costs of replacing or allowing the resignation of fourteen members of his cabinet, including the prime minister, the deputy prime minister, and the chairman of the Economic Planning Board.

Korean political institutions also increased the feasibility of reform. Under the terms of the 1987 constitution, South Korea has a presidential system of government with a unicameral legislature. The unicameral system provides fewer veto gates than is typical in a bicameral system. This should, all else constant, reduce the number of possible roadblocks to reform.[12] In addition to the unicameral legislative process, which may reduce the difficulty of achieving the institutional consensus necessary to meet the feasibility condition, the Korean president has a number of constitutional powers at his disposal. The president may assume the role of agenda setter in the National Assembly. Moreover, he holds a veto over all legislative proposals, and he may act autonomously through decree powers in areas delegated to him by the legislature (article 75). In times of emergency, the president may also be granted broad authority to "preserve the interests of the nation" (article 76; see Maddex 1995, 258). The constitution requires the president to submit the annual budget to the legislature (article 54[2]), which "shall deliberate and decide" upon it (article 54[1]). More important, all legislative proposals are subject to prior examination and amendment by the State Council (article 89), which the president heads and whose members he has a hand in appointing. These formal powers exceed the formal authority of the Mexican and Filipino presidents.

The Korean case is consistent with our hypothesis, as the Kim government desired the reform and could feasibly legislate and implement the policy change. Furthermore, institutional reforms solidified the economic reforms, as those individuals with an interest to obstruct further liberalization lost significant influence in procedural changes.

Philippines

The modern Philippine government took shape when Corazon Aquino assumed the presidency in 1986, when Ferdinand Marcos fled the Philippines in the aftermath of his fraudulent reelection. Once in office,

---

[12] Unicameralism reduces the number of veto gates, but the electoral institutions determine the number of veto players by leading to bipartism versus multipartism and majority coalitions.

Aquino immediately sought broad political and economic reforms in keeping with her campaign promises to right the wrongs of Marcos's rule (Haggard and Kaufman 1989, 72). Marcos had left his country "saddled with huge foreign debts and an economy ill-equipped to compete with its Asian neighbors" (Business Monitor International [BMI 1994b, 21). Privatization of the state-enterprise sector was an important goal of the new, democratic government; more important politically, however, was the need to loosen the economic grip of the beneficiaries of Marcos's system of economic cronyism, under which Marcos' friends and loyalists were granted monopoly property rights in key economic sectors.[13] By enacting liberalizing economic reforms, the democratic government could weaken the influence of Marcos loyalists and undermine support for a return to the Marcos era.

Although reform was clearly desirable to the new leadership, Aquino faced two major feasibility problems with respect to her reform efforts. First, democratic stability was threatened by military participation in several coup attempts between 1986 and 1989, as well as the rebellion by communist and Muslim secessionists. The search for lasting civil peace was an overriding political objective (see EIU, 1993–94, *Philippines*; *EIU, 1994–95, Philippines*; BMI 1994b) that limited the government's ability to enact economic reforms. It meant, in particular, that the military exercised some veto power.

Second, Aquino's own constitutional reforms made further policy changes significantly more difficult. One of Aquino's major political reforms was the establishment of a new constitution that resembles the one crushed by Marcos' 1972 declaration of martial law. The 1987 constitution instituted an American-style presidential system with substantial new controls on executive power (*EIU, 1994–95, Philippines*, 6; BMI 1995). Aquino's failure to build a legislative coalition in Congress exacerbated the gridlock created by multiple veto gates and placed severe limitations on her own authority. Divided government was a "key factor undermining the effectiveness of her government" (BMI 1994b, 24). At the end of her time in the presidency, Corazon Aquino had made only modest progress in economic reform.[14] On the other hand, she was able to hand power to her democratically elected successor, Fidel Valdes Ramos, in a smooth, constitutional transfer in May 1992.

President Ramos won election with only 24 percent of the popular vote. In the Senate, his party took a mere two of twenty-four seats, while the opposition party won a comfortable majority in the Senate

[13] In fact, Marcos "persisted in using his . . . reserves of money and personal loyalty to destabilize the regime" (*EIU Philippines 1993–94* 1994, 6).

[14] Sales of public enterprises had been quite controversial (e.g., Philippine Airlines and the Philippine Shipyard and Engineering Co.).

with fifteen seats. The opposition also won 44 percent of the House of Representatives, but Ramos's Lakas took 25 percent and forged a majority "rainbow coalition." Like Aquino before him, then, Ramos faced a divided government that undermines reform feasibility (BMI 1994b, 7). In the first years of his administration, he concentrated on establishing political stability. While he seems to have achieved a laudable degree of success in that effort, economic reform remains elusive, as implementation of the necessary policy and legislative changes has been fairly slow. So far, Ramos has managed to enact some important reforms, particularly following his allies' success in the May 1995 elections. Trade policy has opened, reversing forty years of import-substitution policies, and foreign investment is now more welcome than before following the legalization of full foreign ownership of companies in some sectors (*EIU, 1993–94, Philippines*; BMI 1995). Ramos's government privatized the state oil company, Petron, in 1994, is selling shares in the National Steel Company, and hopes to sell off its holdings in a number of other firms.[15]

While both Aquino and Ramos had strong motivations for undertaking to reform economic policy, they differed substantially on their ability to move in that direction. Simply put, Aquino was unable to enact reforms, in part because she was forced to concentrate her resources elsewhere to ensure the survival of democracy and in part because the very constitution that she saw to fruition created a divided government. Ramos, by contrast, has been less constrained by threats to democracy, and voters have given him more solid backing in the legislature, allowing him greater policy flexibility. With improved backing in Congress and the apparent strong support of the electorate, he was able to make more significant reform progress.

Mexico

Since the end of the Mexican Revolution, Mexico has experienced little change in the identity of key decision makers. The PRI retains its customary unified government, and hence it continues to control policy making and implementation. Despite the apparent continuity of political authority, however, serious economic reforms began around 1982, during the tenure of President Miguel de la Madrid, precipitated by the Latin American debt crisis. During De la Madrid's presidency, traditional "machine" politicians began to be excluded from the top ranks of

---

[15] These include Philippines National Bank, National Shipping Corporation, Metro Manila Transit Corporation, Philippine National Railways, Manila Hotel, Manila Electric Co., and San Miguel Corporation (BMI 1994b, 86; 1995, 34).

the PRI and replaced by technocrats (Centeno 1994; Centeno and Weldon 1990; Centeno and Maxfield 1989).

As the old core of the party began to take a backseat to the new group of young, technically adept politicians, a near-disastrous schism within the PRI developed. The new generation sought the support of different socioeconomic groups than the older party leaders did. A realignment was imminent (Collier and Collier 1991). While the old PRI depended on the support of labor and peasant organizations, the reforms of De la Madrid, Carlos Salinas, and Ernesto Zedillo targeted other groups at the expense of labor and peasants. To bring about the realignment, the government sought to reform the state-run sectors of the economy, typically by privatizing parastatal firms in each sector. Initially, then, economic crisis made reform more desirable than the status quo. However, crisis also allowed a technocratic group to gain greater control of the PRI. This group appealed to a new constituency, which also favored reform.

Mexico's institutional structure—particularly the electoral rules and presidential authority—enhances the feasibility of reform. Mexico has a presidential system of government with a bicameral legislature. The membership of the Chamber of Deputies is elected by a combination of first-past-the-post (three hundred members) and proportional-representation rules (currently two hundred members). This electoral rule greatly overrepresents any party that wins a plurality, which has historically manufactured majorities for the president's party. For the Senate, each state and the Federal District has a total of four representatives, three of which go to the party whose slate garners the most votes.[16] The Mexican president has both a package veto and a limited line-item veto and may initiate legislation with both houses of Congress.[17] However, unlike in Korea, much of the president's apparent dominance of policy making derives from the president's position as party leader, rather than from his formal authority as head of government. A law that prohibits reelection to elective offices induces tight party discipline, as party members must rely on the president to continue their political careers by nominating them to other positions (see, e.g., Cavarozzi 1994; Cook, Middlebrook, and Molinar Horcasitas 1994; Molinar Horcasitas 1991; Carey 1993).

---

[16] The fourth seat goes to the first candidate of the second-place party (constitutional articles 52–56).

[17] The president can veto part of a bill, but it must be reconsidered in committee. If the committee approves and the floor concurs, the bill is treated as new legislation. If the committee disapproves, the floor can override the veto with a two-thirds margin. It is unclear what happens if the committee and the floor disagree (personal communication with Jeff Weldon).

Reform is usually feasible in Mexico, thanks to the dominance of the PRI. To date, the hierarchical nature of the PRI along with the president's constitutional authorities of appointment and nomination have made implementing new policies unproblematic. In the past, once the leadership of the PRI shifted its policy gears, the party machinery had little trouble steering the policy through Congress and transmitting it to the Mexican bureaucracy. While this ability to change policy quickly allowed the new generation in the PRI to initiate radical changes in the government's role in the economy, it also makes long-term commitment to policy very difficult.[18]

Many of the PRI old guard are still in the party and continue to oppose reform, while the PRI overall continues to lose electoral support, further strengthening the old guard, since declining electoral fortunes are associated with the actions of the technocrats. Reforms that require legislative support in Mexico have therefore slowed. Shortly after Zedillo assumed office, the Salinas administration's image of success collapsed as the new president was forced to devalue the peso and take harsh measures to keep Mexico afloat. These exceptional measures were taken by the administrative fiat of the Central Bank and Ministry of Finance. Other reforms must pass through a larger number of veto gates and have been less in evidence.

India

Particularly after 1991, significant policy-making positions in India were filled by technocratic, reform-minded individuals. However, their influence on policy outcomes has been weaker than in Mexico, and economic policies in India have changed more slowly. This is partially because reform is not entirely desirable to decision makers and less so than was the case in Mexico. In particular, the economic crises that catalyzed reforms in Mexico have been largely absent in India.[19] In addition, reform has not been feasible in India. As in Turkey, discussed below, supporters of reform are not decisive actors and are unable to make sufficient side payments to mute the opposition of their opponents. There are underlying institutional reasons that explain the differences and similarities among these countries.

[18] This is less true under Zedillo, who seems unwilling (or perhaps unable) to play the role of party leader by controlling candidate selection and other internal party matters. Some of his reforms have been heavily modified by Congress, and still others are being held up in committee.

[19] This is, of course, perhaps a tribute to the better management of macroeconomic policy in India than in Mexico.

The Congress Party has lost its postindependence grip on the prime ministership in India only three times and for short periods (1977–1980, 1989–1991, and 1996–). The party long claimed to support economic liberalization. When Narasimha Rao became prime minister in 1991, this rhetoric began to be matched by action (Gould and Ganguly 1993, 222–23). Rao appointed Manmohan Singh, a strong reformer with a Ph.D. in economics, to the post of finance minister, putting him in charge of economic reform and liberalization. Singh initiated a number of policy changes to open up the economy. These included scrapping or loosening controls on the private sector (*EIU, 1993–94, India*, 13) and the removal of quantitative regulations, such as import quotas (ibid., 16). This burst of reform did not extend to public-enterprise reform, nor was the early rapid pace of reform matched later in the 1990s.

There is substantial evidence that the limitations on reform are due, first, to the fact that the party is not unified on reform; some factions of the Congress Party view reform as antithetical to their electoral interests. The resignation of Arjun Singh, Minister of Human Resource Development, is one signal of the disunity of the Congress Party on the issue. He resigned ostensibly over the government's lack of decisiveness in ferreting out corruption. At the same time, he has expressed a desire to "bring the economic liberalization policy in tune with the aspirations of the people and to assuage their apprehensions about it, . . . to give a human face to this policy" (Dahlburg 1994). Other parties share this view and together with the antireform Congress factions are able to block reform.

The political risks of reform to all parties are also increasingly evident. There are many explanations of recent electoral losses by the Congress Party, beginning with critical state elections and culminating in the party's exclusion from the current government. These include reaction to perceived corruption in the Congress Party and the increasing dominance of regional or sectarian interests and the parties that represent them. However, some also take Congress Party losses as evidence that economic reforms are too politically risky and should be proceeding more cautiously (e.g., *Economist* 1994, 17–18). This evidence suggests that India does not fully meet our first reform condition, despite the presence of a finance minister committed to reform.

The feasibility of reform is also problematic. The Congress Party is not as hierarchical as the PRI in Mexico, so it is more difficult for reformers to control the party apparatus. In addition, federalism is much more developed in India than in Mexico, with state governments controlling important enterprises, such as power companies, and authorizing major subsidies, such as those governing electricity and water consumption by rural users. State governments are thus an additional veto gate for specific aspects of continued liberalization (such as power-sector reform). The authority of the state governments is reinforced by the growing influence of regional parties and small, single-member electoral districts that compel national parties to pay close attention to regional concerns (see, e.g., Wallace 1993). These electoral institutions impede the central government from using its budgetary leverage over state governments to induce them to reform more rapidly. Finally, with the increased influence of more regional parties, it is increasingly difficult for single parties to achieve legislative majorities.[20] To the extent that governments are coalition based (as has also become the case in Turkey), additional veto gates in the form of coalition partners arise to impede policy reform.

While these difficulties hinder the prospects for reform, India does enjoy significant advantages over Mexico in sustaining those reforms that do occur. Reforms that are implemented are as difficult to overturn as they were to approve, insulating them from political pressures to reverse them. Indian reforms are therefore likely to enjoy greater credibility when they are eventually enacted.

Turkey

Like Mexico, Turkey in the 1980s and 1990s has felt the presence of reform-minded prime ministers (Turgut Özal and Tansu Çiller) and experienced economic crises that might stimulate reform. However, reform was often undercut or stymied by a more fractious political climate and tighter restrictions on ministerial action than existed in Mexico; that is, for reformers in Turkey, reform has often not been feasible. Turkey's political structure is primarily responsible for this: The country has a parliamentary system with a history of multiparty, democratic governments, albeit punctuated by temporary military regimes. The judiciary has weighed in as an independent force in several economic-policy decisions. This system has given opponents of reform greater leverage than they enjoyed in Mexico.

The most notable reform effort in Turkey occurred in the early 1980s, spurred by economic disaster. Through the end of the 1970s, Turkey

---

[20] India's first-past-the-post electoral system, according to a straightforward application of Duverger's Law (Duverger 1959), might be expected to lead to single-party, majority governments and enhance the chances that India would meet our second reform condition. Our explanation for India's departure from this expected outcome is that the distributional impact of policy change across regions, states, or sectarian groups makes it more difficult for parties to attract membership that crosses these divides.

had followed an import-substituting industrialization strategy. A debt crisis in the late 1970s, when the public sector deficit swelled from less than 2 percent to more than 6 percent of GNP between 1974 and 1979, made the option of not reforming considerably less attractive (Canevi 1994, 182). A military coup in 1980 was followed by sharp measures to curb spending and impose monetary discipline. These policies were pursued under the military government by Turgut Özal; after 1983, when the military withdrew, Özal continued these policies as prime minister. At this time, parliamentary influence over policy making was either nonexistent under the military or muted by the majority control of the Motherland Party, so reform was feasible.

Beginning with local elections in the late 1980s, however, Özal's Motherland Party began to lose support to the opposition True Path and Social Democrat Populist Parties. In 1991, the Motherland Party's parliamentary majority was reduced from 292 seats in the 450-seat parliament to less than a plurality. The center-right True Path Party obtained 178 seats and formed a coalition with the center-left Social Democrat Populist Party (88 seats). Since the late 1980s, there has been no sustained macroeconomic reforms in the country. Even when the leading party figures (Özal or, in the True Path Party, Çiller) favored reform, they could not find coalition partners to back them; in their own parties, there are influential constituencies that oppose reform. The failure of the condition that reform be feasible, therefore, has been a chronic problem for recent economic reform attempts in the country.

The record of privatization-reform attempts provides another demonstration of the lack of reform feasibility in Turkey. However, in the case of privatization, it is doubtful that reform was even desirable to decision makers. The state has always played a significant role in the economy (Saracoglu 1994, 63). It has interests in mining, iron and steel, power generation, chemicals, and textiles (*EIU, 1994–95, Turkey*, 30). The fiscal difficulties that were the primary focus of Özal's reform efforts were intimately related, then, to subsidies to public enterprises. Consequently, Özal's Motherland Party included privatization as an "indispensable element" of its economic platform in the 1980s (Canevi 1994, 188).

He was opposed in privatization efforts by both the True Path and the Social Democrats. At that time, these parties could not defeat the proposals in parliament, but they were able to use the courts to stymie two privatizations that the government had already negotiated with foreign investors (Waterbury 1992, 209). The reason for reform failure could have been the existence of a veto gate opposed to reform—the courts—and opposition from other parties. This would represent another failure to meet our second condition. However, it is also true that even inside the Motherland Party support for reform was limited. John Waterbury notes: "The electoral coalition that has kept the Motherland Party in power does not in any direct sense benefit from the economic reforms. . . . The way Özal has placated various interests is by directing some of the growth in the economy into compensatory payments to select constituents within a narrow coalition" (ibid., 210).

Canevi (1994, 183) observes that the "center right, the center left, the nationalists and the religious conservatives" might have benefited from Turkey's export focus under Özal, but they gained little from privatization and may have even been hurt by it. In 1987, faced with growing political pressures, the Motherland Party "was driven . . . to use public expenditures and the SOE [state-owned enterprise] sector to shore up its narrow coalition" (Waterbury 1992, 211).

It appears that all parties appeal to constituencies who benefit from public enterprises—not surprising considering that state enterprises employ 20 percent of the industrial workforce. Where the True Path and Social Democrat Populist Parties opposed Özal and the Motherland Party's attempts to privatize in the 1980s, in 1991 it was the Motherland Party that strongly supported public-enterprise employees, offering them large wage increases in 1991 in the lead-up to the early parliamentary elections that year (ibid.). Agricultural reform is similarly hampered; in an effort to increase support in the 1987 elections, "Özal pumped over a billion dollars into the countryside through increases in crop purchasing prices" (Waterbury 1989, 53).

The inherent difficulties of reform in Turkey and the tendencies to form coalition governments, which undermine both the desirability and feasibility of reform, have institutional roots. The electoral system is one of proportional representation and encourages multiple parties (five in 1996) and unstable governments. Parties must win between 20 and 25 percent of the district vote and at least 10 percent of the national vote to gain representation in parliament (Turan 1994, 49–50). These rules are sufficient to restrict political competition to a few parties, but, as in India, the net result is to provide significant veto power to smaller interests that would lose under reform efforts. This same system insulates the courts somewhat from political interference, since it is difficult for the parliament to reverse court decisions through legislation. This ensures that the courts as well can act as veto gates for reform.

Abstracting from the significant background role of the military in Turkey, as we have done, there is a substantial similarity in the policy outcomes and the political environment in India and Turkey. While this environment makes reform difficult, it also has the advantage of cementing reform and making it more credible. In Turkey, however, the credibility advantage may be somewhat lessened by the role of the mili-

tary and the apparently more frequent lifting of constitutional protections in the interests of national security. To the extent that the security
rationale for relaxing institutional checks on arbitrary behavior is easily
extended to economic-policy spheres, reform credibility in Turkey may
be less than in India.

China

Political power in China resides in the Communist Party.[21] Leaders are
responsible to each other in a complex web of relationships wherein
leaders in successive tiers of authority are selected by their immediate
subordinates, who are in turn appointed by their leaders (Shirk 1993,
82–86; see also Roeder 1990). This has two important effects with respect to policy change. First, once key policy makers decide on policy
reforms, enactment of those reforms is virtually a foregone conclusion.
Second, no reform is sustainable unless it removes future decision-making power from the government's authority.

China's economy has opened up considerably since the late 1970s.
The key to Chinese economic reform has been a move away from economic planning to marketization (BMI 1994a, 1). This has meant, in
part, that control of many firms has been privatized or has devolved to
municipal or regional political authorities, while towns and villages
have been allowed to undertake significant new economic activities
(known as "township and village enterprises," or TVEs).

Devolving regulatory authority to lower-level authorities tackles two
problems confronting the national government. First, state-owned enterprises are in large part a burden to their owner: They are overstaffed
and inefficient, they face distortionary incentives from their nonmarket
pricing systems, and they are weighed down by burdensome welfare
responsibilities (BMI 1994a, 3). Second, insofar as the government
seems to have realized the inefficiency of economic planning, removing
state enterprises from its direct control helps it commit to abandon
planning in favor of the market. Although the central government has
increased its credibility in the eyes of foreign governments and international investors by decentralizing (see, e.g., BMI 1994a, 127), freedom
from the heavy hand of central government control has not necessarily
translated into increased competition or greater freedom from regulation for firms. Indeed, at lower levels of government, where public officials' opportunities for personal enrichment are limited, the incentives
for public-sector meddling in firms are high, although constrained by

---

[21] We thank Chris Nevitt for discussing with us his current research on post-Leninist
economic reforms. His help on this section was invaluable.

previously nonexistent cross-jurisdiction private-enterprise competition.[22] This suggests two things: First, the central government's ceding of control over public enterprises does not necessarily imply privatization; and second, privatization and privatized firms will operate according to political exigencies, not market ones (see Lieberthal and Oksenberg 1988; Oi 1990).

Leaders have both the incentive to attract investment and to get rid of onerous liabilities and the ability to privatize or devolve state enterprises. However, the limits to this strategy are clear: The largest and most obsolete state-owned enterprises, mostly industrial, remain with the central government, since lower-level governments have neither the resources nor the desire to shoulder the subsidies required to keep the businesses afloat.

Conclusion

While the degree of success at liberalization has varied significantly across countries, political factors determine systematically when a country will reform and whether that reform will succeed and be sustained. A first necessary condition is that liberalization must be preferred to the status quo by the political leadership. This desirability must originate in either a change in the political leadership, a change in the government's socioeconomic coalition, or a modification in the value of the status quo. For every case of reform discussed above, we can clearly identify at least one of these situations. In Chile, for example, the 1973 coup d'etat replaced Allende—a leader supported by a working-class social coalition—with Pinochet, who was supported by the middle and upper classes. We can easily interpret the reforms following the coup as a redirection of policy away from an interventionist-state status quo toward policies that benefited Pinochet's constituent groups. The reenergized liberalization following Chile's 1982 debt crisis and recession demonstrates the desirability of reform for a different set of reasons: Not a shift in power but rather a devaluation of the status quo resulted in the need for the same group of leaders to restimulate the economy through liberalization.

We can also identify cases where the desirability condition is met, but no reform occurs, as in Turkey and the Philippines. This is the case because we have posited the existence of another necessary condition:

[22] A recent example of Chinese authorities' ability to change unilaterally the terms of a contract can be seen in that case of the McDonald's restaurant in Beijing. McDonald's, which claims to have a twenty-year land-use lease for the site of the restaurant, which opened in 1992, has been given an eviction notice to make way for a new commercial and residential development.

TABLE 8.5
Summary of Case Studies

Country	Necessary Condition 1: Desirability	Sufficient Regime change? Coalition realigned? Change in value of status quo?	Necessary Condition 2: Feasibility	Sufficient
Chile	1973: yes	regime change	1973: yes	dictator, so uni-
	1982: yes	debt crisis, ex-ternal crisis	1982: yes	fied veto gates
South Korea	1992: yes	regime change	1992: yes	held both veto gates; weak op-position
Philippines	1986: yes	regime change, external crisis	1986: no	divided veto, civil unrest
	1992: yes	same proreform regime	1992: yes	unified veto, less unrest
Mexico	1994: yes	debt, inflation external crisis	1994: yes	PRI controls unified veto
India	1996: no	change in lead-ership to non-reformers	1994: no	regional and ethnic splits
Turkey	1980: yes	coup changes leadership	1980: yes	dictatorship, unified veto
	1991: no	coalition split on reform	1991: no	split coalition government
China	yes	internal change in value of sta-tus quo policies	yes	unified party control of veto gates

Reform must be politically feasible. In other words, reform-oriented leadership must have some meaningful control over the agenda and oc-cupy the institutional veto gates. If a veto player's constituents oppose reform, then—due to the electoral connection in democratic states—we expect that actor to veto any policy changes that are contrary to the interests of her socioeconomic coalition.[23] Therefore, we argue that lib-eralization will not occur unless policy makers who favor reform con-trol the political resources to enact and implement policy change. Table 8.5 summarizes the case studies in terms of whether the seven nations have satisfied the two key necessary conditions for reform.

[23] Some authors assert that a similar process is at work in authoritarian states (see the discussion of the electorate in Roeder 1990).

The case studies illustrate the fundamental importance of political desirability and political feasibility to reform outcomes. While some institutional structures may hinder policy change by making the attainment of decisive political control more difficult, other structures may make reform more likely by providing incentives for leaders to abandon the status quo. Therefore, it is important to consider political institutions when we assess a developing nation's potential for successful reform. We believe that by specifying the necessary conditions above, we have taken a step toward a systematic understanding of when economic liberalization can flourish.

9

Afterword

PAUL W. DRAKE AND MATHEW D. MCCUBBINS

IN THE LAST two centuries, many countries around the globe have established liberty, democratized, and opened free markets. Moreover, the previous two decades have seen an unprecedented upswing in individual political and economic liberty in nations as different as Argentina and Taiwan, as distant as Chile and Poland, and as previously illiberal as South Korea and Russia. While citizens in each of these countries have made important gains in their abilities to control their own political and economic destinies, the end results of these current liberalizing policies may not be democracies and free markets. Many additional liberalizing steps may be necessary for the full development of democracy and free markets.

Further, it is important to remember that the swing toward liberty is not unidirectional. Previous waves of liberalization eventually led to retrenchment, where tyrannies and dictatorships replaced democracies or free markets. Indeed, the pendulum may swing toward liberalization for a time, but the inexorable gravity of political power may cause the upward swing to stall or even retreat.

The authors in this volume have recounted the pendulous swings of liberty. Together, they have demonstrated that the prerequisites of liberalization are that a sovereign desire liberal reforms and that he or she possesses the capabilities to achieve those reforms. When reforms occurred, there is plausible reason to believe that the prerequisites were met.

But the search for the necessary conditions of liberalization are perhaps misplaced, as they are, in practice, often insufficient and difficult to identify and measure. Thus, the authors here sought to identify sufficient conditions for liberalization, asking, "When will liberalization begin, or, alternatively, when will a sovereign's desire and capability together be sufficient for liberalization to proceed?"

Most of the authors explained how, in varying situations, a sovereign makes the trade-off between maintaining control on the one hand and increasing productivity through liberalization on the other hand. North and Weingast, for example, show that a sovereign's need for capital impels him or her to abdicate some power to ensure the credibility of a commitment to the owners of capital. This abdication, in turn, leads to liberalization. Rogowski focuses on the need of a sovereign to extend representation to other mobile factors of production in order to ensure that these assets do not leave the country. Drake explains how the need to gain trading and investing partners in an increasingly connected liberal world economy, combined with the collapse of Soviet and U.S. support for many nonliberal regimes, induced authoritarians to undertake liberalizing reforms.

Another set of authors focus on the role of the military in liberalization. Haggard and Kaufman examine how economic conditions affect the level of factionalism in domestic politics, and how the level of factionalism, in turn, creates incentives for the sovereign to liberalize. Loveman isolates the influence of institutions on the likelihood of both military intercession into politics and military exit from politics. Heller, Keefer, and McCubbins discuss a variety of conditions that are sufficient to explain the presence or absence of liberalizing reforms in a number of developing countries.

These explorations should be thought of as suggestions of sufficient conditions. We have not specified the circumstances under which these conditions are in fact sufficient for an increase in individual liberty and when they are not. For example, when will the need for a sovereign to make credible commitments lead him down the path of liberalizing reforms, as opposed to employing alternative, illiberal strategies (e.g., confiscatory taxation)?

Furthermore, these studies examined only upward swings in the pendulum, not the conditions whereby liberal societies pursue illiberal policies. But, as Loveman reminds us, regimes may vacillate between liberal and illiberal policies and reforms. Thus, it may be critical to specify when a sovereign will be expected to continue a liberalizing strategy as opposed to reversing or circumscribing the process of reform. What economic, institutional, and cultural conditions facilitate the transformation of a regime to a democracy and retard moves back to authoritarianism? What are the forces that cause the pendulum to swing up, and what pulls it back down? What brings about liberal and illiberal equilibriums in the pendulum's arc? Such questions reflect the boundaries of our current knowledge.

Further study needs to more completely analyze the sufficient conditions for liberalization as well as the long-term viability of moves toward democratization. In addition, future empirical work should further evaluate the hypotheses suggested here. When such work is undertaken, we will improve our understanding of the process of liberalization.

References

Alchian, Armen A., and Harold Demsetz. 1972. "Production, Information Costs, and Economic Organization." *American Economic Review* 62:777–95.

Alfonso, Juan Maestre. 1989. *Constituciones y Leyes Políticos de America Latina, Filipinas y Guinea Ecuatorial, II, Los Regímenes de Seguridad Nacional, I, Chile, Uruguay.* Seville: Escuela de Estudios Hispano-Americanos de Sevilla.

Alt, James E., and Robert C. Lowry. 1994. "Divided Government, Fiscal Institutions, and Budget Deficits: Evidence from the States." *American Political Science Review* 88:811–28.

Amnesty International. 1988. *Honduras Autoridad Civil-Poder Militar, Violaciones de los Derechos Humanos en la Década de 1980.* London: Amnesty International Publications.

Anderson, B. L. 1970. "Money and the Structure of Credit in the 18th Century." *Business History* 85:90.

Anderson, Perry. 1974. *Lineages of the Absolutist State.* London: NLB.

Arat, Zehra F. 1988. "Democracy and Economic Development: Modernization Theory Revisited." *Comparative Politics* 20 (October): 21–36.

Arendt, Hannah. 1951. *The Origins of Totalitarianism.* New York: Harcourt, Brace.

———. 1966. *The Origins of Totalitarianism.* Rev. ed. New York: Harcourt, Brace, and World.

Arrow, Kenneth A. 1951. *Social Choice and Individual Values.* New Haven: Yale University Press.

Ashton, Robert. 1960. *The Crown and the Money Market, 1603–1640.* Oxford: Clarendon Press.

Ashton, T. S. 1955. *An Economic History of England.* London: Methuen.

Auth, José. 1994. "Elecciones presidenciales y parlamentarias de 1993." *Estudios Públicos* 62 (fall): 339–61.

Baldez, Lisa, and John Carey. 1997. "Budget procedure and fiscal restraint in post-transition Chile." In Political institutions and determinants of public policy: when do institutions matter? ed. Stephan Haggard and Mathew McCubbins. Typescript.

Ballesteros, Enrique Bernales. 1993. "La Constitución Autoritaria de 1993." *Análisis Internacional* 4:15–28.

Baloyra, Enrique. 1987. *Comparing New Democracies: Transition and Consolidation in Mediterranean Europe and the Southern Cone.* Boulder: Westview Press.

Barro, Robert. 1987. "Government Spending, Interest Rates, Prices, and Budget Deficits in the UK, 1701–1918." *Journal of Monetary Economics* 20:221–48.

————. 1991. "Economic Growth in a Cross Section of Countries." *Quarterly Journal of Economics* 106:407–43.

Barro, Robert J., and Jong-Wha Lee. 1993. "International Comparisons of Educational Attainment." *Journal of Monetary Economics* 32:363–94.

Bates, Robert H. 1981. *Markets and States in Tropical Africa: The Political Basis of Agriculture Policies.* Berkeley and Los Angeles: University of California Press.

————. 1988a. "Governments and Agricultural Markets in Africa." In *Toward a Political Economy of Development: A Rational Choice Perspective,* ed. Robert H. Bates. Berkeley and Los Angeles: University of California Press.

————. 1988b. "The State and Development: Taiwan, Argentina, and Central America." In *Toward a Political Economy of Development: A Rational Choice Perspective,* ed. Robert H. Bates. Berkeley and Los Angeles: University of California Press.

Bates, Robert H., and Anne O. Krueger. 1993. *Political and Economic Interactions in Economic Policy Reform: Evidence from Eight Countries.* Cambridge: Blackwell.

Bates, Robert H., and Da-Hsiang Donald Lien. 1985. "A Note on Taxation, Development, and Representative Government." *Politics and Society* 14:53–70.

Bednar, Jenna, William Eskridge, and John Ferejohn. 1994. A political theory of federalism. Typescript.

Bergquist, Charles, Ricardo Peñaranda, and Gonzalo Sánchez. 1992. *Violence in Colombia.* Wilmington, Del.: Scholarly Resources.

Bethell, Leslie, ed. 1995. *The Cambridge History of Latin America.* Vol. 7, part. 2. New York: Cambridge University Press.

Bethell, Leslie, and Ian Roxborough. 1992. *Latin America between the Second World War and the Cold War, 1944–1948.* Cambridge: Cambridge University Press.

Bien, David. 1987. "Offices, Corps, and a System of State Credit: The Uses of Privilege under the Ancient Regime." In *The French Revolution and the Creation of Modern Political Culture,* vol. 1. ed. K. Baker. New York: Pergamon.

Blakemore, Harold. 1986. *South America, Central America, and the Caribbean.* London: Europa Publications.

Bolivia: Neoliberalismo y Derechos Humanos. 1988. Bolivia: Comisión Andina de Juristas.

Boström, Mikael. 1989. "Political Waves in Latin America." *Ibero Americana Nordic Journal of Latin American Studies* 19:3–19.

Bratton, Michael, and Nicolas van de Walle. 1994. "Neopatrimonial Regimes and Political Transitions in Africa." *World Politics* 46:453–89.

Braun, R. 1975. "Taxation, Sociopolitical Structure, and State-Building: Great Britain and Brandenburg-Prussia." In Tilly 1975.

Bruneau, Thomas C. 1982. *The Church in Brazil.* Austin: University of Texas Press.

Buchanan, James, and Geoffrey Brennan. 1981. *Reason of Rules.* Cambridge: Cambridge University Press.

Bullow, Jeremy, and Kenneth Rogoff. 1989. "A Constant Recontracting Model of Sovereign Debt." *Journal of Political Economy* 97:155–78.

Burn, A. R. 1982. *A Pelican History of Greece*. Baltimore: Penguin.

Business Monitor International. 1994a. *China 1994*. London: Business Monitor International.

———. 1994b. *Philippines 1994*. London: Business Monitor International.

———. 1995. *Philippines 1995*. London: Business Monitor International.

Butler, David, and Donald Stokes. 1976. *Political Change in Britain*. 2d ed. New York: St. Martin's.

Callaghy, Thomas M., and John Ravenhill. 1993. *Hemmed In: Responses to Africa's Economic Decline*. New York: Columbia University Press.

Canevi, Yavuz. 1994. "Turkey." In *The Political Economy of Policy Reform*, ed. John Williamson. Washington, D.C.: Institute for International Economics.

Carey, John Michael. 1993. "Term Limits and Legislative Representation." Ph.D. diss., University of California, San Diego.

———. 1994. "Shirking and the Last Term Problem: Evidence for a Party-Administered Pension System." *Public Choice* 81:1–22.

Carey, John M., and Matthew S. Shugart. 1995. "Incentives to Cultivate a Personal Vote: A Rank Ordering of Electoral Formulas." *Electoral Studies* 14: 417–39.

Carothers, Thomas. 1991. *In the Name of Democracy: U.S. Policy toward Latin America in the Reagan Years*. Berkeley and Los Angeles: University of California Press.

Carr, Barry, and Steve Ellner. 1993. *The Latin American Left: From the Fall of Allende to Perestroika*. Boulder: Westview Press.

Carter, Jimmy. 1982. *Keeping Faith*. New York: Bantam Books.

Carter, Miguel. 1991. *El papel de la iglesia en la caída de Stroessner*. Asunción, Paraguay: RP Ediciones.

Castañeda, Jorge G. 1993. *Utopia Unarmed: The Latin American Left after the Cold War*. New York: Knopf.

Cavarozzi, Marcelo. 1994. "Mexico's Political Formula, Past and Present." In Cook, Middlebrook, and Horcasitas 1994.

Cavarozzi, Marcelo, and Manuel Antonio. 1989. *Garretón, Muerte y resurrección: Los partidos políticos en el autoritarismo y las transiciones del Cono Sur*. Santiago: Facultad Latinoamericana de Ciencias Sociales.

Caviedes, Cesar. 1991. *Elections in Chile: The Road toward Redemocratization*. Boulder: Lynne Rienner.

Centeno, Miguel Angel. 1994. *Democracy within Reason: Technocratic Revolution in Mexico*. University Park, Pa.: Pennsylvania State University Press.

Centeno, Miguel Angel, and Sylvia Maxfield. 1989. "The Marriage of Finance and Order: Origins and Implications of Change in the Mexican Political Elite." Paper presented at the conference, "Mexico: Contrasting Visions," New York City, April.

Centeno, Miguel Angel, and Jeffrey A. Weldon. 1990. "The New *Científicos*: Technocratic Elites in Mexico." Paper presented at the annual meeting of the American Sociological Association, New York City, August.

Central Intelligence Agency. 1993. *World Factbook*. Washington, D.C.: Central Intelligence Agency.

———. 1994. *World Factbook*. Washington, D.C.: Central Intelligence Agency.

Cerdas-Cruz, Rodolfo, Juan Rial, and Daniel Zovatto, eds. 1992. *Elecciones y Democracia en America Latina, 1988–1991.* San José, Costa Rica: IIDH-CAPEL.

Chalmers, Douglas A., Maria do Carmo Campello de Souza, and Atilio A. Boron. 1992. *The Right and Democracy in Latin America.* New York: Praeger.

Chalmers, Douglas A., and Craig H. Robinson. 1982. "Why Power Contenders Choose Liberalization: Perspectives from South America." *International Studies Quarterly* 26:3–36.

Chandaman, C. D. 1975. *The English Public Revenue: 1660–1688.* Oxford: Clarendon Press.

Clague, Christopher, Philip Keefer, Stephen Knack, and Mancur Olson. 1997. "Democracy, Dictatorship, and the Institutions Supportive of Economic Growth." In *Institutions and Economic Development: Growth and Governance in Less-Developed and Post-Socialist Countries,* ed. Christopher Clague. Baltimore: Johns Hopkins University Press.

Clapham, John. 1945. *The Bank of England: A History.* Vol. 1, *1694–1797.* New York: Macmillan.

Collier, Ruth Berins. 1982. *Regimes in Tropical Africa: Changing Forms of Supremacy, 1945–1975.* Berkeley and Los Angeles: University of California Press.

Collier, Ruth Berins, and David Collier. 1991. *Shaping the Political Arena: Critical Junctures, the Labor Movement, and Regime Dynamics in Latin America.* Princeton: Princeton University Press.

Conaghan, Catherine M., and James M. Malloy. 1994. *Unsettling Statecraft: Democracy and Neoliberalism in the Central Andes.* Pittsburgh: University of Pittsburgh Press.

Cook, Maria Lorena, Kevin J. Middlebrook, and Juan Molinar Horcasitas. 1994. "The Politics of Economic Restructuring in Mexico: Actors Sequencing and Coalition Change." In *The Politics of Economic Restructuring: State-Society Relations and Regime Change in Mexico,* ed. Maria Lorena Cook, Kevin J. Middlebrook, and Juan Molinar Horcasitas. San Diego: Center for U.S.-Mexican Studies, University of California, San Diego.

Corbo, Vittorio, Rolf Lüders, and Pablo T. Spiller. 1995. The institutional foundations of economic reforms: the case of Chile. Typescript, Universidad Católica de Chile and the University of California, Berkeley.

Cox, Gary W., and Mathew D. McCubbins. 1991. "Divided Control of Fiscal Policy." In *The Politics of Divided Government,* ed. Gary W. Cox and Samuel Kernell. Boulder: Westview.

———. 1993. *Legislative Leviathan: Party Government in the House.* Berkeley and Los Angeles: University of California Press.

Crouzet, F. 1967. "England and France in the Eighteenth Century." In *Causes of the Industrial Revolution in England,* ed. Max Hartwell. London: Methuen.

Cust, Richard. 1987. *The Forced Loans and English Politics.* Oxford: Oxford University Press.

Dahl, Robert A. 1971. *Polyarchy: Participation and Opposition.* New Haven: Yale University Press.

———. 1973. *Regimes and Oppositions*. New Haven: Yale University Press.

———. 1982. *Dilemmas of Pluralist Democracy*. New Haven: Yale University Press.

———. 1989. *Democracy and Its Critics*. New Haven: Yale University Press.

Dahl, Robert A., and Edward R. Tufte. 1973. *Size and Democracy*. Stanford: Stanford University Press.

Dahlburg, John-Thor. 1994. "No. 2 Man's Resignation Weakens Indian Leader." *Los Angeles Times*, 25 Dec. A12.

Danopoulos, Constantine. 1988. *The Decline of Military Regimes*. Boulder: Westview Press.

Deane, Phyllis. 1979. *The First Industrial Revolution*. 2d ed. Cambridge: Cambridge University Press.

Dean, Warren. 1970. "Latin American Golpes and Economic Fluctuations, 1823–1966." *Social Science Quarterly* 51:70–80.

Demsetz, Harold. 1967. "Toward a Theory of Property Rights." *American Economic Review* 57:347–59.

Diamond, Larry. 1988. Democracy in Latin America: U.S. and other external influences. Unpublished ms. Stanford.

———. 1992. "Economic Development and Democracy Reconsidered." *American Behavioral Scientist* 35:450–99.

Diamond, Larry, Juan Linz, and Seymour Martin Lipset, eds. 1988. *Democracy in Developing Countries*. Boulder: Lynne Rienner.

Diamond, Larry, and Marc F. Plattner, eds. 1993. *The Global Resurgence of Democracy*. Baltimore: Johns Hopkins University Press.

Dickson, P. G. M. 1967. *The Financial Revolution in England*. London: Macmillan.

Di Palma, Giuseppe. 1990. *To Craft Democracies: An Essay on Democratic Transitions*. Berkeley and Los Angeles: University of California Press.

Downing, Brian. 1992. *The Military Revolution and Political Change, Origins of Democracy, and Autocracy in Early Modern Europe*. Princeton: Princeton University Press.

Downs, Anthony. 1957. *An Economic Theory of Democracy*. New York: Harper.

Drake, Paul W. 1993. Obstacles to policy changes in Chile. Typescript, University of California, San Diego.

Drake, Paul W., and Iván Jaksic, eds. 1991. *The Struggle for Democracy in Chile*. Lincoln: University of Nebraska Press.

———. 1995. *The Struggle for Democracy in Chile*. Rev. ed. Lincoln: University of Nebraska Press.

Drake, Paul W., and Eduardo Silva, eds. 1986. *Elections and Democratization in Latin America, 1980–85*. San Diego: Center for Iberian and Latin American Studies.

Drake, Paul W., and Arturo Valenzuela. 1989. "The Chilean Plebiscite: A First Step Toward Redemocratization." *LASA Forum* 19(4):18–36.

Dubin, Jeffrey A., and R. Douglas Rivers. 1988. SST: A user's manual. Pasadena, Calif.: California Institute of Technology, mimeograph.

Duverger, Maurice. 1959. *Political Parties*. 2d ed. London: Methuen.

Economist. 1994. "The Trouble with Democracy, Part 2." 17 Dec. 17–18.

Economist Intelligence Unit Country Profile, 1992–93, Korea. 1993. London: EIU.

Economist Intelligence Unit Country Profile, 1993–94, India. 1994. London: EIU.

Economist Intelligence Unit Country Profile, 1993–94, Philippines. 1994. London: EIU.

Economist Intelligence Unit Country Profile, 1994–95, Philippines. 1995. London: EIU.

Economist Intelligence Unit Country Profile, 1994–95, Turkey. 1995. London: EIU.

Ekelund, Robert B., and Robert D. Tollison. 1981. *Mercantilism as a Rent-Seeking Society.* College Station: Texas A&M University Press.

Ekiert, Grzegorz. 1991. "Democratization Processes in East Central Europe: A Theoretical Reconsideration." *British Journal of Political Science,* 21:285–313.

Europa World Yearbook. 1991. London: Europa Publications.

———. 1993. London: Europa Publications.

———. 1994. London: Europa Publications.

Fagen, Richard R., ed. 1979. *Capitalism and the State in U.S.–Latin American Relations.* Stanford: Stanford University Press.

Feldstein, Martin. 1995. "Global Capital Flows: Too Little, Not Too Much." *The Economist,* 24 June, 72–73.

Feldstein, Martin, and Charles Horioka. 1980. "Domestic Saving and International Capital Flows." *Economic Journal* 90:314–29.

Fiorina, Morris. 1992. *Divided Government.* New York: Macmillan.

Fisk, H. 1920. *English Public Finance.* New York: Bankers Trust Co.

Flake, Gordon. 1994. "The Republic of Korea: The Korean Economy in 1993." *Korea's Economy 1994.* Washington, D.C.: Korea Economic Institute of America.

Forrest, W. G. 1966. *The Emergence of Greek Democracy: 800–400 B.C.* New York: McGraw-Hill.

Fossedal, Gregory A. 1989. *The Democratic Imperative: Exporting the American Revolution.* New York: Basic Books.

Frieden, Jeffry A. 1991. *Debt, Development, and Democracy: Modern Political Economy and Latin America, 1965–1985.* Princeton: Princeton University Press.

———. 1991. "Invested Interests: The Politics of National Economic Policies in a World of Global Finance." *International Organization* 45: 425–51.

Friedman, David. 1977. "A Theory of the Size and Shape of Nations." *Journal of Political Economy* 85:59–78.

Frohmann, Alicia. 1993. Chile: external actors and the transition to democracy. Unpublished ms. Santiago.

Fukuyama, Francis. 1992. *The End of History and the Last Man.* New York: Maxwell Macmillan International.

Gallardo, Lt. Col. Juan M., and Lt. Col. Edmundo O'Kuingttons Ocampo. 1992. "El Rol de las Fuerzas Armadas en la Sociedad, Doctrina Militar en el

REFERENCES   **187**

Acontecer Político de SudAmerica." *Military Review* 72, Edición Hispan-
américana (Nov.–Dec.): 14.
Gasiorowski, Mark. 1993. Economic crisis and political regime change: an
event history analysis. Unpublished ms. Department of Political Science, Loui-
siana State University.
Gastil, Raymond D. 1986. *Freedom in the World: Political Rights and Civil
Liberties, 1985–1986.* New York: Greenwood Press.
Geddes, Barbara. 1994. *The Politician's Dilemma: Building State Capacity in
Latin America.* Berkeley and Los Angeles: University of California Press.
Gerchunoff, Pablo, et al. 1992. *Las privatizaciones en la Argentina.* Washing-
ton, D.C.: Banco Interamericano de Desarrollo.
Gettleman, Marvin E., et al. 1981. *El Salvador: Central America and the New
Cold War.* New York: Grove Press.
Gillespie, Charles G. 1987. "From Authoritarian Crises to Democratic Transi-
tions." *Latin American Research Review* 52:165–84.
———. 1991. *Negotiating Democracy: Politicians and Generals in Uruguay.*
Cambridge: Cambridge University Press.
Gilpin, Robert. 1987. *The Political Economy of International Relations.* Prince-
ton: Princeton University Press.
Ginsberg, Benjamin. 1982. *The Consequences of Consent: Elections, Citizen
Control, and Popular Acquiescence.* Reading, Mass.: Addison-Wesley.
Glain, Steve. 1994. "Shackled 'Tiger': South Korean Leader Struggles to Free up
a Regulated Economy." *Wall Street Journal,* 30 March, A1, A10.
Godoy Arcaya, Oscar. 1994. "Las elecciones de 1993." *Estudios Públicos* 62
(fall): 301–37.
Goodman, Louis W., Johanna S. R. Mendelson, and Juan Rial, eds. 1990. *The
Military and Democracy: The Future of Civil-Military Relations in Latin
America.* Lexington, Mass.: Lexington Books.
Gould, Harold A., and Sumit Ganguly. 1993. "Introduction to Part Two." In
India Votes, ed. Harold A. Gould and Sumit Ganguly. Boulder: Westview
Press.
Gourevitch, Peter A. 1978. "The Second Image Reversed." *International Orga-
nization* 32:881–912.
———. 1979. "The Re-emergence of 'Peripheral Nationalisms': Some Compar-
ative Speculations on the Spatial Distribution of Political Leadership and Eco-
nomic Growth." *Comparative Studies in Society and History* 21:303–22.
———. 1986. *Politics in Hard Times: Comparative Responses to International
Economic Crises.* Ithaca: Cornell University Press.
Grofman, Bernard, and Arend Lijphart, eds. 1986. *Electoral Laws and their
Political Consequences.* New York: Agathon Press.
Gunnemark, Erik V. 1991. "Countries, Peoples, and Their Languages: The Geo-
linguistic Handbook." Dallas: Summer Institute of Linguistics.
Hachette, Dominique, and Rolf Luders. 1992. *Privatization in Chile: An Eco-
nomic Appraisal.* San Francisco: ICS Press.
Hachette, Dominique, Rolf Lüders, Guillermo Tagle, Héctor Ottone, Catalina
Le Blanc, Pilar Vicuña, and Sergio Cobo. 1992. *Seis casos de privatización en
Chile.* Washington, D.C.: Banco Interamericano de Desarrollo.

Hadenius, Alex. 1992. *Democracy and Development*. New York: Cambridge University Press.

Haggard, Stephan, and Robert R. Kaufman. 1989. "Economic Adjustment in New Democracies." In Nelson et al. 1989.

———. 1995. *The Political Economy of Democratic Transitions*. Princeton: Princeton University Press.

Haggard, Stephan, and Robert Kaufman, eds. 1992. *The Politics of Economic Adjustment: International Constraints, Distributive Conflicts, and the State*. Princeton: Princeton University Press.

Hall, Robert E., and Charles I. Jones. 1996. "The Productivity of Nations," version 2.0.0 (18 October). Available at http://www.stanford.edu/~chadj/.

Halperín Donghi, Tulio. 1969. *Historia contemporánea de América Latina*. Madrid: Alianza.

Handelman, Howard, and Thomas G. Sanders, eds. 1981. *Military Government and the Movement Toward Democracy in South America*. Bloomington: Indiana University Press, 1981.

Hanushek, Eric A., and John E. Jackson. 1977. *Statistical Methods for Social Scientists*. Orlando, Fla.: Academic Press.

Hartlyn, Jonathan, Lars Schoultz, and Augusto Varas. 1992. *The United States and Latin America in the 1990s: Beyond the Cold War*. Chapel Hill: University of North Carolina Press.

Hayek, Friedrich A. 1960. *Constitution of Liberty*. Chicago: University of Chicago Press.

Heller, William B. 1995. Legislative insitutions, parliamentary process, and cabinet coalitions: structure and policy in postwar Italy and western Europe. Ph.D. thesis. Department of Political Science, University of California, San Diego.

Helliwell, John F. 1994. "Empirical Linkages Between Democracy and Economic Growth." *British Journal of Political Science* 24:225–48.

Herman, Edward S., and Frank Brodhead. 1984. *Demonstration Elections*. Boston: South End Press.

Hermet, Guy, and Richard Rose. 1978. *Elections without Choice*. New York: Macmillan.

Herz, John H. 1982. *From Dictatorship to Democracy: Coping with the Legacies of Authoritarianism and Totalitarianism*. Westport, Ct.: Greenwood Press.

Hicks, John. 1969. *A Theory of Economic History*. Oxford: Clarendon Press.

Higley, John, and Richard Gunther. 1992. *Elites and Democratic Consolidation in Latin America and Southern Europe*. New York: Cambridge University Press.

Hill, B. W. 1976. *The Growth of Parliamentary Parties: 1689–1742*. Hamden: Allen and Unwin.

Hill, C. 1980. *Century of Revolution, 1603–1714*. 2d ed. New York: W. W. Norton.

Hirschman, Albert O. 1970. *Exit, Voice, and Loyalty*. Cambridge, Mass.: Harvard University Press.

Hirst, Derek. 1986. *Authority and Conflict: England, 1603–1658*. Cambridge, Mass.: Harvard University Press.

Hobbes, Thomas. 1950. *Leviathan*. New York: Cambridge University Press.

Hoffman, Philip. 1988. Taxes, fiscal crises, and representative institutions: the case of early modern France. Unpublished ms., California Institute of Technology, Pasadena, Calif.

Homer, Sidney. 1963. *A History of Interest Rates*. New Brunswick, N.J.: Rutgers University Press.

Huber, John D. 1992. "Restrictive Legislative Procedures in France and the United States." *American Political Science Review* 86:675–87.

Hume, David. *The History of England*. Indianapolis: Liberty Fund.

Huntington, Samuel P. 1968. *Political Order in Changing Societies*. New Haven: Yale University Press.

———. 1984. "Will More Countries Become Democratic?" *Political Science Quarterly* 99(2):193–218.

Huntington, Samuel P. 1991. *The Third Wave: Democratization in the Late Twentieth Century*. Norman: University of Oklahoma Press.

Ilkin, Selim. 1994. "Privatization of State Economic Enterprises." In *Politics in the Third Turkish Republic*, ed. Metin Heper and Ahmet Evin. Boulder: Westview Press.

Inkeles, Alex, ed. 1991. *On Measuring Democracy*. New Brunswick, N.J.: Transaction Books.

Issacs, Anita. 1993. *Military Rule and Transition in Ecuador*. Pittsburgh: University of Pittsburgh Press.

Jackson, Robert H., and Carl G. Rosberg. 1985. "Democracy in Tropical Africa: Democracy Versus Autocracy in African Politics." *Journal of International Affairs* 38(2):293–305.

Jaquette, Jane S. 1989. *The Women's Movement in Latin America: Feminism and the Transition to Democracy*. Boston: Unwin Hyman.

Johnson, Carlos Molina, Lt. Col. 1987. *Algunas de las Razones del Quiebre de la Institucionalidad Política*. Santiago: Estado Mayor del Ejército.

Johnson, John J. 1958. *Political Change in Latin America: The Emergence of the Middle Sectors*. Stanford: Stanford University Press.

Jones, J. R. *Revolution of 1688 in England*. New York: Norton, 1973.

Joslin, D. M. 1954. "London Private Bankers, 1720–1785." In *Essays in Economic Hisory*, vol. 2, ed. E. M. Carus-Wilson. New York: St. Martin's Press.

Jowitt, Ken. 1992. *New World Disorder: The Leninist Extinction*. Berkeley and Los Angeles: University of California Press.

Kahler, Miles. 1986. *The Politics of International Debt*. Ithaca: Cornell University Press.

Karl, Terry Lynn. 1990. "Dilemmas of Democratization in Latin America." *Comparative Politics* 23:1–22.

Karst, Kenneth L., and Keith S. Rosenn. 1975. *Law and Development in Latin America, A Case Book*. Berkeley and Los Angeles: University of California Press.

Katzenstein, Peter. 1985. *Small States in World Markets: Industrial Policy in Europe*. Ithaca: Cornell University Press.

Kaufman, Robert R. 1990. "Stabilization and Adjustment in Argentina, Brazil, and Mexico." In Nelson, ed. 1990.

Keir, David. 1966. *The Constitutional History of Modern Britain Since 1845.* London: Black.

Kenyon, John. 1985. *Stuart England.* 2d ed. New York: Penguin.

Keohane, Robert, and Helen Milner, eds. 1996. *Internationalization and Domestic Politics.* New York: Cambridge University Press.

Kindleberger, Charles P. 1951. "Group Behavior and International Trade." *Journal of Political Economy* 59:30–46.

———. 1984. *Financial History of Western Europe.* London: Allen and Unwin.

Klarén, Peter F., and Thomas J. Bossert. 1986. *Promise of Development: Theories of Change in Latin America.* Boulder: Westview Press.

Klein, Benjamin, Robert C. Crawford, and Armen A. Alchian. 1978. "Vertical Integration, Appropriable Rents, and the Competitive Contracting Process." *Journal of Law and Economics* 21:297–326.

Krugman, Paul R. 1991. *Geography and Trade.* Cambridge, Mass.: MIT Press.

Kuczynski, Pedro-Pablo. 1988. *Latin American Debt.* Baltimore: Johns Hopkins University Press.

Lake, David A. 1992. "Powerful Pacifists: Democratic States and War." *American Political Science Review* 86:24–37.

Laver, Michael, and Norman Schofield. 1990. *Multiparty Government.* Oxford: Oxford University Press.

Laver, Michael, and Kenneth Shepsle. 1990. "Coalitions and Cabinet Government." *American Political Science Review* 84:873–90.

Lernoux, Penny. 1989. *People of God: The Struggle for World Catholicism.* New York: Viking.

Levine, Daniel H. 1979. *Churches and Politics in Latin America.* Beverly Hills: Sage Publications.

———. 1988. "Paradigm Lost: Dependence to Democracy." *World Politics* 40:377–94.

———. 1992. *Popular Voices in Latin American Catholicism.* Princeton: Princeton University Press.

Lieberthal, Kenneth G., and Michel Oksenberg. 1988. *Policy Making in China: Leaders, Structures, and Processes.* Princeton: Princeton University Press.

Lieuwen, Edwin. 1961. *Arms and Politics in Latin America.* New York: Praeger.

Lijphart, Arend. 1984. *Democracies: Patterns of Majoritarian and Consensus Government in Twenty-One Countries.* New Haven: Yale University Press.

Lipset, Seymour Martin. 1959. "Some Social Requisites of Democracy: Economic Development and Political Legitimacy." *American Political Science Review* 53:69–105.

———. 1960. *Political Man: The Social Bases of Politics.* Garden City, N.Y.: Doubleday.

Lipset, S. M., K.-R. Seong, and J. C. Torres. 1991. A comparative analysis of social requisites of democracy. Unpublished paper. Hoover Institution, Stanford University.

Londregan, John, and Kenneth Poole. 1990. "Poverty, the Coup Trap, and the Seizure of Executive Power." *World Politics* 42:151–83.

Loveman, Brian. 1991. "Misión Cumplida? Civil-Military Relations and the

Chilean Political Transition." *Journal of InterAmerican Studies and World Affairs* 33(3):35–74.

———. 1993. *The Constitution of Tyranny: Regimes of Exception in Spanish America*. Pittsburgh: University of Pittsburgh Press.

———. 1994. "Protected democracies and military guardianship: political transitions in Latin America, 1979–1993." Unpublished ms.

Loveman, Brian, and Thomas M. Davies, Jr. 1989. *The Politics of Antipolitics: The Military in Latin America*. Lincoln: University of Nebraska Press.

Lowenthal, Abraham F. 1990. *Partners in Conflict: The United States and Latin America in the 1990s*. Rev. ed. Baltimore: Johns Hopkins University Press.

Lowenthal, Abraham F., ed. 1991. *Exporting Democracy: The United States and Latin America*. Baltimore: Johns Hopkins University Press.

Lowenthal, Abraham F., and J. Samuel Fitch, eds. 1986. *Armies and Politics in Latin America*. Rev. ed. New York: Holmes and Meier.

Lynch, John. 1973. *The Spanish American Revolutions, 1808–1826*. New York: Norton.

Macaulay, Lord. 1914. *The History of England*. Vol. 5. London: Edward amd Charles Dilly.

MacEwan, Arthur. 1988. "Transitions from Authoritarian Rule." *Latin American Perspectives* 15(3):115–130.

MacLeod, Dag. 1993. Worker rights in a global economy. Masters thesis, University of California, San Diego.

Maddex, Robert L. 1995. *Constitutions of the World*. Washington, D.C.: CQ Press.

Maddison, Angus. 1995. *Explaining the Economic Performance of Nations: Essays in Time and Space*. Brookfield, Vt.: E. Elgar.

Mainwaring, Scott. 1986. *The Catholic Church and Politics in Brazil, 1916–1985*. Stanford: Stanford University Press.

Mainwaring, Scott, Guillermo O'Donnell, and J. Samuel Valenzuela. 1992. *Issues in Democratic Consolidation: The New South American Democracies in Comparative Perspective*. Notre Dame: University of Notre Dame Press.

Mainwaring, Scott, and Alexander Wilde. 1989. *The Progressive Church in Latin America*. Notre Dame: University of Notre Dame Press.

Maitland, F. W. 1908. *Constitutional History of England*. Cambridge: Cambridge University Press.

Malloy, James M., and Mitchell A. Seligson, eds. 1987. *Authoritarians and Democrats: Regime Transition in Latin America*. Pittsburgh: University of Pittsburgh Press.

Maniruzzaman, Talukder. 1987. *Military Withdrawal from Politics: A Comparative Study*. Cambridge, Mass.: Ballinger.

March, James G., and Herbert A. Simon. 1958. *Organizations*. New York: Wiley.

Martin, David. 1990. *Tongues of Fire: The Explosion of Protestantism in Latin America*. Cambridge: Basil Blackwell.

Mathias, Peter. 1983. *The First Industrial Nation*. 2d ed. London: Methuen.

May, Thomas Erskine. 1964. *Erskine May's Treatise on Law, Privileges, Pro-

ceedings, and Usage of Parliament. 17th ed. Ed. Barnett Cocks. London: Butterworth.

Mayhew, David R. 1974. *Congress: The Electoral Connection.* New Haven: Yale University Press.

McCubbins, Mathew D. 1991a. "Government on Lay-Away: Federal Spending and Deficits under Divided Party Control." In *The Politics of Divided Government,* ed. Gary W. Cox and Samuel Kernell. Boulder: Westview Press.

———. 1991b. "Party Governance and U.S. Budgets: Divided Government and Fiscal Stalemate." In *Politics and Economics in the Eighties,* ed. Alberto Alesina and Geoffrey Carliner. Chicago: University of Chicago Press.

McCubbins, Mathew D., Roger G. Noll, and Barry R. Weingast. 1987. "Administrative Procedures as an Instrument of Political Control." *Journal of Law, Economic, and Orgnaization* 3:243–77.

———. 1989. "Structure and Process, Politics and Policy: Administrative Arrangements and the Political Control of Agencies." *Virginia Law Review* 75:431–82.

McKelvey, Richard D. 1976. "Intransitivities in Multidimensional Voting Models and Some Implications for Agenda Control." *Journal of Economic Theory* 12:472–82.

McNeill, William. 1983. *Pursuit of Power.* Chicago: University of Chicago Press. Blackwell.

McNollgast. 1992. "Positive Canons: The Role of Legislative Bargains in Statutory Interpretation." *Georgetown Law Journal* 80:705–42.

McSherry, Patrice. 1992. "Military Power, Impunity and State-Society Change in Latin America." *Canadian Journal of Political Science* 25:463–88.

Milgrom, Paul R., Douglass C. North, and Barry R. Weingast. 1990. "The Role of Institutions in the Revival of Trade: The Law Merchant, Private Judges, and the Champagne Fairs." *Economics and Politics* 2:1–23.

Milkis, Sidney M. *The President and the Parties: The Transformation of the American Party System since the New Deal.* New York: Oxford University Press.

Milner, Helen. 1988. *Resisting Protectionism: Global Industries and the Politics of International Trade.* Princeton: Princeton University Press.

Mitchell, B. R. 1988. *British Historical Statistics.* Cambridge: Cambridge University Press.

Moe, Terry. 1984, "The New Economies of Organization." *American Journal of Political Science* 28:739–77.

Moffett, Matt. 1994. "Seeds of Reform: Key Finance Ministers in Latin America Are Old Harvard-MIT Pals." *Wall Street Journal,* 1 August, A1, A6.

Molinar Horcasitas, Juan. 1991. *El tiempo de la legitimidad: Elecciones, autoritarismo y democracia en México.* Mexico: Cal y Arena.

Moodie, Graeme C. 1971. *The Government of Great Britain.* London: Methuen.

Moore, Barrington, Jr. 1966. *The Social Origins of Dictatorship and Democracy: Lord and Peasant in the Making of the Modern World.* Boston: Beacon Press.

Morales, Héctor Alejandro Gramajo. 1989. *Tesis de la Estabilidad Nacional.* Guatemala: Editorial del Ejército.

Munck, Gerardo. 1993. "Beyond Electoralism in El Salvador: Conflict Resolution Through Negotiated Compromise." *Third World Quarterly* 14:75–93.

Muñoz, Heraldo V. 1986. *Las relaciones exteriores del gobierno militar chileno.* Santiago: PROSPEL-CERC, Ediciones del Ornitorrinco.

———. 1992. *El fin del fantasma: Las relaciones interamericanas después de la guerra fría.* Santiago: Hachette.

Muñoz, Heraldo V., and Carlos Portales. 1987. *Una amistad esquiva: Las relaciones de Estados Unidos y Chile.* Santiago: Pehuen.

Muravchik, Joshua. 1986. *The Uncertain Crusade: Jimmy Carter and the Dilemmas of Human Rights.* Lanham, Md.: Hamilton Press.

———. 1991. *Exporting Democracy: Fulfilling America's Destiny.* Washington, D.C.: AEI Press.

Nelson, Joan M. 1989. "The Politics of Pro-Poor Adjustment." In Nelson et al. 1989.

Nelson, Joan M. 1992. *Encouraging Democracy: What Role for Conditioned Aid?* Washington, D.C.: Overseas Development Council.

Nelson, Joan M. 1994a. "Overview: How Market Reforms and Democratic Consolidation Affect Each Other." In Nelson 1994.

Nelson, Joan M., ed. 1990. *Economic Crisis and Policy Choice: The Politics of Adjustment in the Third World.* Princeton, N.J.: Princeton University Press.

Nelson, Joan M., and Stephanie Eglington. 1992. *Encouraging Democracy: What Role for Conditional Aid?* Washington D.C.: Overseas Development Council.

Nelson, Joan M., et al. 1989. *Fragile Coalitions: The Politics of Economic Adjustment.* Washington, D.C.: Overseas Development Council.

Nelson, Joan M., et al. 1994. *Intricate Links: Democratization and Market Reforms in Latin America and Eastern Europe.* New Brunswick, N.J.: Transaction Books.

Nichols, Glenn O. 1989. English government borrowing before the financial revolution. Unpublished ms., Anderson College, Anderson, S.C.

North, Douglass. 1981. *Structure and Change in Economic History.* New York: W. W. Norton.

North, Douglass C. 1990. *Institutions, Institutional Change, and Economic Performance.* New York: Cambridge University Press.

North, Douglass C., and Barry R. Weingast. 1989. "Constitutions and Commitment: The Evolution of Institutions Governing Public Choice in Seventeenth-Century England." *The Journal of Economic History* 49:803–32.

Notestein, Wallace. 1924. *The Winning of the Initiative by the House of Commons.* London: Oxford University Press.

Nunn, Frederick. 1983. *Yesterday's Soldiers: European Military Professionalism in South America, 1890–1940.* Lincoln: University of Nebraska Press.

O'Brien, Philip, and Paul Cammack. 1985. *Generals in Retreat: The Crisis of Military Rule in Latin America.* Dover, N.H.: Manchester University Press.

O'Donnell, Guillermo. 1973. *Modernization and Bureaucratic-Authoritarian-*

ism: Studies in South American Politics. Berkeley: Institute of International Studies, 1973.

O'Donnell, Guillermo, Philippe C. Schmitter, and Laurence Whitehead, eds. 1986. *Transitions from Authoritarian Rule.* Baltimore: Johns Hopkins University Press.

Ogg, David. 1955. *England in the Reigns of James II and William III.* Oxford: Oxford University Press.

Oi, Jean C. 1990. "The Fate of the Collective after the Commune." In *Chinese Society on the Eve of Tiananmen: The Impact of Reform,* ed. Deborah Davis and Ezra Vogel. Cambridge, Mass.: Harvard University Press.

Olson, Mancur. 1971. *The Logic of Collective Action: Public Goods and the Theory of Groups.* Cambridge, Mass.: Harvard University Press.

Oppenheim, Lois Hecht. 1993. *Politics in Chile: Democracy, Authoritarianism, and the Search for Development.* Boulder: Westview Press.

Ordeshook, Peter C. 1993. "Some Rules of Constitutional Design." *Social Philosophy and Policy* 10:198–232.

Özbudun, Ergun. 1988. "The Status of the President of the Republic under the Turkish Constitution of 1982: Presidentialism or Parliamentarism?" In *State, Democracy, and the Military: Turkey in the 1980s,* ed. Metin Heper and Ahmet Evin. Berlin: Walter de Gruyter.

Pastor, Robert A., ed. 1989. *Democracy in the Americas: Stopping the Pendulum.* New York: Holmes and Meier.

Perkins, H. J. 1968. "The Social Causes of the British Industrial Revolution." *Transactions of the Royal Historical Society* 18:1–25.

Pindyck, Robert S., and Daniel L. Rubinfeld. 1991. *Econometric Models and Economic Forecasts.* 3d ed. New York: McGraw-Hill.

Piñera, José. 1994. "Chile." In *The Political Economy of Policy Reform,* ed. John Williamson. Washington, D.C.: Institute for International Economics.

Pinkney, Robert. 1990. *Right-Wing Military Government.* London: Pinter.

Pion-Berlin, David. 1989. *The Ideology of State Terror, Economic Doctrine, and Political Repression in Argentina and Peru.* Boulder: Lynne Rienner.

Pollard, A. F. 1926. *The Evolution of Parliament.* London: Longmans, Green, and Co.

Posición Constitucional de las Fuerzas Armadas en Iberoamérica y en España. 1992. Seville: Tecnos.

Powell, E. 1966. *The Evolution of the Money Market: 1385–1915.* London: Cass.

Pressnell, L. S. 1960. "The Rate of Interest in the 18th Century." In *Studies in the Industrial Revolution,* ed. L. S. Pressnell. London: Athlone Press.

Price, W. 1906. *English Patents of Monopoly.* Boston: Houghton Mifflin.

Pridham, Geoffrey. 1991. *Encouraging Democracy: The International Context of Regime Transition in Southern Europe.* Leicester: Leicester University Press.

———, ed. 1984. *The New Mediterranean Democracies: Regime Transition in Spain, Greece, and Portugal.* Totowa, N.J.: Frank Cass.

Przeworski, Adam. 1991. *Democracy and the Market: Political and Economic Reforms in Eastern Europe and Latin America.* New York: Cambridge University Press.

Puryear, Jeffrey M. 1992. Building democracy: foreign donors and Chile. Conference papers, no. 57, Columbia University.

———. 1994. *Thinking Politics: Intellectuals and Democracy in Chile, 1973–1988*. Baltimore: Johns Hopkins University Press.

Ramseyer, J. Mark, and Frances M. Rosenbluth. 1995. *The Politics of Oligarchy: Institutional Choice in Imperial Japan*. New York: Cambridge University Press.

Remmer, Karen L. 1985. "Redemocratization and the Impact of Authoritarian Rule in Latin America." *Comparative Politics* 17:1–25.

———. 1989. *Military Rule in Latin America*. Boston: Unwin Hyman.

———. 1991a. *Military Rule in Latin America*. 2d ed. Boulder: Westview Press.

———. 1991b. "New Wine or Old Bottlenecks? The Study of Latin American Democracy." *Comparative Politics* 23:479–96.

Rial, Juan. 1990. *Las Fuerzas Armadas en los Años 90, Una Agenda de Discusión*. Montevideo: Peitho.

Rich, Robert, Jr., and Eric L. Johnson. 1993. "Democratic Transition in Korea: The 1992 Elections." *Korea's Economy 1993*. Washington, D.C.: Korea Economic Institute of America.

Riker, William. 1962. *A Theory of Political Coalitions*. New Haven: Yale University Press.

Rock, David. 1994. *Latin America in the 1940s: War and Postwar Transitions*. Berkeley and Los Angeles: University of California Press.

Roeder, Philip G. 1990. Reforming the constitution of Stalinism: Gorbachev's institutional problem. Paper presented at the annual meeting of the American Political Science Association, Washington, D.C., 30 Aug.–Sept. 2.

Rogowski, Ronald. 1989. *Commerce and Coalitions*. Princeton: Princeton University Press.

Romualdi, Serafino. 1967. *Presidents and Peons: Recollections of a Labor Ambassador in Latin America*. New York: Funk and Wagnalls.

Root, Hilton L. 1989. "Tying the King's Hands: Credible Commitments and Royal Fiscal Policy During the Old Regime." *Rationality and Society* 1:240–58.

Root, Hilton, and Daniel Ingberman. 1987. Tying the king's hands. Unpublished ms., University of Pennsylvania, Philadelphia, Pa.

Rosenau, James. 1969. *Linkage Politics: Essays on the Convergence of National and International Systems*. New York: Free Press.

Rouquié, Alain. 1987. *The Military and the State in Latin America*. Trans. Paul E. Sigmund. Berkeley and Los Angeles: University of California Press.

Rueschemeyer, Dietrich, Evelyne Huber Stephens, and John D. Stephens. 1992. *Capitalist Development and Democracy*. Chicago: University of Chicago Press.

Rustow, Dankart A. 1970. "Transitions to Democracy." *Comparative Politics* 2:337–63.

———. 1990. "Democracy: A Global Revolution?" *Foreign Affairs* 69(4): 75–91.

Saracoglu, Rüsdü. 1994. "Liberalization of the Economy." In *Politics in the Third Turkish Republic*, ed. Metin Heper and Ahmet Evin. Boulder: Westview Press.

Sargent, Thomas. 1986. *Rational Expectations and Inflation*. New York: Harper and Row.

Schmitter, Philippe C., and Terry Karl. 1991. "What Democracy Is . . . and Is Not." *Journal of Democracy* 2:75–88.

Schoultz, Lars. 1981. *Human Rights and United States Policy toward Latin America*. Princeton: Princeton University Press.

Schuman, Michael. 1996. "South Korea Voters Deliver a Defeat to Ruling Party." *The Wall Street Journal*, 12 April, A8.

Schumpeter, Joseph. 1962. "Fiscal Crises and the Tax State." In *Classics in the Theory of Public Finance*, ed. Richard A. Musgrave and Alan T. Peacock. London: Macmillan.

Shirk, Susan L. 1993. *The Political Logic of Economic Reform in China*. Berkeley and Los Angeles: University of California Press.

Shugart, Matthew Soberg, and John Carey. 1992. *Presidents and Assemblies: Constitutional Design and Electoral Dynamics*. Cambridge: Cambridge University Press.

Sigmund, Paul E. 1990. *Liberation Theology at the Crossroads: Democracy or Revolution?* New York: Oxford University Press.

———. 1991. *The United States and Democracy in Chile*. Baltimore: Johns Hopkins University Press.

Silva, Eduardo. 1991. Capitalist coalitions and economic policymaking in authoritarian Chile, 1973–1988. Ph.D. diss., University of California, San Diego.

Sistemas Electorales y Representación Política en LatinoAmerica. 1986. 2 vols. Madrid: Fundación Friedrich Ebert / ICI.

Skidmore, Thomas E. 1993. *Television, Politics, and the Transition to Democracy in Latin America*. Baltimore: Johns Hopkins University Press.

Smith, Brian. 1982. *The Church and Politics in Chile*. Princeton: Princeton University Press.

Smith, Peter H. 1991. "Crisis and Democracy in Latin America." *World Politics* 43:608–34.

Smith, William C., Carlos H. Acuña, and Eduardo A. Gamarra. 1994a. *Democracy, Markets, and Structural Reform in Contemporary Latin America: Argentina, Bolivia, Brazil, Chile, and Mexico*. New Brunswick, N.J.: Transaction Books.

———. 1994b. *Latin American Political Economy in the Age of Neoliberal Reform: Theoretical and Comparative Perspectives for the 1990s*. New Brunswick, N.J.: Transaction Books.

Spalding, Hobart A,. Jr. 1977. *Organized Labor in Latin America*. New York: New York University Press.

Spiller, Pablo T., and Luis Viana Martorell. 1994. How should it be done? Electricity regulation in Argentina, Brazil, Uruguay, and Chile. Typescript, University of California, Berkeley.

Stallings, Barbara. 1987. *Banker to the Third World: U.S. Portfolio Investment in Latin America, 1900–1986*. Berkeley and Los Angeles: University of California Press.

———. 1993. "The New International Context of Development." *Items* 47:1–6.

Stallings, Barbara, and Robert Kaufman, eds. 1989. *Debt and Democracy in Latin America*. Boulder: Westview Press.

Stepan, Alfred. 1971. *The Military in Politics: Changing Patterns in Brazil*. Princeton: Princeton University Press.

———. 1988. *Rethinking Military Politics: Brazil and the Southern Cone*. Princeton: Princeton University Press.

Stepan, Alfred, ed. 1989. *Democratizing Brazil: Problems of Transition and Consolidation*. New York: Oxford University Press.

Stephens, Evelyne Huber. 1989. "Capitalist Development and Democracy in South America." *Politics and Society* 17:281–352.

———. 1990. "Democracy in Latin America: Recent Developments in Comparative Historical Perspective." *Latin American Research Review*, 25:157–76.

Stoll, David. 1990. *Is Latin America Turning Protestant? The Politics of Evangelical Growth*. Berkeley and Los Angeles: University of California Press.

Stolper, Wolfgang Friedrich, and Paul A. Samuelson. 1941. "Protection and Real Wages." *Review of Economic Studies* 9:58–73.

Stone, Alec. 1992. *The Birth of Judicial Politics in France: The Constitutional Council in Comparative Perspective*. New York: Oxford University Press.

Stone, Lawrence. 1965. *The Crisis of the Aristocracy, 1558–1641*. Oxford: Clarendon Press.

Strom, Kaare. 1990. *Minority Government and Majority Rule*. Cambridge: Cambridge University Press.

Swatos, William H. 1995. *Religion and Democracy in Latin America*. New Brunswick, N.J.: Transaction Books.

Szoboszlai, Gyorgy. 1992. *Flying Blind: Emerging Democracies in East-Central Europe*. Budapest: Institute for Social Sciences.

Taagepera, Rein, and Matthew Soberg Shugart. 1989. *Seats and Votes: The Effects and Determinants of Electoral Systems*. New Haven: Yale University Press.

Tiebout, Charles. 1956. "A Pure Theory of Local Expenditures." *Journal of Political Economy* 64:416–24.

Tilly, Charles. 1975. "Reflections on the History of European State-Making." In *The Formation of National States in Western Europe*, ed. Charles Tilly. Princeton: Princeton University Press.

Tocqueville, Alexis de. [1835]. *Democracy in America*. New York: Vintage Books.

Tsebelis, George. 1995. "Decision Making in Political Systems: Veto Players in Presidentialism, Parliamentarianism, Multicameralism, and Multipartism." *British Journal of Political Science* 25:101–29.

Tullock, Gordon. 1987. *Autocracy*. Dordrecht: Kluwer Academic Publishers.

Turan, Ilter. 1994. "Evolution of the Electoral Process." In *Politics in the Third Turkish Republic*, ed. Metin Heper and Ahmet Evin. Boulder: Westview Press.

United Nations Development Program. 1992. *Human Development Report 1992*. New York: Oxford University Press.

United States Marine Corps Small Wars Manual. 1987. NAVMC 2890. [1940]

Urrutia, Miguel. 1991. *Long-Term Trends in Latin American Economic Development*. Washington, D.C.: Johns Hopkins University Press.

Valenzuela, Arturo. 1978. *The Breakdown of Democratic Regimes, Chile.* Baltimore: Johns Hopkins University Press.

Valenzuela, J. Samuel. 1989. "Labor Movements in Transitions to Democracy: A Framework for Analysis." *Comparative Politics* 21:445–73.

Vanhanen, Tatu. 1990. *The Process of Democratization, A Comparative Study of 147 States, 1980–88.* New York: Crane Russak.

Varian, Hal R. 1992. *Microeconomic Analysis.* 3d ed. New York: W. W. Norton.

Veitch, John M. 1986. "Repudiations and Confiscations by the Medieval State." *Journal of Economic History* 46 (March): 31–36.

Villanueva, Víctor. 1973. *Ejército Peruano, Del Caudillaje Anárquico al Militarismo Reformista.* Lima: Editorial Juan Mejía Baca.

Wallace, Paul. 1993. "The Regionalization of Indian Electoral Politics, 1989–90: Punjab and Haryana." In *India Votes*, ed. Harold A. Gould and Sumit Ganguly. Boulder: Westview Press.

Wallerstein, Immanuel. 1974. *The Modern World-System*, vol. 1. New York: Academic Press.

Walter, Knut, and Philip J. Williams. 1993. "The Military and Democratization in El Salvador." *Journal of InterAmerican Studies and World Affairs* 35:39–87.

Waterbury, John. 1989. "The Political Management of Economic Adjustment and Reform." In Nelson et al. 1989.

———. 1992. "The Heart of the Matter? Public Enterprise and the Adjustment Process." In Haggard and Kaufman, eds. 1992.

Weber, Max. 1968. *Economy and Society.* 3 vols. ed. Guenther Roth and C. Wittich. New York: Bedminster Press. [1922]

Weingast, Barry R. 1995. "The Economic Role of Political Institutions: Market-Preserving Federalism and Economic Development." *Journal of Law, Economics, and Organization* 11:1–31.

Weingast, Barry R., and William Marshall. 1988. "The Industrial Organization of Congress; or Why Legislatures, Like Firms, Are Not Organized as Markets." *Journal of Political Economy* 96:132–63.

Weinstein, Martin. 1988. *Democracy at the Crossroads.* Boulder: Westview Press.

Welch, Claude E., Jr. 1987. *No Farewell to Arms? Military Disengagement from Politics in Africa and Latin America.* Boulder: Westview Press.

———. 1992. "Military Disengagement from Politics: Paradigms, Process, or Random Events." *Armed Forces and Society* 18:323–42.

Weldon, Jeffrey A. In press. "The Logic of *Presidencialismo* in Mexico." In *Presidentialism and Democracy in Latin America*, ed. Scott Mainwaring and Matthew Soberg Shugart. Cambridge: Cambridge University Press.

White, Lynn. 1962. *Medieval Technology and Social Change.* Oxford: Oxford University Press.

Wiarda, Howard. 1979. *Critical Elections and Critical Coups: State, Society, and the Military in the Process of Latin American Development.* Athens, Ohio: Ohio University Center for International Studies.

Wilkie, James W., and David Lorey. 1987. *Statistical Abstract of Latin America*, vol. 25. Los Angeles: UCLA Latin American Center Publications.

Willems, Emilio. 1967. *Followers of the New Faith: Future, Change, and the Rise of Protestantism in Brazil and Chile.* Nashville: Vanderbilt University Press.

Williamson, Jeffrey G. 1983. "Why Was British Growth so Slow During the Industrial Revolution?" *Journal of Economic History* 64:687–712.

Williamson, Oliver E. 1975. *Markets and Hierarchies, Analysis and Antitrust Implications: A Study in the Economics of Internal Organization.* New York: Free Press.

———. 1985. *The Economic Institutions of Capitalism: Firms, Markets, Relational Contracting.* New York: Free Press.

World Bank. 1993. *World Development Report 1993: Investment in Health.* Oxford: Oxford University Press.

———. 1995. *Bureaucrats in Business: The Economics and Politics of Government Ownership.* Washington, D.C.: The World Bank.

Index

Absolutism, 21, 22n, 45
Accountability, 96, 129
Africa, 74n, 79, 81, 92, 95, 102–3, 103n, 104, 104n, 107, 112
Agenda setting, power of, 147, 153, 153n, 155–58, 166, 177
Albania, 73
Alfonsín, Raúl, 128
Allende, Salvador, 160–61, 176
Aquino, Corazon, 166–68
Argentina, 73–74, 82, 84, 87, 93, 97, 100–101, 105–6, 106n, 107, 110, 115n, 116n, 117n, 118, 118n, 119, 121, 122n, 123–28, 130, 132–35, 138, 139n, 141–45, 179
Armed forces, 11, 78, 85–87, 90, 93–95, 98–99, 104–12, 114–19, 121–29, 136–39, 150, 161, 165, 167, 172–75, 180. *See also* Military guardianship; Standing army
Ashton, Robert, 34
Ashton, T. S., 39, 41
Asia, 11–12, 74n, 79, 79n, 81, 93, 96, 167
Australia, 48
Authoritarian regime(s), 3–5, 11, 52, 68, 73–74, 76, 80, 82–83, 85–86, 90–98, 102–14, 119, 121, 123, 126, 131, 136, 138, 148, 159, 177n, 179–80
Authoritarian withdrawals. *See* Transitions to democracy
Aylwin, Patricio, 88–89, 163

Bahrain, 48
Bargain(s) *or* bargaining, 4, 13, 21, 26, 93, 96–97, 126, 154, 157–58
Belgium, 58, 68
Bicameralism. *See* Legislature(s): structure of
Bolivia, 73–74, 100–101, 105, 107, 115n, 116n, 117n, 118n, 119, 121, 122n, 123, 127–28, 132–35, 137–38, 140–45
Borrowing, government, 15, 17, 23, 31, 33–38

Brazil, 73–74, 76, 83, 87, 93, 99, 100–102, 105–8, 110, 115n, 116n, 117, 117n, 118, 118n, 122n, 123–24, 126–28, 131–35, 139n, 140–45
Britain. *See* England
Budgets, government, 7, 14, 17, 22–26, 30, 31, 33–34, 36–38, 44–45, 151, 153n, 155, 173. *See also* Borrowing, government
Bulgaria, 73
Bureaucratic-authoritarianism, 95, 107
Bullow, Jeremy, 20
Business interests. *See* Investors

Canada, 48
Canevi, Yavuz, 174
Castro, Fidel, 136
Checks, institutional. *See* Veto power(s)
Chile, 10–11, 70, 73–74, 74n, 76, 80, 81n, 86–91, 93, 97, 100–106, 109–10, 116n, 118, 123, 126–28, 131, 133–38, 139n, 140–41, 143–44, 146, 148, 159–61, 161n, 162–63, 176, 177, 179
China, 148, 159, 159n, 160n, 175–76, 176n, 177
Chun Doo Hwan, 109–10, 164
Church, Catholic, 78–79, 84, 88–90, 116n
Çiller, Tansu, 172–73
Civil society, organization of, 1, 4, 12, 75, 77, 80, 84, 87, 90, 93, 96, 103–5, 108, 112, 114, 167. *See also* Working-class organization
Coalition(s), 6–7, 27, 32, 90, 96, 104–5, 111, 123, 147, 149–52, 154–55, 157, 158, 162–63, 167, 172, 174, 176–77
Colombia, 74, 84, 115n, 117n, 119, 119n, 121, 128, 133–35, 138, 140–45
Communism *or* communist movements, 73, 77, 81–83, 86, 88, 119, 139n, 167
Constituents *or* constituencies, 19, 21, 28, 148–50, 154, 156, 160, 162, 169, 173–74, 176–77
Constitution(s), 19, 120, 126, 136, 137, 138, 164, 167

Conversion costs, 53–55

Costa Rica, 74, 80, 115n, 121, 128, 133–35, 139n, 140–42, 144

Costs and benefits, 5–8, 18, 80, 85–86, 89–91, 94, 96–98, 105, 126, 147, 150, 154, 157–58, 166. *See also* Conversion costs; Risks; Transaction costs

Coup(s), 115, 155n, 116–17, 117n, 119, 121–25, 127–28, 135, 139, 147, 160, 164, 167, 173, 177

Credible commitment, 9–17, 19, 30–31, 33, 38–39, 158, 180

Credible threat, 30–31, 125

Cuba 74, 82, 115n, 117n, 118–19, 124, 132–36, 138

Czechoslovakia, 73, 100–101

Dahl, Robert, 94, 126

De la Madrid, Miguel, 168–69

De Rosas, Juan Manuel, 130, 130n

Dean, Warren, 115n

Deane, Phyllis, 40

Debt crisis, 76–77, 87, 90, 146, 150–51, 160, 168, 173, 176–77

Democracies , 3–5, 9, 11, 44, 48–49, 52, 56, 57n, 58–59, 61–69, 72, 72n, 73, 73n, 74–78, 80–91, 94, 97, 98n, 102, 103, 108, 111, 113, 116, 119, 120, 121, 129, 129n, 130–31, 134–39, 139n, 148–49, 160, 163–64, 167, 177, 179–80. *See also* Protected democracy

Democratization. *See* Transitions to democracy

Development, level of. *See* Socioeconomic modernization, level of; Wealth, national

Dictator(s), 5, 81–82, 84–87, 91, 94, 113, 160, 173

Dictatorship(s). *See* Authoritarian regime(s)

Divided government, 8–9, 11, 98–99, 104–9, 114, 125, 167–68, 171, 177, 180

Dominant-party governments, 74, 93–94, 104–5, 112–14, 119, 124, 171

Dominican Republic, 74, 80, 115n, 117n, 118, 118n, 132–35, 141, 143, 145

Domino effect, 72, 74, 85–86, 92

Downing, Brian, 116n

Duverger, Maurice, 173n

East Germany, 73, 109

Eastern Europe 70, 73, 79, 81, 82, 85, 88, 89, 90, 92, 94, 102, 104, 109, 112

Economic crisis, 11, 74, 76, 87, 91–93, 96–99, 102–11, 113, 114, 122–23, 146–47, 150–51, 169–70, 172, 177. *See also* Inflation

Economic performance, 7, 12, 16, 18, 21, 39, 42, 45, 46, 47, 75, 86, 90, 93, 96–97, 99, 100–102, 111, 113, 146, 148

Economic reform. *See* Liberalization: economic; Structural adjustment

Ecuador, 73–74, 80, 83, 100–101, 115n, 116n, 117n, 118, 118n, 123, 127–28, 132–34, 138, 140, 142–43, 145

Education, 11, 49, 55, 57, 57n, 59, 61, 62, 63–69, 75, 119, 120, 125, 139

Ekelund, Robert, 31–32

El Salvador, 73–74, 83, 100–101, 115n, 116n, 117n, 118–19, 127–28, 133–35, 138, 140–45

Electoral rules, 153–55, 161, 161n, 162–63, 166n, 169, 172n, 174

Elites, 4–5, 71, 77, 93, 94, 96, 98–99, 103, 105, 108, 110, 113–14, 153

Emigration, 49, 53, 54, 57n, 58n, 180. *See also* Exit

England, 10, 13–15, 17–18, 21–47, 52, 72, 82–83, 124–25, 127, 150, 154, 156

Equilibrium, 49, 53 55–57, 57n

Estonia, 73

Exit, 49, 52–53, 55n, 57, 57n, 59, 60, 62, 66, 69

Federalism, 156, 171

Feminism, 84, 90

Fitch, J. Samuel, 116

Foreign pressure. *See* Imperial factors; United States government; Western Europe

France, 5, 14–15, 26n, 27, 31, 33, 35, 37, 43, 45–46, 58, 72, 135, 157

Franchise, 48, 58, 58n, 59n, 66, 68, 120–21, 131–36

Freedoms. *See* Rights

Frei Montalva, Eduardo, 137

Frei Ruiz-Tagle, Eduardo, 163

Game theory, elements of, 14, 20–21

Gasiorowski, Mark, 102

Gastil, Raymond, 48, 59n

Gastil political freedom index, 58–64, 64n
Geopolitical factors. *See* Imperial factors
Germany, 68, 76, 157
Ghana, 100–101
Glorious Revolution, 15, 17, 21, 29–30, 33, 37, 39, 40, 43–45
Government structure, 153, 155, 166–67, 169, 172
Greece, 73, 76, 100–101
Growth. *See* Economic performance
Guatemala, 73, 74, 79, 81n, 100–101, 115n, 116n, 117n, 118, 118n, 123, 127–28, 133–35, 138, 139n, 141–43, 145

Haiti, 73, 74, 81, 115n, 117, 117n, 143, 145
Hirschman, Albert O., 52, 69
Hobbesian war, 8–9
Holland, 37, 60, 68
Honduras, 73–74, 100–101, 115n, 116n, 117n, 118, 118n, 119, 123, 127, 133–35, 138n, 141–42, 144
Human capital. *See* Education
Human rights, 79–80, 82–84, 88–90, 126, 128
Hungary, 73, 100–101
Huntington, Samuel, 131, 148

Ideology, 4, 11, 32, 72–74, 82–85, 87–88, 90–91, 119, 121, 138, 139n, 147, 149
Imperial factors, 72, 74, 78–83, 111, 121, 180
Incentives, 6, 14, 17–21, 71, 79, 86, 92, 97, 146–48, 150, 170, 175–76, 178, 180
India, 60, 94, 148, 159, 170, 170n, 171–72, 174–75
Individualism, 78, 85
Indonesia, 112
Inflation, 37, 99, 101–2, 146, 150, 155, 177
Institutional change, 17, 28–33, 35, 39, 43–44, 46, 161–63, 165, 167
Institutional structures. *See* Institutions
Institutions, 6, 8, 10, 12, 16–19, 21, 26–29, 31, 38–39, 43–47, 86, 93, 95, 104, 108–9, 111–14, 116–17, 122–25, 127–28, 147–49, 153–58, 161–63, 166, 169, 172, 174, 177–78, 180. *See also*

Constitution(s); Electoral rules; Federalism; Government structure; Institutional change; Judiciary; Legislature(s)
International factors, 4, 11, 70–91, 119, 127, 190
Investors, 18, 34, 44, 55–57, 69, 96–97, 103,105, 107–8, 111–12, 114, 158

Japan, 146
Judiciary: dependence of, 26–27, 156; independence of, 10, 13, 15, 17, 28, 30, 32–33, 156–57, 157n, 172–74. *See also* Star Chamber

Kim Young Sam, 164, 165, 165n, 166
Knowledge, 149, 152–53, 161n
Korea, South, 73, 93, 96–97, 100–102, 105–6, 109–11, 148, 159, 163–66, 169, 177, 179

Labor movement(s). *See* Working-class organization
Languages, knowledge of, 54, 57, 57n, 60, 61, 62, 64–65, 67–68
Latin America, 11–12, 70–86, 90, 92–97, 103–4, 107, 110, 115–45, 151, 160, 168
Latvia, 73
Legislature(s): role of, 8–10, 13, 15, 17, 29, 30, 32, 155, 161, 163; structure of, 155–56, 166, 166n. *See also* Parliament, English
Legitimacy, 12, 74, 77, 80, 96, 114, 119, 121–24, 126–27, 130–31, 137
Legitimating myth *or* mission. *See* Legitimacy
Liberalization: 5–12, 44, 149–59, 162, 180; conditions for, 8–9, 12, 122, 146–53, 157, 159, 176–79; definition of, 3–4; economic, 4, 12, 116, 146–48, 159, 160, 163–65, 165n, 167–70, 170n, 171–79; political, 4, 72, 116, 117, 119, 139, 148, 167, 179. *See also* Transitions to democracy
Liberties. *See* Rights
Lieuwen, Edwin, 115n
Linguistic expertise. *See* Languages, knowledge of
Lipset, Seymour Martin, 67n, 94–95, 103, 112
Lithuania, 73

Macaulay, Lord, 35
Marcos, Ferdinand, 106, 166–67
May, Erskin, 32
Menem, Carlos, 128
Mexico, 73n, 74, 83, 93, 104–5, 112–13, 115, 119, 124, 133–35, 140–45, 148, 151, 159, 166, 168–72, 177
Middle East, 48, 66, 79, 81, 102, 112
Middle-income countries, 93, 95, 103–4, 112
Military guardianship, 118–24, 126–27, 129, 136–37, 139
Monarch, 10–11, 13–17, 20, 22–35, 37–39, 43–45
Moore, Barrington, 116n

Napoleon Bonaparte, 130
National security (internal), 118, 122, 122n, 123, 128, 136–39, 175. See also Order, internal
Neoliberalism, 77–78, 83, 86–87, 90, 107
New economics of organization, 19n
Nicaragua, 73, 74, 74n, 81n, 115n, 117n, 118, 124, 132–35, 138n, 142, 144
Nichols, Glenn, 34
Nigeria, 100–101
North, Douglass, 49, 50n, 52

O'Donnell, Guillermo, 4, 95, 98
Opposition, 4, 28–29, 43, 71, 78–79, 82–84, 86–87, 89–93, 97–98, 104–5, 108–9, 111–13, 129, 138–39, 147, 158, 165–66, 173, 177
Order, internal, 6–8, 86, 90, 116n, 122, 122n, 123, 128, 131, 136–38, 167–68
Özal, Turgut, 110, 172–74

Panama, 73–74, 81, 115n, 117n, 119, 133–35, 140, 142, 144–45
Papacy. See Church, Catholic
Paraguay, 73–74, 100–101, 104, 115n, 116n, 117, 117n, 118, 133–35, 139n, 140–41, 143–45
Park Chung Hee, 109
Parliament, English, 8, 17, 22–33, 35, 43–45
Parliamentarism. See Government structure
Parties, political, 83, 87–89, 114, 126, 154, 161–62, 164, 169–75. See also Dominant-party governments

Path dependence, 116, 116n, 117
Perón, Juan, 124
Peru, 73–74, 76, 80, 83, 87, 93, 95, 100–101, 105–6, 115n, 116n, 118, 118n, 119, 121, 123, 124, 127–28, 132–36, 138, 140–42, 144–45, 151
Philippines, 73, 76, 87, 93, 100–101, 105–9, 148, 159, 166–68, 176–77
Pinochet, Augusto, 86–91, 109–10, 124, 136, 160–61, 161n, 162–63, 176
Plato, 136
Poland, 73, 100–101, 104, 179
Political learning, 85, 87–88
Population size, 54, 62–65, 68, 151
Portugal, 72–73, 76, 100–101
Presidentialism. See Government structure
Presnell, L. S., 40
Principal-agent relations, 56, 67
Protected democracy, 134–39
Protest(s). See Civil society, organization of
Protestantism, 85, 90
Przeworski, Adam, 9
Punishment, 6, 125, 127–28

Ramos, Fidel Valdes, 167–68
Rao, Narasimha, 171
Regime change, 71–74, 76, 90, 102, 150, 152, 177. See also Transitions to democracy
Regime(s) of exception, 137–38
Representative government. See Democracies
Repression, 4, 6, 7–8, 86, 97–98, 98n, 99, 103, 105, 108–9, 115, 118, 120, 126–29
Retribution. See Punishment
Revenues, government. See Borrowing, government; Budgets, government
Revolution or revolutionary movements, 4, 5, 15, 45–46, 74–75, 77, 88, 124, 135–36, 138. See also Glorious Revolution
Rights: political, 3–5, 7, 29–32, 39, 43–44, 129–30, 136, 138–39; property, 7, 11, 13–16, 21, 23–26, 28–32, 39, 43, 44, 46, 47, 167. See also Human rights
Risks, 7, 24, 38, 43, 86, 146, 149
Rogoff, Kenneth, 20
Roh Tae Woo, 164–65
Romania, 73, 100–101, 104

Rouquié, Alain, 122
Rule of law, 6–7, 67, 129
Ruler. *See* Sovereign
Rules of the game. *See* Institutions
Russia, 73, 81, 89, 179

Salinas, Carlos, 169–70
Saudi Arabia, 48
Scandinavian countries, 60, 68
Schmitter, Philippe C., 4, 98
Self-enforcing limits, 13, 19, 21, 31, 44
Self-interest, 5, 12, 44, 49, 97
Senegal, 100–101, 146
Singapore, 97, 104
Singh, Arjun, 171
Singh, Manmohan, 171
Social movements. *See* Civil society, organization of
Socioeconomic modernization, level of, 75, 92–95. *See also* Wealth, national
Sovereign, 3, 5–14, 16, 18–20, 49, 54n, 124, 179–80; preferences of, 5–8, 14, 19–20, 31, 89, 91, 113, 126, 146–48, 150–51, 153, 157, 160, 163
Soviet Union, 73n 78, 80, 82, 88, 90, 94, 102, 156
Spain, 21–22, 26n, 27, 43, 72–73, 76, 100–101
Stability, political. *See* Order, internal
Standing army, 14, 27, 43
Star Chamber, 27–29, 44, 156
State: neoclassical theory of, 49, 50n, 51–52, 55; size of, 68–69; strength of, 148. *See also* Institutions; Monarch; Sovereign
Structural adjustment, 96, 99, 102, 107–11, 113
Suffrage. *See* Franchise
Switzerland, 52, 68

Taiwan, 73, 93, 96–97, 104–5, 112–13, 179
Technology, 75, 85, 90, 151
Tiebout, Charles, 69
Thailand, 93, 99, 100–103, 105, 107
Tocqueville, Alexis de, 5, 135–36
Tollison, Robert, 31–32
Transaction costs, 8, 14, 19, 46, 49n
Transitions to democracy, 5, 11, 15, 31, 49, 66, 70–71, 73–74, 76, 78–92, 94, 95, 97–102, 105, 108, 111, 113–22,

124–129, 129n, 130, 131, 133–34, 136, 138–39, 160, 179, 180; terms of, 92, 105, 109, 111, 114, 125–28
Turkey, 73, 93, 100–103, 105, 110, 148, 159, 170, 172–77

Unicameralism. *See* Legislature(s): structure of
Unions. *See* Working-class organization
United States, 48, 52, 66, 76–78, 153, 156
United States government, 72, 79, 80–81, 83, 86–87, 90, 120, 128, 131
Uruguay, 73, 74, 76, 87, 93, 97, 100–101, 103, 105–7, 107n, 110, 115, 116n, 121, 123–38, 133–35, 141–42, 144

Vatican. *See* Church, Catholic
Veitch, John, 20
Venezuela, 74, 115n, 117n, 119, 121, 133–35, 140, 142–44
Veto power(s), 9, 27, 29–32, 44, 106n, 111, 121, 153–63, 165n, 166, 166n, 167, 169, 169n, 170, 172–75, 177
Voice, 56, 69
Voting rights. *See* Franchise

War(s), effects of, 10, 14, 20, 37, 45, 67, 72, 82, 91, 119, 124–25, 127–28
Washington (D.C.). *See* United States government
Waterbury, John, 174
Wealth, national, 49, 54, 55, 57, 57n, 59, 60n, 61–69. *See also* Socioeconomic modernization, level of
Weber, Max, 50n, 85
Western Europe, 78–79, 82, 90
Whitehead, Laurence, 4
Wiarda, Howard, 115n
Williamson, Jeffrey, 46n
Williamson, Oliver, 19, 55n, 56, 56n, 69
Women's participation, 84, 132–33
Working-class organization, 77–82, 86–87, 90, 97, 98n, 103, 111–12, 147, 150, 160

Yugoslavia, 73

Zambia, 104
Zedillo, Ernesto, 169–70